ILLUSTRATED HISTORY OF THE DOUGLAS CAMP-MEETING

B. L. Fisher Library Camp Meeting Series ; vol. 2.
Series editor: Robert A. Danielson, Ph.D.

Illustrated History

Of

Douglas Camp Meeting

by

Rev. Edward Davies

Author of "The Life of Bishop Taylor," "The Gift of the Holy Ghost," and "The Believer's Handbook on Holiness," etc.

Introduction By Rev. E.M. Levy, D.D.

How goodly are thy tents, O Jacob, and thy tabernacles, O Israel.

First Fruits Press
Wilmore,
Kentucky c2016

Illustrated history of Douglas Camp Meeting.
By Edward Douglas.

First Fruits Press, ©2016
Previously published jointly by McDonald, Gill & Co. and Holiness Book Concern, ©1890.

ISBN: 9781621716358 (print), 9781621716419 (digital), 9781621716426 (kindle)

Digital version at http://place.asburyseminary.edu/firstfruitsbooks/13/

First Fruits Press
B.L. Fisher Library
Asbury Theological Seminary
204 N. Lexington Ave.
Wilmore, KY 40390
http://place.asburyseminary.edu/firstfruits

Davies, Edward, 1830-
   Illustrated history of Douglas Camp Meeting / by Edward Douglas ; introduction by E.M. Levy. -- Wilmore, Kentucky : First Fruits Press, ©2016.

          xviii, 97 pages, [9] leaves of plates : portraits, illustrations ; 21 cm.-- (B.L. Fisher Library camp meeting series ; volume 2)
          Reprint. Previously published: Boston : McDonald, Gill & Co. ; Reading, Mass. : Holiness Book Concern, ©1890.
          ISBN - 13: 978-16217176358 (pbk.)
          1. Douglas Camp Meeting. 2. Camp-meetings--Massachusetts. I. Title. II. B.L. Fisher Library. Camp meeting series ; volume 2.

BV3799.D68 D38 2016   269

Cover design by John Ramsay

asburyseminary.edu
800.2ASBURY
204 North Lexington Avenue
Wilmore, Kentucky 40390

First Fruits
THE ACADEMIC OPEN PRESS OF ASBURY SEMINARY

First Fruits Press
The Academic Open Press of Asbury Theological Seminary
204 N. Lexington Ave., Wilmore, KY 40390
859-858-2236
first.fruits@asburyseminary.edu
asbury.to/firstfruits

ILLUSTRATED HISTORY

OF

DOUGLAS CAMP MEETING.

BY

REV. EDWARD DAVIES.

Author of " The Life of Bishop Taylor," " The Gift of the Holy Ghost," and " The Believer's Handbook on Holiness," etc.

INTRODUCTION BY REV. E. M. LEVY, D.D.

How goodly are thy tents, O Jacob, and thy tabernacles, O Israel."

BOSTON:

McDONALD, GILL & CO.,

36 BROMFIELD STREET.

HOLINESS BOOK CONCERN, READING, MASS.

Press of the *Christian Witness*, Boston, Mass.

PREFACE.

THE readers of this book will hardly realize the time and expense that it has cost me to gather together and set in order the facts contained in this book. But it has been a labor of love. It has enabled me to live over again those heavenly times at Douglas, and has been a love feast to my soul, as I have no doubt it will be to many. Others might have done better, but I have done what I could to immortalize the memory of those glorious sermons, testimonies, songs, and services at Douglas Camp Meeting for the past fifteen years; also to keep up the memory of the dear ministers and their sermons, who have crossed the flood, such as B. W. Gorham, F. B. Joy, and F. B. Dickinson. Dr. E. M. Levy has kindly written the introduction, and otherwise helped me very much. Dea. Morse and Bros. McDonald and Gill have been very kind and helpful. Many thanks to them all.

I send forth this book in honor of my faithful wife, who helped me much during my fifteen years in the ministry, and has been equally faithful during my eighteen years in the work of an evangelist.

Read this book with prayer for the author and for yourself, and God will make it a blessing.

EDWARD DAVIES.

READING, MASS.

CONTENTS.

CONTENTS.

CHAPTER VII.

CAMP MEETING OF 1890.

CHAPTER VIII.

INTRODUCTION.

THE modern camp meeting has a Scriptural support in the Feast of the Tabernacles. In the twenty-third chapter of Leviticus there is an account of this interesting festival: " Also in the fifteenth day of the seventh month, when ye have gathered in the fruit of the land, ye shall keep a feast unto the Lord seven days: on the first day shall be a sabbath, and on the eighth day shall be a sabbath. And ye shall take you on the first day the boughs of goodly trees, branches of palm trees, and the boughs of thick trees, and willows of the brook; and ye shall rejoice before the Lord your God seven days. And ye shall keep it a feast unto the Lord seven days in the year. It shall be a statute forever in your generations: ye shall celebrate it in the seventh month. Ye shall dwell in booths seven days; all that are Israelites born shall dwell in booths: that your genera-tions may know that I made the children of Israel to dwell in booths, when I brought them out of the land of Egypt."

The Feast of Tabernacles was the most joyous of all festive seasons in Israel, and was the third great annual festival, at which all Israel was to appear before the Lord at the place which He should choose. It fell on the fifteenth of the seventh month, or Tishri, corresponding to Septem-ber or the beginning of October. It was a time of year when the hearts of all the people would naturally be full of thankfulness, gladness, and expectancy. The fruits of the earth had been gathered, and a season of rest prevailed before the coming on of the rainy season, after which a new crop was to be planted in the prepared soil. It was thus a thanksgiving occasion, and "the voice of rejoicing was heard in the tabernacles of the righteous." "Because the Lord thy God shall bless thee in all thine increase, and in all the works of thine hands, therefore thou shalt surely rejoice, thou, and thy son, and thy daughter, and thy man-servant, and thy maid-servant, and the Levite, the stranger, and the fatherless, and the widow, that are within thy gates."

In the Mishnah, according to Edersheim, and other Hebrew writers, minute details are given as to the con-struction of the "booths." They must be real "booths," constructed of boughs of living trees, and solely for the purposes of this festival. Hence they must be high enough, yet not too high, not more than thirty feet; three of the sides must be of boughs, completely covered, yet not so shaded as not to admit sunshine and air, nor yet so open as not to have sufficient shade.

It is needless to enter into further details, except to say that these booths, and not their houses, were to be the regular dwellings of all in Israel, and that during the entire period they were to eat, sleep, meditate, pray, in short, entirely live in them.

Very beautiful and impressive must have been this scene, The entire nation leaving their houses, every family apart, and for eight days, including two Sabbaths, finding physical and spiritual refreshment in worship, under the protection of the leaves of fragrant trees and the pure air of heaven.

The origin of our "feast of tabernacles," while not of divine authority, grew, no doubt, out of the condition of society. In all ages there have been open-air meetings for worship. The Scotch Covenanters, we know, in times of persecution, met in secluded valleys and behind the shelter of the rocks. Here the faithful pastor broke for them the Bread of Life, and commended them to the care of Him who is "a shelter from the storm, and a rock in a weary land."

In after times also, when peace had spread her dove-like wings over the country, similar meetings were held. So great were the crowds attending the annual communion seasons, that both the preaching and the administration of the Lord's Supper had to be held in the church-yards and under the shade of trees. The sturdy and devout Scotch-men would come with their families from far and near, and, for many days at a time, would with great reverence listen to sermons of three hours in delivery, "nor thought the season long."

In our own country the Puritans, perhaps from necessity, held many of their religious services in the open air, while the immortal Whitefield delivered most of his sermons in the streets and in the fields. The early Methodists did the same. One of these, with fiery eloquence and divine unction preached, for many weeks, every Lord's Day, in the vicinity of Philadelphia, under spreading oak trees, using a sugar hogshead for his pulpit. By these means thousands were converted to God.

Rev. William McDonald, in *The Christian Witness*, published an account of the rise and progress of camp meetings. It appears, from this interesting sketch, that Rev. James McGready, of Scotch-Irish descent, a native of Pennsylvania, moved, with his parents, when quite young, to North Carolina, and, while yet a youth, united with the Presbyterian Church. He was sent, in the fall of 1785, to his native State to be educated, and at the school which finally became the Jefferson College.

He was licensed to preach, Aug. 13, 1788. It was not until he had been engaged in the ministry for some time that he came to the sad conclusion that he was without an experimental knowledge of Christ. Making this discovery, he sought God with all his heart, and in doing so found peace by believing, during the administration of the Lord's Supper. Soon after this remarkable change, he returned to North Carolina. The fire within him burned hotly, and his earnest discourses and pointed appeals aroused the opposition of unconverted professors and obstinate unbelievers. It is said that some of "the base sort" went to his church, broke down the seats, burnt the pulpit, and left a letter addressed to him, written in blood, requiring him to leave the country at the peril of his life.

But, nothing daunted by these threats, on the following Sabbath morning he took his stand in the door of his dismantled church, and preached a sermon of great power, warning the wicked to "flee from the wrath to come." He continued laboring here for souls until 1796, when he removed to Kentucky, and became pastor of three congregations, — Muddy River, Jasper River, and Red River.

His whole soul was on the stretch for sinners. He secured a pledge from his members that they would spend one half hour every Saturday, at sunset, and every Sabbath morning at sunrise, in pleading with God for a revival of His work and the salvation of souls. As might be expected, during the following year a gracious work commenced at the Jasper River Church. In 1799 the work spread to such an extent that he found it necessary to seek the assistance of other devoted and earnest ministers. The revival spread more and more in 1800. It prevailed over so vast a region of country that it was called the revival of 1800. This great awakening became largely catholic in spirit, and was participated in by members of various denominations.

At this time was held the first real camp meeting ever known in modern times. The place was Jasper River, Logan County, Ky., during the month of July, 1800. The circumstances were very simple. A family had just arrived in the County from Carolina, and were anxious to attend one of Mr. McGready's meetings, but could not see their way clear to do so, because of the distance and the fact of their being strangers. A female member of the family suggested that, as they had encamped in their wagon on their long journey, they might do the same while attending the revival meetings. They consequently, with wagon and provisions, started for the meeting, camping near the church.

This suggested to other families the method by which they also could attend. So at the next meeting several other families followed their example. This simple arrangement suggested to Mr. McGready the idea of camp meeting, which he appointed at Jasper River, and announced that the people would be expected to camp on the ground. They did so, and for shelter used their wagon covers and cloth tents.

The first camp meeting continued from Friday to the following Tuesday, and resulted in the conversion of forty-five souls. The people came in crowds, many from a distance of twenty, fifty, and even one hundred miles.

This was the origin of camp meetings in this country. For some reason they very soon passed out of the hands of the Presbyterians, and within a few years have been conducted by the Methodists, although the Baptists and other denominations have occasionally used the same method for special summer services.

The early camp meetings of the Methodists were seasons of marvellous power. Father Boehm gives some account of the work in his day. Speaking of a camp meeting on the Eastern shore of Maryland, he says: "There were one hundred and forty-six conversions in one day, and seventy-eight wholly sanctified. Another day there were one hundred and forty-six conversions, and one hundred and twenty-two wholly sanctified. Peter Van Nost preached at eight o'clock, and there were eighty-one converted and sixty-eight sanctified that evening. On Thursday following there were two hundred and sixty-four converted and fifty-five sanctified. There were one thousand converted and nine hundred and sixteen sanctified during this one camp meeting."

In the Baptist Encyclopædia an account is given of a remarkable revival of religion that swept over the State of Georgia in the year 1824, resulting in the addition of from fifteen to twenty thousand souls to the Baptist churches alone. This work of salvation originated in an open-air meeting held by the Antioch Church, in Morgan County. During a sermon preached by Rev. Adiel Sherwood of Connecticut, the Holy Spirit fell first upon the preacher and then upon the people, and nearly four thousand sinners cried out in great anguish of soul. The scene was beyond description, and the results of this baptism of the Holy Ghost and of fire were realized by the churches of all denominations in the State for many years.

It is a very significant fact that the camp meetings held for the spread of scriptural holiness have been preeminently successful in the conversion of sinners, as well as in the sanctification of believers. Sermons that search out and uncover the carnality remaining in believers, and that proclaim God's remedy for the removal of all sin, are sure to convict sinners. The argument is conclusive: "And if the righteous scarcely be saved, where shall the ungodly and the sinner appear?"

The following pages will give the reader some striking illustrations of this statement. The origin of the National Holiness Association, as also of Douglas Camp Meeting, may have been small and insignificant, but eternity alone can tell the story of what God has wrought by these agencies in quickening formal churches, sanctifying believers, and converting sinners. The streams flowing from these fountains of holy influence have touched many lands, making fertile the barren soil and filling human spirits with gladness. The narrative is an interesting one, and will be read with profit and delight long after the present actors on the scene have passed from earth to heaven.

In the year 1858, a young man, of large business prospects, impenitent and worldly, was, through the power of the Holy Spirit, converted to God. The change was radical. At once he became an earnest worker in the field of Christian labor. Business, family, pleasure, and money were held as secondary to the conversion of his friends and neighbors. He preached to men in their homes, on the streets, and in the shops, beseeching them to turn from sin and seek God. His zeal was tireless, his consecration sincere, and his joy in the service of his Master was without cessation. And yet there was unrest in his soul. The discovery of lingering carnality awakened great anxiety and caused many tears to flow. Within two months after his conversion we find him with a deep hunger in his soul after holiness. Night after night we see him in earnest conversation with his precious Christian mother. But even she could not help him now. "George," she would say to his passionate yearnings, "you are seeking something that you cannot hope to enjoy this side the grave."

Some one — to this day he has not discovered who — sent

him a copy of "The Guide to Holiness." With over-
flowing tears he read its pages of Christian experience.
Hastening again to his mother's home, "Here, mother,"
he exclaimed, "somebody has got the experience I so much
desire." Together, like St. Augustine and Monica, this
mother and son would sit until the midnight hour, reading,
conversing, weeping, and praying.

In July, 1870, Mother Morse went to the Hamilton (Mass.)
Camp Meeting. Her precious son had started the desire in
her soul also for the same salvation, and she was destined
to enter into the Beulah Land before him. In that meeting this "elect lady" sought and obtained the blessing of
entire sanctification. Returning home the happy possessor
of the priceless pearl of heart purity, she was able now
to encourage and instruct the son she so fondly loved.

In November of the same year, a holiness convention was
held at New Bedford, Mass.; mother, son, and daughter were
present. During the services, George went to the altar
seeking the experience of "perfect love;" but when the
invitation was given to the unconverted, he would leave
the altar and go through the congregation, persuading
sinners to go forward and seek God's forgiveness. The
second day, Nov. 15, 1870, after the afternoon services,
with his mother and sister, all in earnest conversation and
prayer, he went to the bridge, from which a fine view may
be had of the bay. Here the little company halted, and
for a time no one broke the silence. The evening shadows
were beginning to fall around them. It was now five o'clock.
Looking down the bay toward the light-house, with his
heart yearning for "the second blessing," he had reached
the end of all self effort. A deep, solemn stillness rested
upon his soul. Just then, as the light-house keeper lighted
his lamp, and its cheering rays darted over the bosom of

the great deep, the light of Heaven fell upon the soul of His servant. Instantly all gloom disappeared; the witness of the Spirit came as clear and unmistakable to his sanctification, as it had come to his justification. And "the anointing abideth in him unto this day."

Such is the story of one that God has used, and is still using, for the advancement of His kingdom in the world. Douglas is only one of many agencies set in motion by this man of God who, "through sanctification of the Spirit and belief of the truth, was made meet for the Master's use, and prepared unto every good work."

Edgar M. Levy.

DOUGLAS CAMP MEETING.

CHAPTER I.

"Come Holy Ghost, my heart inspire ;
  Attest that I am born again ;
Come, and baptize me now with fire,
  Nor let thy former gifts be vain :
I cannot rest in sins forgiven ;
Where is the earnest of my heaven ? "

FOR several years I have felt that a history of this great camp meeting should be written. For, though this camp had a very small beginning it is safe to say, that it has not been equalled in power and glory by any camp in New England in the same time.

It is located on the New York and New England railroad, forty-eight miles from Boston, and fourteen miles from Putnam, Conn. It is in the State of Massachusetts, and is not far from the railroad station.

In the summer of 1875 J. W. Coolidge, Evangelist, of the Congregational Church, and Luther Wing, of the Methodist Church, held a small camp meeting on the other side of the road from the present camp. The meeting was held for the promotion of holiness, and the conversion of sinners. Among those that were present, we may mention : Dea. George M. Morse and

I. T. Johnson, Evangelist; Dr. C. B. Robbins, of Worcester; Ex-governor Berry, of N. H., a Methodist who was in office at the time of the late war. Also several recent converts from the Catholic Church in Putnam. Also, Deacons Lovering and Carver of the Baptist Church, Putnam; and Deacon Stoddard of the Congregational Church, in Douglas. Rev. F. D. Blakeslee, D.D., President of the East Greenwich Seminary (R.I.), preached on the sabbath of the camp, and Miss Charlotte Holmes, a Quakeress, of Burrillville, R. I., also preached at that camp on the sabbath. Her sermon was in the morning and made a profound impression. Dr. Blakeslee carried the congregation by storm in the afternoon.

The social services during the sabbath were conducted by Deacon Morse and I. T. Johnson, and quite a company were converted during the day. The first convert of the camp meeting was a French Catholic, named Peter Dion, who has since become a missionary among the French. This conversion stirred up much opposition, which was manifest on every side.

The following brethren were also present and helped in the social and public services, pointing sinners to Christ, and encouraging believers: viz., Rhoades Allen, Dea. Wm. Stone, Joseph Cundall, Deacon Fenn, Dea. T. P. Botham, Dea. F. Lovering, all of Putnam, and E. M. Hough of East Douglas.

God honored that meeting with his gracious presence. There were so many converted or sanctified, that there was a general desire that there should be another camp meeting held in that vicinity, next year, and as Dea. Morse was a business man of means, and was such an earnest worker, he was desired to take the lead in the enterprise. Feeling that he might glorify God in this work, he purchased several acres of land, and erected several buildings, including a dining-hall, office, and dormitory, also a number of tents.

The camp meeting in 1876, was under the care of Dea. Morse, I. T. Johnson, and other laborers, both lay and clerical. The presence of the Lord was manifested, sinners were converted, and believers sanctified by the power of God. Charles Nichols, a Congregational evangelist from Boston, took a generous part in these early meetings. The meeting increased in favor with God and man. The people in all the region round were interested, and came to the services. There was no Tabernacle at that time, so in rainy weather, the services were held in the pavilion in front of the office, in the tents, and sometimes in the dining-hall.

The services were held on the line of entire santification for believers, and true repentance and faith in Christ, for the salvation of sinners. " The power of the Lord was present to heal."

All these premises were owned by Dea. George M. Morse, who is a mill owner and manufacturer from Putnam, Conn., where he lives in a large mansion, where his cotton mills are located, where he earns the money which he so freely spends for God and suffering humanity, and where his large family of nine children have been born, who are branching out in many directions.

Deacon Morse is a vigorous man, of medium stature and of peaceable disposition. He was converted as follows : —

After he had lived in sin about forty years, he promised his mother to read the Bible through if she would send him one in large print. While engaged in reading his Bible he was called to sit up all night and watch with the dead body of a neighbor's child. At the midnight hour, all alone, God met him as he read the following stanzas, which he found, that night, in that Bible, which his mother no doubt put in. The stanzas are said to have been written by Mrs. Phœbe Palmer. As he read them the Holy Spirit applied them to his heart and he burst into tears, and cried like a child.

> " Remember, love, who gave you this
> When other days shall come —
> When she who had thy earliest kiss
> Sleeps in her narrow home.
> Remember, 'twas a mother gave
> The gift to one she'd die to save.
>
> That mother sought a pledge of love,
> The holiest for her son;
> And from the gifts of God above
> She chose a godly one.
> She chose for her beloved boy
> The source of life, and light, and joy.
>
> And bade him keep the gift — that when
> The parting hour should come,
> They might have hope to meet again,
> In her eternal home.
> She said his faith in that would be
> Sweet incense to her memory.
>
> And should the scoffer in his pride,
> Laugh that fond gift to scorn,
> And bid him cast that pledge aside
> That he from youth had borne —
> She bade him pause and ask his breast
> If he, or she, had loved him best.

DEACON MORSE'S CONVERSION.

> A parent's blessing on her son
>   Goes with this holy thing;
> The love that would retain the one
>   Must to the other cling.
> Remember, 'tis no idle toy
> A mother's gift — remember, boy.''

This incident led to his conversion. Mothers pray on, for your wayward boys.

After he had been soundly converted, he was deeply convicted of inbred sin, and felt his need of entire sanctification. He could not rest till he had the precious blessing of a clean heart. This wonderful and complete salvation not only enlarged his heart but also increased his benevolence. He began to study various ways of doing good to his fellow-men.

He found a true friend and fellow laborer in I. T. Johnson, Evangelist, of Oxford Mass., whom God has been pleased to honor with the salvation of many souls, in many places, for many years. Brother Johnson has done excellent service on this ground from its beginning, and has a fine cottage on the ground.

The secretary of the first two camp meetings on this ground was Stillman Morse, son of Deacon Morse. Then W. F. Davis of Oxford, took this office for a number of years. They both did good service. I very well remember the early camp meetings on this ground.

They were small, but full of power, and accomplished much good. Souls were converted, including some French Catholics, some of whom have become efficient workers in the cause of the kingdom of Christ; and one, at least, has become a minister of the Lord Jesus.

Rev. George Hughes was an early attendant at this

glorious camp, for Deacon Morse was led to seek entire
santification through reading " The Guide to Holiness."
God has given Brother Hughes much power in preaching on this encampment. He is a minister of the old-
fashioned sort, whose faith in God is full and complete,
and who preaches with and by " the Holy Ghost sent
down from heaven." I remember how he preached one
year upon, " Blessed are they that hunger and thirst
after righteousness, for they shall be filled." He was
caught away by the Spirit, and carried the people with
him. He was also an honored and faithful member of
" The National Camp Meeting Association " for a number of years, and is one of the editors of " The Guide to
Holiness," which is always full of the sweetness of the
gospel of the Son of God. For a number of years I had
charge of the children's meetings on these grounds, and
many were converted to God. I. T. Johnson would
generally hold, at the stand, a large and successful
revival service immediately after dinner on Sunday,
when the masses were there. He is a plain-spoken,
earnest, and successful worker. I must not forget to
mention Mrs. Susan B. Morse, the mother of Deacon Morse.
She was indeed the mother of the camp, while her son was
the father of it. She had a fervent spirit of piety, and
and took a great interest in this camp and helped to
pay its expenses for many of the earlier years. But
on June 17, 1881, the Master called, and she went from
the toils and sufferings of earth, to the rest and joys of
heaven. Her good works were many, and her memory
is blessed. She " rests from her labors and her works
do follow her." She was the worthy mother of a noble

son, for whom she prayed many years before he was converted, and when he was far away from God. Her prayers prevailed, and her heart greatly rejoiced. Mrs. George M. Morse has taken a great interest in the camp meetings, and otherwise rendered excellent service in advising with her husband about it. I must also make special mention of the indispensable man of the camp, William B. Stone, who for so many years has been the caterer, has done such splendid service in feeding the multitudes, and whose disposition has been so even that he could maintain his temper under many provocations. No wonder that so many people came from Providence and other places when they could have both a spiritual and a temporal feast at the same time. Among them I must make special mention of Dea. Gulliver of Providence, and his excellent wife. They were so full of faith and the Holy Ghost that we were all glad to meet them. The deacon died. His widow still delights to come to Douglas.

A lovely stream of pure water winds its crooked way through Douglas Camp Ground, and the tents are on each side of the stream. It reminds us of the valley of the Jordan, on a small scale. The land rises in front of the preacher's stand, so that thousands of people can sit in sight within speaking distance. There is a heavy growth of pine trees that make a lovely shade. It is beautiful for situation, and is already a joy to all New England.

Mrs. N. J. Hill of East Douglas attended the first camp meeting. She walked from East Douglas to the camp on a very hot day. She and Luther Wing were the only persons in town at that time that enjoyed full salvation. She has been a faithful attendant ever since.

Dea. Morse told us that when at Round Lake National Camp Meeting in 1872, he met a one-armed man in the woods; he began to preach to him "Jesus," and wept over him. He was converted and became a minister, after finishing his education at Drew Theological Seminary. Bro. Tilley tells a similar experience in Delaware, where a tramp was entertained and saved, and became a local preacher.

At the first camp meeting on this ground, the power of God came down so that, in one of the social meetings in the men's pavilion, everybody was saved. A Frenchman ran out of the meeting and down to the office. Bro. Morse's son, Stillman, asked him how the meeting was going. He replied, "I stay till they catch 'em six. Then I leave." It is thought that there were thirty souls converted that night.

I am glad to learn that Zaccheus A. Ballard was at the first camp meeting. He says Mr. Coolidge was a devout man, and much concerned for the salvation of souls.

Mrs. Amanda Smith, who has labored so many years in Africa, was an earnest and very acceptable worker at some of these earlier camp meetings.

Engraved by Litner

Yours Truly,
W. Mc Donald.

CHAPTER II.

"OH that the Comforter would come,
  Nor visit as transient guest,
But fix in me His constant home,
  And keep possession of my breast,
And make my soul His loved abode,
  The temple of indwelling God!"

NATIONAL CAMP MEETING AT DOUGLAS, 1879.

THESE National Camp Meetings have a mighty influence throughout the world. I have attended many of them, and can testify to the power of God as it has been marvellously displayed at these meetings. The National Camp Meeting at Douglas was under the charge of Rev. William McDonald, because Rev. J. S. Inskip, the President, was holding a National Camp Meeting in the West at the same time. They sent each other fraternal greetings by telegraph during the meetings, and it was quite refreshing to get the glad news from each other in that way.

Revs. W. H. Boole, Charles Munger, J. A. Wood, J. N. Short, George Pratt, and Joshua Gill, of the National Association, were present at Douglas, and many other dear ministers of God; and Christian workers in abundance, including Rev. Bros. D. J. Griffin, King, Davies, and Livesey. Perfect harmony prevailed. Many were converted, reclaimed, or fully sanctified.

A poor drunkard was present, and could hardly give attention to the preaching; but Dea. Morse knew the man, and how important it was that he should be saved. We had a season of prayer, and Dea. Morse offered one of his mighty, wrestling, and prevailing prayers, for which he is noted. God answered prayer; the drunkard was sobered and saved, and lived for God two years, and died in the faith of God. A large tabernacle had been erected, where the services were held in rainy weather, and at other times.

There were some wonderful scenes of power at this National Meeting. Indeed, such was the faith of the people in God, at this camp, that no ordinary blessing could satisfy them. The preaching was kept fully on the line of "holiness to the Lord." Surely, these were among the times that the prophet wrote about, when "holiness to the Lord" should "be upon the bells of the horses, and the pots in the Lord's house" should "be like the bowls before the altar. Yea, every pot in Jerusalem and in Judah shall be holiness unto the Lord of hosts."

Indeed, so fully did the distinction between regeneration and entire sanctification prevail among the people, that one of the boys that had been converted in the children's meeting, when giving his testimony a few days after, said, "I know I have been converted, but I have not that other blessing."

He knew he was not wholly sanctified, as the people were around him. And so did many more, who could not rest till they obtained that great boon of heaven. Christians of all churches entered into this blessed state, and went home to tell of the wonderful story of Jesus, and His perfect and wonderful love.

At this camp meeting the New England Association for the Promotion of Holiness was organized. Rev. Wm. McDonald was elected president, and Bros. Pratt, Munger, Stratton, Livesey, Cilley, and Malcolm were vice-presidents.

Bro. McDonald has had charge of nearly all the camp meetings at Douglas since that time. He was also vice-president of the National Association for the Promotion of Holiness, of which Rev. J. S. Inskip was the honored president. These two mighty men of God have travelled at least 50,000 miles together, and held some of the most glorious camp meetings that mortals ever attended. Glorious men, each of them, but very different in their temperaments.

John S. Inskip was aggressive and fiery: Wm. McDonald was more conservative and sober. The one was the engine, the other was the balance-wheel, and one was just as essential as the other. Indeed, it is hard to see how one of them could have succeeded without the other.

The New England Association did much good, and held a number of good camp meetings. Rev. J. A. Wood was a very efficient member, and has been made a great blessing by his able sermons and vigorous exhortations and fine discriminations. McDonald and Wood make a good, steady, and vigorous pair, and were always reliable and ready for any emergency.

The camp meeting of 1880 at Douglas was a season of great power. Bro. McDonald was away, and Rev.

G. Pratt of Maine, a wonderful man of God, was to take charge of this meeting, but illness kept him away. So Dea. Morse led the camp meeting in a very successful and acceptable manner. The influence of the last year's meeting had gone out far and wide, and the people came in great numbers. Other buildings had been erected for the increasing crowds; still it was hard to accommodate them all.

The burden was upon my heart for the children. Meetings were appointed, and the seal of heaven was upon these meetings from the beginning. The last service among the children was marvellous in the eyes of angels and of men. At this time John S. Inskip, Wm. McDonald, and J. A. Wood were on their way round the world.

After Rev. G. Hughes' wonderful sermon, Mrs. Clark of New York was overwhelmed with the power of God, and fell at the altar before the Lord, and many felt the shock of divine power. The altar service continued till eleven P.M. It was a glorious time. The last meeting of the camp was in the line of assimilation with the image of God. We were crying out to God for the image of Christ to be stamped upon us. Many received the answer to their prayers. The glory of God covered the camp. Thus closed the heavenly camp meeting of 1880. There was an excellent set of sermons preached at this camp meeting, and they were a great blessing to the people.

The camp meeting of 1881 commenced Aug. 2. Much prayer had been offered concerning this camp meeting, and the power of God was there from the beginning. Rev. Wm. McDonald was in charge, and opened the first service with a discourse upon "The Baptism of the Holy Ghost," at the close of which the people flocked to the altar. It was a time of great humiliation before the Lord, and was a good preparation for the rest of the camp meeting. Bros. McLean, Simmons, Wood, Short, Gill, Munger, Dr. Steele, the writer, and many others were present, including Dr. Charles Cullis of Boston. The sermons were full of holy power and heavenly unction.

Rev. John Allen of Farmington, Me., was called "Camp Meeting John Allen," was at this meeting. He was filled with the Spirit, and made a great blessing to the people. He was present at every camp meeting here until God called him to his eternal reward. He was quite a preacher when the Spirit was upon him, and preached with great acceptance. He died in his ninety-third year, Aug. 30, 1887, on the East Livermore camp ground, Me., the day after he preached there; and "ceased at once to work and live." Rev. John Allen was an excellent man of God. He attended three hundred and seventy-four camp meetings.

Misses Cassie and Lois Smith of Pawtucket, R.I., were efficient workers at this meeting. Bro. Alderman of Hyde Park, Mass., had charge of several services.

Perfect harmony prevailed, and the tide of salvation rose higher and higher, until Jordan overflowed all its banks. All classes rushed to the altar as soon as they were invited; and some of the quiet people, who have a great sense of propriety, were so overpowered by the Spirit, that they would fall down before the Lord at the altar; others shouted for joy.

The Sunday morning love feast almost excelled everything we had ever had at even a National camp meeting. Two hundred testified for God in eighty minutes, and the testimonies were clear and strong, and very definite. One hundred witnessed for Christ by rising, that had no time to speak. God was there in great power.

Dr. Charles Cullis of Boston preached an excellent sermon after the love feast, from John 2: 7. Many were blessed of God under the word.

Mrs. W. McDonald held some precious mother's meetings, and Mrs. J. A. Wood held a series of meetings for young ladies. Mrs. Dr. Levy led the children's meetings.

In these days of power it was very common for a little group, here and there, to go up the side of the hill or down in some valley, and hold a prayer meeting for a special blessing upon the services. How many times I have known Bros. Griffin and Thomas to do so! Who can tell the power of united and believing prayer? I hope this custom will be kept up, for the good of those who pray, as well as of those that they pray for.

As Bros. McDonald and Wood had returned from India, and had seen William Taylor's missions, and as the missionary fire always burned at this camp, a subscription was taken of $114 for the Taylor missions. These missions in India, with those of Dr. William Butler, have become so very prosperous that there are now three annual conferences of the Methodist Episcopal Church in India. This camp meeting closed in a blessed manner, and the people were determined to come again.

CAMP MEETING OF 1882.

With such a record the year before, no wonder that the rumor went out, and the people needed no persuasion to come to this camp, and they were on hand at the early part of the meeting, not for recreation, but for God and salvation.

A larger tabernacle had been erected by Dea. Morse, at a large expense, and hundreds of good chairs had been provided for the public good. Revs. J. A. Wood and William McDonald spoke in the first meeting, and the glory of God rested upon the people for half an hour, and a sacred awe filled the place. It was past ten o'clock at night when this meeting closed.

The preaching during the whole ten days was full of point and of power. Inbred sin was assailed on every side, and the power of the gospel was present to heal. So that "Where sin abounded, grace did much more abound." Rev. G. Hughes preached twice with much power; so did Dr. Levy. Rev. B. W. Gorham was there, and preached three times, with the unction from the Holy One. Dr. W. F. Mallalieu, now a bishop, preached on "The Pentecostal Baptism." The people were moved and melted under the words. Rev. E. A. Withey, evangelist, preached a precious sermon. He and his wife and four children have since then spent more than five years in Bishop Taylor's missions in Africa. When some one told the bishop that Bro. Withey prayed too much for Africa, the bishop said, "That will help to make up for those who do not pray enough." Bro. Withey is presiding elder of the Angola District.

Rev. John Parker of New York has attended all the camp meetings from the beginning, except the last, and is always a joy and delight. He is so full of heavenly sunshine that everybody is glad to see him; and although he only stays a few days, he is called on once or twice to edify and bless the people by his luminous and instructive sermons and his heavenly songs. His social qualities are very attractive.

Rev. J. S. Inskip made his only visit to this ground on the last three days of this meeting. He was in excellent health and spirits, and preached as only he could preach when the Holy Ghost rested upon him. He was pre-eminently a man of God, full of faith and of the Holy Ghost. He too has joined the blood-washed. He died at Ocean Grove, N.J., March 7, 1884. His last song was, "The Sweet By and By." Just before he died, with a face beaming with celestial light, he shouted, "Victory! triumph! triumph!" These were his last words. Blessed man of God!

Rev. David Updegraff of Ohio preached a blessed sermon on Sabbath afternoon. Bros. McDonald, Wood, Short, Bray, King, Alderman, and others preached at this camp meeting with divine energy. The Sabbath love feasts were, as usual, seasons of power. As many as four testimonies were given in a minute. They were such clear-cut testimonies that they sparkled like diamonds. Many wondered where so many precious gems came from. Many of them since then have gone to their heavenly rest. I must not forget to mention another true yoke-fellow, who for many years has taken charge of the office work and had a general oversight of the temporalities of the camp meetings, — James B. Bowen. He is a man of solid physical proportions, of a genial temper, good judgment, long-suffering patience, and great endurance, who has endeared himself to all the people and is an indispensable man.

CAMP MEETING OF 1883.

This blessed camp meeting commenced July 24, with an informal service in the evening. Many were waiting before the Lord for the manifestation of the divine presence, and they were not disappointed. It was a meeting of unusual power. The promised Comforter was in the midst, and the camp meeting went on with great power from day to day. Rev. W. Bray and Dr. Daniel Steele preached on Wednesday. Rev. G. W. McDonald of Woodstock, N.B., J. A. Wood, and D. J. Griffin preached on Thursday. Revs. J. N. Short, B. F. Joy, and J. M. Leonard preached on Friday. Rev. G. E. Fuller, Dr. E. M. Levy, and G. Hughes preached on Saturday. Sunday was a great day, as usual. There was a glorious love feast in the morning, after which Rev. W. McDonald preached. Rev. John Parker preached at 2.30, and Rev. B. W. Gorham in the evening. God enabled each of them to preach in the Holy Ghost, and eternal good was done. About five thousand persons were in attendance, and positive results were achieved in the salvation of sinners and the sanctification of believers.

Dr. Daniel Steele preached his remarkable sermon on " The Holy Ghost the Conservator of Orthodoxy," which

was edifying in a high degree. Many Baptist brethren from New Brunswick were among the earnest
seekers. Rev. H. C. McBride and wife were made a
great blessing. Rev. G. Hughes and wife and son
were blessed and made a blessing.

The tide of salvation rose higher and higher from
day to day, till it reached a higher point than ever
before at Douglas. There were twenty-six sermons
preached by twenty ministers, including Rev. A. E.
Withey. Six of them preached twice. Bro. I. T.
Johnson conducted a number of noon and 6 P.M.
meetings, and God made them a great blessing. The
death of Dr. Palmer of New York was the topic of
one service. He was a man of God, full of faith and
of the Holy Ghost. Two hundred testimonies were
given at the second love feast. They were as rich
as if sent from the skies. Dea. Morse was all
ablaze with divine glory. God helps him because he
keeps his commandments; out of a million dollar's
worth of property under his care, he will not allow
repairs to be made on the Sabbath. Nearly $800
were raised for missions. Rev. B. S. Taylor, then of
Vermont, was made a great blessing.

CHAPTER III.

"WHERE is the indubitable seal
    That ascertains the kingdom mine?
That powerful stamp I long to feel, —
    The signature of love divine;
Oh, shed it in my heart abroad,
Fulness of love, of heaven, of God!"

PEN AND INK PICTURES.

REV. WILLIAM MCDONALD, so many years the president of this meeting, is also the President of the National Camp Meeting Association, since the death of J. S. Inskip. He is one of the editors of *The Christian Witness*, in connection with Revs. J. Gill and G. A. McLaughlin. He is well beloved by thousands all over the nation. He is now past seventy years of age and is ripening for eternal glory, but still wields his pen with great power.

Rev. Joshua Gill has had charge of the book stand at Douglas for many years; is one of the most laborious and successful business managers in all New England, an incisive and stirring preacher, an excellent singer, and one of the leading authors of that unequalled song book called "Songs of Joy and Gladness," which has already had a sale of three hundred fifty-five thousand copies.

Rev. J. A. Wood has done excellent service at Douglas for many years. He is the author of that

VILLAGE ON THE WEST COAST OF AFRICA.   A PALAVER TREE.

blessed book called "Perfect Love," and its companion
book called "Purity and Maturity."

Bishop W. Taylor has been made a great blessing
at Douglas for a number of years. His preaching is so
plain and practical, and also scriptural, and his spirit is
so genial, and his faith in God and man so strong and
steady, that it is an inspiration to be in his company.
He has just returned from his episcopal tour in Africa,
and is in vigorous health. Thousands of dollars have
been collected at Douglas for his mission work. This
leads us to notice more fully that the missionary
fire burns at Douglas.

Indeed, this may be called a missionary camp meeting;
for many have been called of God to the mission field on
these grounds. Among the rest we are glad to mention
Rev. Amos E. Withey and wife, and four lovely children
who were often at this camp. They were among the first
company that went out to Africa in 1885, under Bishop
Taylor, and have done such excellent work in various
parts of the province of Angola. And the children, that
many were sure would die, have stood the climate better
than the adults, and can speak several languages, and
are making excellent missionaries. The oldest daughter
died in Africa. I shall never forget the time when Miss
Effie Brannen of Boston felt it her duty to go to Africa.
She had a mighty conflict with self and Satan. She
knew her parents would oppose, but Christ called, and she
could not refuse. When she gave up all, the fire of God
flamed through her whole body, soul, and spirit. Her
very countenance was all aglow with the divine glory.
We subscribed money to send her to an academy, but the
committee at New York said, "Send her on; she will

learn in Africa." The Mariner's Bethel Church of East
Boston, of which Dr. L. B. Bates is pastor, and of which
she was a member, gave Miss Brannen an excellent
outfit. She sailed from New York and reached Africa
in due season, and did good service for God. She became the wife of W. P. Dodson, one of Taylor's best
missionaries. But her health failed and God called her
home. She wears a martyr's crown in glory, and is far
better off with her body in Africa and her soul in
paradise, than though she had returned from Africa.
Bro. Dodson would not leave his post of duty.
Heaven will afford a grand reunion and a glorious
coronation.

SEASONS OF SPIRITUAL POWER AT DOUGLAS.

I have seen many altar services at Douglas that were
most glorious, that would run on hour after hour, so
that it was almost impossible to close them.

> " Heaven came down our souls to greet,
> And glory crowned the mercy seat."

We had an ever memorable altar service at the stand
one night after Rev. G. Hughes had preached upon the
spirit of martyrdom for Christ. The Spirit came down
in such power that many fell before the Lord. Mrs.
Clarke, evangelist from New York, was overpowered,
and fell into the straw declaring she would be a martyr
for the Holy Ghost. Many were filled with the Spirit.
Others were transformed into the divine likeness.

Many a time Bros. Griffin and Thomas and others

would go into the woods and wait before God, hour after hour, in united earnest prayer, and simple, childlike faith. At other times Dea. Morse would have the burden of prayer upon him, and would take hold of God, by faith, till the heavens gave way. Then others would be moved in the same blessed way.

Some of these seasons of power were near the dining hall, when, as we left the hall, some one began to sing, and the people gathered round. The power of God would fall upon us. Some one would exhort and others would pray. Sometimes sinners would come forward for prayers, to find Christ. Sometimes a fully baptized man or woman would go on the hill near the hall and begin to preach. Sinners and saints would gather, and eternal good be done. The fire would spread from soul to soul, until many felt the power and the glory. Sometimes these seasons of power would be at the station, when the dear ones were going away, who were so full of faith and fire that they could not contain. The passengers on the train were amazed, and many passengers were convicted while these baptized ones were singing or telling their experience as the train moved on. Sometimes there were shouts of victory.

Douglas Camp Meeting is Undenominational.

Dea. Morse and his devoted mother and many more were Baptists, including Dr. Levy of Philadelphia; Bros. McDonald, Gill, and a host of others are Methodists; but they all feel perfectly at home at Douglas. Indeed, they are so baptized into one Spirit that you cannot tell one from the other. They all beautifully blend like the colors of the rainbow, and all shine in the white light of the Sun of Righteousness.

Many successful Christian workers have been raised up or helped at this camp meeting. Besides I. T. Johnson, of whom I have spoken, I may mention the two Davis boys from Oxford, who from a small beginning have made good ministers of the Lord Jesus. Also F. B. Thomas, who has become quite a successful evangelist, and who, by the aid of Dea. Morse and others, went with his family to New Zealand, and preached the glorious gospel in those ends of the earth. He and his family suffered much during the seventeen thousand mile voyage. But the Lord delivered them, and gave them the victory again and again, both on the land and on the sea. Bro. Thomas is still in the harvest field working with power.

The Influence of this Camp Meeting

Has already been felt in the ends of the earth, as we have already shown. It has also had a great influence upon the cities and towns of this vicinity. Hundreds have been converted, and I trust as many have been fully sanctified. "Holiness to the Lord" has been constantly on the banner and in the sermons and in the songs, until this whole region has felt the power. The people in this section are delighted to listen to the preaching of those excellent ministers that this camp meeting brings together. Miss Lizzie O. Smith of Willimantic, Conn., has been made a blessing to the camp, and the camp has been made a blessing to her. Her book has been read with interest and profit.

No Speculation at Douglas Camp Meeting.

As Dea. Morse has owned all the real estate and personal property of this camp meeting, there can be no speculation in corner lots. The people go to worship God, and build each other up in holiness. They make this their great business. The baggage is hauled to and from the station free of expense, and Dea. Morse has held himself responsible for the expenses of the camp, and has paid out hundreds of dollars, if not thousands, from his own pocket, for this purpose. No wonder that the blessing of God is on this whole institution!

Dea. Morse has charity for all. The Lord has taught him not to despise any man. He seems to know how to do with all classes, and knows how to utilize the peculiarities of the various workers so as to make the most of them all. Dea. Morse lay at the point of death some years ago at Pitman Grove, N.J., when Bros. Withey and Griffin came to my room, and we offered "the prayer of faith," and God raised him up. We felt that we could not give him up; that his work was not done. After he recovered he told me that his soul entered the spirit world. He passed into eternity's dawn, but God spared him to his large family, and to the church. Dea. Morse had charge of the Silver Lake Camp Meeting, Vt., this summer. By the manifestation of perfect love and Christian benevolence, he endeared himself to all. Many were in tears when he departed. He wept himself. Long may his life be spared!

DOCTRINES TAUGHT AT DOUGLAS CAMP MEETING.

The leaders of this meeting believe the teachings of the Bible, in relation to human depravity, that all men are born in sin, and shapen in iniquity. That "the heart is," by nature, "deceitful above all things, and desperately wicked"; and that after a man is truly regenerated by the Holy Ghost, still he has the remains of this depravity in him, and that it manifests itself in many ways, and tends to weaken his faith, damp the ardor of his love, becloud his spiritual vision, hinder his usefulness, and mar the peace of his soul. It manifests itself in pride; in self-will, often giving him a will contrary to the divine will, leading him to do something that is pleasing to nature that is not pleasing to God.

They have found, by experience, that these evils of the heart are not to be extracted by growth in grace. Yea, this depravity hinders the growth in grace. They teach, also, that soon after a man is truly converted, by proper instruction he may be led on to entire sanctification, or perfect love, and then go on his way rejoicing in perfect victory over the world, the flesh, and the devil; that amid all the trials of life he can walk and talk with God continually.

They teach that it is dangerous to live in any state below that of perfect love, for to refuse to be fully saved, when God commands it, is to forfeit even our assurance of our peace with God. They believe that all true Christians may have the blessed experience referred to by the poets : —

Speak the second time, " Be clean,"
    Take away my inbred sin;
Every stumbling-block remove,
    Cast it out by perfect love.

Break off the yoke of inbred sin,
    And fully set my spirit free;
I cannot rest till pure within, —
    Till I am wholly lost in Thee.

Therefore they think it best to have camp meetings and conventions at which this wonderful salvation shall be kept constantly before the minds of the people, and they be urged to press constantly after it. This is the very design of the Douglas Camp Meeting; and it is safe to say that this camp would never have existed if Dea. Morse had not obtained this experience in his own soul.

They believe, that after you are fully sanctified you can still go on to greater degrees of perfection; that in this world we may be " Changed . . . from glory to glory, even as by the Spirit of the Lord "; that while our feet touch the earth, our hearts may be in heaven and our treasures there also. In this way we may the better glorify God and benefit our fellow men.

They believe and teach that we may cease from groaning after this fulness and begin to glory in it, and continue in this glorying until God calls them to His everlasting kingdom. They contend for the glorious *liberty* expressed as follows : —

Oh, come and dwell in me,
    Spirit of power within,
And bring the glorious liberty
    From sorrow, fear, and sin!

The seed of sin's disease,
  Spirit of health, remove —
Spirit of finish'd holiness,
  Spirit of perfect love.

Hasten the joyful day
  Which shall my sins consume,
When old things shall be done away
  And all things new become.

I want the witness, Lord,
  That all I do is right,
According to Thy will and Word,
  Well pleasing in Thy sight.

I ask no higher state;
  Indulge me but in this,
And soon or later, then translate
  To Thy eternal bliss.

And again they sing, —

Breathe, oh, breathe Thy loving Spirit
  Into every troubled breast!
Let us all in Thee inherit,
  Let us find that second rest.

Take away our bent to sinning,
  Alpha and Omega be;
End of faith, as the beginning,
  Set our hearts at liberty.

They also cry out for the perfect *love* of God as expressed by the poet: —

The thing my God doth hate,
  That I no more may do;
Thy creature, Lord, again create,
  And all my soul renew:

My soul shall then, like Thine,
  Abhor the thing unclean,
And, sanctified by love divine,
  Forever cease from sin.

That blessed law of Thine,
   Jesus, to me impart;
The Spirit's law of life divine,
   Oh, write it on my heart!

Implant it deep within,
   Whence it may ne'er remove, —
The law of liberty from sin,
   The perfect law of love.

Thy nature be my law,
   Thy spotless sanctity;
And sweetly every moment draw
   My happy soul to Thee.

Soul of my soul, remain!
   Who didst for all fulfil,
In me, O Lord, fulfil again
   Thy Heavenly Father's will.

They are crying out to God for the *rest* which the
Bible teaches and the poet sets forth : —

Lord, I believe a rest remains
   To all Thy people known;
A rest where pure enjoyment reigns,
   And Thou art loved alone:

A rest where all our souls' desire
   Is fix'd on things above;
Where fear and sin and grief expire,
   Cast out by perfect love.

Oh that I now the rest might know,
   Believe, and enter in!
Now, Saviour, now the power bestow,
   And let me cease from sin.

Remove this hardness from my heart;
   This unbelief remove;
To me the rest of faith impart,—
   The Sabbath of Thy Love.

And when they have attained that perfect love and glorious liberty and heavenly rest, they go on singing, each one for themselves, —

> I have entered the valley of blessing so sweet,
>   And Jesus abides with me there;
> And His Spirit and blood make my cleansing complete,
>   And His perfect love casteth out fear.
>
> There is peace in the valley of blessing so sweet,
>   And plenty the land doth impart,
> And there is rest for the weary, worn travellers' feet,
>   And joy for the sorrowing heart.
>
> There is love in the valley of blessing so sweet,
>   Such as none but His bloodwashed may feel,
> When heaven comes down, redeemed spirits to greet,
>   And Christ sets His covenant seat.

Some people cannot understand how they can be fully saved in the midst of so much sin and temptation. The following statements of Bishop William Taylor will be a blessing to many.

BISHOP TAYLOR ON INSTINCTS AND PASSIONS.

" The simple instincts are not under the direct control of the will, and hence are not essentially changed by the work of the Holy Sanctifier in the heart. The appetites and passions growing out of those instincts do come within the power of the will, and hence must be controlled and kept in harmony with one conscientious standard of righteousness. When an appeal is made by Satan, or any other agency, to any instinct of my nature, the first conscious instinctive emotion is

EDGAR M. LEVY.

not a moral action, for it is outside the province of the will. The appeal is indeed made to the will, through the persuasive medium of the instinct; and now I must meet it promptly at the very threshold of the citadel of my moral nature, and inquire — First, Is it right? If I conscientiously settle the question in the affirmative, then I thank God for affording me this source and means of enjoyment. Second, How far is this right? — for lawful gratifications may be carried on to an unlawful extent and hence become sinful. I then fix the line, and say to appetite or passion, so far shalt thou go and no farther. A mistake in judgment need not affect the purity of the heart; but the purity of the heart, on the other hand, will not exempt us from the legitimate penalties of other laws, other than the moral law of my conscience, which may be broken through that mistake."

Others may be perplexed how they can maintain this exalted state if they should ever reach it. To such I recommend the following hymn of Capt. Kelso Carter.

> Standing on the promises of Christ, my King,
> Through eternal ages let His praises ring ;
> Glory in the highest, I will shout and sing,
> Standing on the promises of God.

> CHORUS : Standing, standing, standing on the
> promises of Christ, my Saviour;
> Standing, standing, I am standing on
> the promises of God.

> Standing on the promises I cannot fail
> When the howling storms of doubt and fear assail;
> By the living Word of God I shall prevail,
> Standing on the promises of God.

Standing on the promises I now can see
Perfect, present cleansing in the blood for me,
Standing in the liberty that Christ makes free,
    Standing on the promises of God.

Standing on the promises of Christ, my Lord,
Bound to Him eternally with love's strong cord,
Overcoming daily with the Spirit's sword,
    Standing on the promises of God.

Standing on the promises I cannot fall,
Listening every moment to the Spirit's call,
Resting in my Saviour as my all in all,
    Standing on the promises of God.

These people believe that the very God of peace can sanctify them wholly, and then preserve them, spirit, soul, and body, blameless unto the coming of our Lord Jesus Christ. (1 Thess. 5: 23, 24.) They believe that we can walk with God, like Enoch, and have the testimony that we please Him, and be ready to be translated any day when the Lord shall call. They believe that they may be filled with all the fulness of God. (Eph. 3: 16–19.)

HOLINESS CONVENTIONS AT PUTNAM.

The interest in the Douglas Camp Meeting and the great theme of holiness has led Dea. Morse to hold holiness conventions at Putnam. They continue about four days, and are held in the hall fitted up by the deacon, or in the church. These conventions have a salutary influence over the community, and bring together many of the saints of the Most High.

Rev. J. J. Woodbury and family, of the New England Conference, have always had a tent at this camp meeting, and have always had a lively interest in the well being of the camp and people. He died suddenly at Turner's Fall, Mass., April 21, 1885. "He walked with God, and was not, for God took him" to rest in his Father's house. The widow and daughter still remain. His daughter, Mary, is a successful evangelist and a powerful woman in prayer and exhortation.

The missionary fire of this camp meeting sent Miss Rose Williams into Bishop Taylor's work in South America for several years. She returned in broken health, but is recovering. She is a fine singer and a good worker for Christ.

Dea. Levi Stoddard, an excellent Christian man, was a member of the committee of arrangements for many years. He died in peace, in Douglas, in the summer of 1888. I shall never forget that Dr. Levy asked the privilege of holding a five o'clock P. M. meeting to be comprised of Baptists and Congregationalists exclusively. The meeting was appointed, not to draw any invidious distinctions, nor to mar the beautiful harmony of Christians of all evangelical churches, but simply to ascertain to what extent the doctrine and experience of holiness had spread among these two leading denominations in New England. I am glad to record that the large tabernacle was crowded at the appointed hour, and about three hundred rose to testify to this blessed experience, and many gave utterance to the fulness of their joy.

The meeting made a profound impression, and was characterized by great tenderness, and showed to all how "holiness to the Lord" was spreading in all the churches, and this glorious camp meeting was helping on this blessed work.

Dr. Mary R. Myers, a graduate of the Boston University, was present at a number of these camp meetings, and caught the missionary spirit that she afterward manifested so gloriously in going out to Africa with the first company that sailed under the direction of Bishop Taylor. She was married on the coast of Africa to C. L. Davenport, one of the missionaries, by Bishop Taylor, and was stationed a number of years at Dondo, two hundred and forty miles up the Coanza River, and did excellent service both as a medical doctor and faithful missionary. She was beloved of all. She died in holy triumph at Dondo, in the midst of her extensive usefulness. Her grave, in that lovely valley of the Coanza River, is a monument of the love of Jesus in a human heart.

J. G. Covley of Norwich has attended many of these camp meetings. He was editor of a newspaper for many years, and experienced entire sanctification at his home eight years ago. He had the assurance in him that he should never lose this great blessing, for God loved him with an everlasting love.

Mrs. Celia Smith of Providence, R.I., came to this camp in 1883, with Gilbert Irons and wife, and John Lamond and wife. They were so filled with the Spirit that they determined to have a small Douglas Camp Meeting in Providence. They held meetings from house to house, until the meetings were settled at the home of Sister Smith, at 58 Wilson Street, where they have been held weekly ever since, and have been a fountain of blessedness all the time.

Mrs. H. H. Bennett of Warren, Mass., came to this

camp in 1886. She was so wonderfully emptied of self and so gloriously filled with God that heaven came down to earth. The glory of God has filled her soul ever since, even under severe trials.

I am very happy to record the many pleasant times that we have had with J. H. Atwater and his amiable wife, from Providence, R.I. They are choice spirits, filled with perfect love. They belong to the people called Friends. They are friends, indeed, of all that love our Lord Jesus Christ. They are always welcome, and their testimony is well received because they are true to God all the year round.

Thomas Lankton of Hartford delighted to be at this camp, and though he was lame and aged, his heart was young. His little book has been made a blessing. He enjoyed entire sanctification.

CHAPTER IV.

"Thy power I pant to prove,
   Rooted and fix'd in love;
Strengthen'd by Thy Spirit's might,
   Wise to fathom things divine,
What the length and breadth and height,
   What the depth of love like Thine."

Douglas Camp Meeting, 1884.

This meeting opened July 29. The tide of salvation was high at the start, for so many were blessed the year before that the largest company was present on the first evening. Rev. William McDonald read the thirty-fifth chapter of Isaiah, and made a few opening remarks, then called upon Bro. Gorham to lead in prayer. He prayed like a man full of the Holy Ghost, as he often did, and the power of God came upon the people. Other earnest prayers were offered, and testimonies were given. There was so much of the presence of God manifested that some said, "This camp meeting begins where some camp meetings close." The grounds were in excellent order for the crowd that thronged the place. This was, indeed, the largest camp meeting ever held on this ground.

There was a large company of ministers present, and they all entered heartily into the work. Dr. Watson preached the first sermon with his usual power and spirituality. Rev. E. I. D. Pepper editor of *The Christian Standard*, preached in the afternoon. Many were blessed under the word. He is one of the sweetest spirited men in the holiness ranks, yet he can utter the plainest truths without fear. Rev. J. A. Wood preached in the evening, and God was with him.

Bros. Short, Simmons, and Griffin preached the next day, and Dr. Levy, Bishop Mallalieu, and Bro. Gorham preached the next day, which was Friday. Dr. Herr Baptist of Norwich, Conn., and Dr. Watson and George Hughes preached on Saturday.

The love feast on Sunday was led by Rev. N. P. Alderman, and was of the glorious kind. One hundred and ten spoke in forty-five minutes, and were followed by a powerful sermon by William McDonald. Dr. Watson and Bishop Taylor also preached the same day.

The social meetings were led by Bros. Leonard, Coon, Davies, Bray, Ballentine, Sprague, Joy, J. H. Mansfield, Alderman, Withey and Johnson. Bro. Gorham led the eight o'clock meeting on Wednesday and read Isa. 40, and brought out the fact that "love is the essence of all religion, and is the mightiest influence in the universe." He said, "We want the fire of God all through us; if you get in the habit of going back and forth, it will take seven archangels to hold you up. I am justified, sanctified, and satisfied." Rev. F. B. Joy, a Baptist, was present, and was made a blessing to many. Bro. Short said in the eight o'clock meeting, "I died hard. Let people get down and stay there till they die, and they will get the baptism of the

Holy Ghost." Dea. Morse said he was "saved tremendously."

Dr. Levy preached from 1 Thess. 5: 23, and said : "Justification by faith was rescued by Luther from the rubbish of Romanism. We now want to rescue sanctification by faith from the neglect of the present age. Not by works but by faith ; the cleansing stream is at our feet. It takes but a little time to plunge in and be cleansed."

Bishop Taylor preached from 1 John 4: 16, 17. He said, "I dwell in the air, and the air dwells in me. When sin is in man, the Spirit is left out; but let sin out, and you do not have to ask the Spirit to come in, any more than you do the air when you raise the window. When you entered the kingdom of God you had to submit, and you can stay in the kingdom only on the same terms. I came to God as a felon, legally dead; but now I have rights and have something to bring. The eleventh commandment is love. I am to present my body as a living sacrifice, exercising perfect submission and perfect faith."

Bishop Taylor gave an account of his self-supporting missions on Monday, and a collection of $216 was taken besides the $500 given by Dea. Morse. The crowd was so great that about sixty had to go to East Douglas to stay on Saturday and Sunday nights. The feast was so exceedingly rich that the people could not stay away.

Rev. J. A. Wood, in his sermon on Heb. 4: 3, said : "We have rest through faith; the streets of heaven begin below. Christ brings peace by saving us from sin, which is the only disturbing element in the universe ; conversion is the greatest work God ever does for the soul. This perfect soul rest is not exemption from physical or mental suffering. Entire sanctification takes the carnal bent out of the will."

Rev. J. Gill preached from 1 Cor. 7: 6, and said, "Moral impurity consists in outward transgression and inward depravity. The gospel provides a remedy for both. The atonement furnishes the ground, and the Holy Spirit the agent. The processes are: first, the washing of regeneration; second, sanctification. By these processes a man morally impure becomes morally pure, and adjusted to God's law."

At 1.30 P.M., Bro. Johnson gave a Bible reading on the Holy Ghost. At 6.30 P.M. Miss Elizabeth Sisson spoke of her mission work in India.

At 1.30 P.M., on Wednesday, Bro. Devinaw, a converted Catholic, gave an address which included an account of his work among the Catholics in Illinois. He is now pastor of the First French M. E. Church in America.

The closing sermon of this marvellous meeting was by Bro. Wood, from Col. 3: 5–8. To obtain sanctification, and the witness of it, is not a hard thing but an easy thing, when we ask it with all the heart.

Dea. Morse followed with a rousing testimony of his experience, which produced a profound impression. Bros. Johnson, Hatch, and Gorham also spoke. These testimonies were followed by a blessed season of prayer; and thus ended the largest, and many think the best, meeting up to that time on this ground.

CAMP MEETING OF 1885.

This meeting commenced July 30. The first meeting was for consecration, and was led by W. McDonald. Rev. J. A. Wood preached the first sermon from Matt. 5: 1–12. The same heavenly power was present, for the people had not forgotten the blessed meeting of last year. Rev. B. W. Gorham preached in the afternoon from Matt. 6: 22, 23. Capt. R. Kelso Carter preached from Gen. 9: 25. The love feast was led by Rev. W. McBray, and was of the same usual heavenly order. The love feast was followed by a sermon by President McDonald, from Heb. 6: 1–3. Bro. Short preached in the afternoon, and Bro. Gorham in the evening. Rev. F. B. Dickinson, late of Norwich, Conn., then of Somerville, Mass., had entered into the experience of entire sanctification, and preached a blessed sermon from Num. 9: 16. This glorious, young, and most promising minister of the Baptist Church, was like a flaming meteor, and illumined the moral heavens where he shone. But alas! like a meteor he vanished away, after a short sickness at Somerville. There was a large crowd and much sorrow at his funeral. Rev. John Parker preached from 1 Pet. 1: 15 and Heb. 12: 14. Rev. D. O. Fox, returned missionary from India, was present, and preached from Matt. 5: 48.

It is wonderful how much is crowded into a single day at this camp. Beside the early morning meeting, which is well attended, there is a very large meeting at 8.30, running straight into the 10 o'clock preaching service, followed by an altar service, and closing just in time enough for dinner. Then at 1.30 comes the mothers' meeting and the children's meeting and a public service at the stand. Another sermon at 3, and a service of song and testimony at 6.30, and a sermon, followed by an altar service, at 7.30. And this tremendous high pressure is kept up for ten days, till heaven, earth, and hell are moved. Bishop Taylor's missions were remembered in a public meeting, led by the president, and $1,251 was raised for these missions. Rev. A. McLean preached a very profitable sermon. He is always a welcome worker. The closing services were of thrilling interest.

CAMP MEETING OF 1886.

This camp meeting opened Tuesday, July 27. The first service was led by President McDonald. Rev. A. Hartt, evangelist, led the singing, as he has done for a number of years. Rev. F. B. Joy offered the opening prayer. The leader read a portion of the third chapter of Hebrews, and said : " Israel was guilty of many and great sins, but her greatest sin was that of unbelief. The great sin of the present age is unbelief. It is the sin of sins. The great sin of the Church is unbelief. This is worse than worldliness or any other sin. Mlutitudes of church members declare they do not believe that God can do what He has promised in His Word. They cannot enter in because of unbelief. Let this be a *faith* meeting. Put away unbelief. I fear there is a latent unbelief lingering about even some holiness people. Are we ready to throw ourselves overboard? The power of God does not come except by believing God. Put away unbelief. By simple faith we conquer. Who is willing to part company with unbelief forever?"

More than one hundred came forward to be filled with faith and with the Holy Ghost. After a season of silent prayer, Bros. Short and Davies led in vocal prayer. The testimonies that followed showed that God had answered prayer. So this heavenly meeting began where it left off last year. Indeed, there is a kind of family feeling in this camp, so that all the meetings have the family resemblance. Most of the speakers reported the past year as the best of their lives.

The ministers and people were all ready for their full share of the work, and of the blessings of the camp, and faith was in lively exercise. Dr. A. Lowrey of " The Divine Life," preached the first sermon. He is stout and ruddy, with gray hair, and venerable in appearance. He offered prayer, and read the thirty-fifth chapter of Isaiah and preached from the eighth verse. His introduction was a beautiful description of the grandeur of the Holy Land. Free salvation and full salvation were the topics of his discourse. His discussion was clear, convincing, and spiritual. He would not use the word "holiness" as an adjective, by saying "holiness camp meetings" or "holiness literature"; he would not say "holiness gospel"; but " God's thundering legion for the spread of holiness." He concluded with three deductions : —

1. Nothing is legitimate in church, Sunday school, or religious machinery, that does not involve holiness.

2. Holiness is the very heart of Christianity itself.
3. Holiness is the great necessity of the Church.
It was a blessed and memorable service.

H. L. Hastings of Boston was on his way home, and stayed long enough to take charge of the 1.30 meeting at the stand, and gave a very impressive talk, full of points. He concluded that the eighth chapter of Romans is better to live in than the seventh.

Bro. Short stirred the people greatly by his afternoon sermon, on 1 John 3 : 22 : " And whatsoever we ask, we receive of him," etc.

President McDonald, in the evening service answered this question : " How may we know the leadings of the Holy Spirit from the other leadings and impressions ? "

Answer. " The Holy Spirit always leads us on the line of the Word of God. Impressions may or may not lead in that way, but the Holy Spirit always leads that way. 1. The Spirit witnesses with our spirits that we are the children of God. 2. He leads us into all truth. 3. He brought to the disciples remembrance whatsoever Christ had said.

" Some think they may be so led by the Spirit as not to need the Bible any more. They forget that the Bible is the work of the Holy Ghost. The great work that the Holy Spirit does outside of His subjective work in the heart, is to open our eyes to understand the Scriptures."

Rev. G. N. Ballentine preached in the evening from Mal. 3 : 10 : " Prove me now herewith." " God has done His best to save every soul, and now He challenges us to prove Him. Heaven's windows are

large, and He has promised to open them wide if we
will bring all the tithes into the store house. Bring
in all, adjust yourselves to God perfectly, and stay
there forever. Then comes the fulness of the blessing."

Rev. J. A. Wood preached on Thursday, from Acts
5 : 1. The subject was, "The Baptism of the Holy
Ghost."

"1. What is it? " This baptism is the free communication of the divine personality of God. The Holy
Ghost is a person. And this baptism is as available
now as in the days before the pentecost.

"2. Notice the *results* of this baptism. It is the
communication of the fulness of God to the soul — a
fulness of peace, joy, and power. It is the dynamite
within us that removes all sin, and brings in all purity,
all meekness, all humility, all patience. It takes us
with all our idiosyncracies, and fits the soul for God's
use." This was an excellent sermon and produced a
lasting effect. Many came to the altar seeking this
fulness.

Thus this camp meeting went on from day to day,
increasing in the divine power, and leading hundreds
into the fountain of cleansing. I have not space
to quote other sermons, but they were all on the same
line of entire sanctification for all believers. Many
sinners and backsliders were led to Christ. Dea.
Morse had charge of the last service, and one man was
converted. Thus the saints of God were ready to go
forth in Christ's name to do His will.

Mr. Thomas Kennedy from Ware, Mass., and his
family, have been regular attendants upon this camp,

and have been greatly blessed. They were formerly from England. They are a happy, devoted family.

George E. Tilley, Jamaica, N.Y., came to this camp meeting affected with malaria, almost sick enough to be at home. As he stood upon the bridge not far from the dining hall, looking up the stream, and snuffing the balmy air, he said to himself, "This must be paradise, and this the river of the water of life." While standing there, his sickness left him. He was so baptized with the Holy Ghost that he went home and began to lead souls to Christ, and has helped to establish a Methodist Church at Floral Park, and another at Morris Park, and has become a local preacher, and has led many souls to Christ.

CHAPTER V.

"Ah! give me this to know,
    With all Thy saints below;
Swells my soul to compass Thee,
    Pants in Thee to live and move;
Fill'd with all the Deity,
    All immersed and lost in love. "

THE CAMP MEETING OF 1887.

THIS heavenly meeting began Thursday, July 28. Dea. Morse looked young and fresh. Bros. Johnson, Bowen, and Stone were at their posts of honor and service. There was a large body of ministers present at the beginning. An impromptu meeting was held in the tabernacle in the afternoon. The camp fires were already kindled, and one man was sanctified.

Dr. E. M. Levy and Rev. Joshua Gill had charge of this camp meeting, and were greatly aided in their work by the Holy Spirit. Dr. Reddy preached in the evening from Acts 19: 2: " Have ye received the Holy Ghost since ye believed?" This was his first sermon at Douglas. He was well received, and made a deep impression. He said: " The Lord's taking possession of the tabernacle and of the temple were symbols of His taking possession of His spiritual Church at the pentecost. The pentecostal baptism

Sincerely yours

B. Weed Gorham

is a sample of the bestowment of this gift upon the
Church. This gift comes after conversion, and con-
sumes inbred sin and fills the heart with perfect
love."

B. W. Gorham astonished the people by the fire and
fervor that he put into the meeting at half-past eight.

On Friday Bro. Ballentine preached at half-past ten,
from, " The Word of God is not Bound." He showed
us the what, when, and how of entire sanctification in
a faithful manner.

Bro. Hughes gave us one of his glorious sermons
on the "Transfiguration of Christ," which suggests:
1. Immaculate purity; 2. Transcendent love; 3. Super-
lative light. It was as Christ prayed that the fashion
of His countenance was changed. So it may be with
us. The transforming power rested upon a number
in the altar service.

Rev. William McDonald preached the next day
half-past ten; text, Heb. 4: 1, 11. He told us of
the rest, and how to obtain it; Canaan could not be
the type of heaven —

(1) Because there were many enemies there. Not so
in heaven.

(2) Besides, heaven is in the distance, but we that
believe do now enter into this blessed rest. We may
rest from internal discordance and from undue anxiety or anxious solicitude.

There is no future to a child of God, to one fully
saved from sin. The future is now; moment by
moment. The best time to enter this rest is immediately after conversion.

Rev. L. B. Wilson, M.D., of Baltimore, preached at half-past two, from Ps. 40 : 8 : "I delight to do thy will, O my God." "Many think that the oft-repeated idea of this psalm refers particularly to Christ. I think it applies much better to human nature. Some people delight to do some of the will of God. We must accept God's will as an entirety, yea; we must 'delight' to do that will, and shall, when our hearts are right. The position of the Psalmist is possible to us all."

In the evening L. T. Brown preached from Rev. 3 : 20, claiming that this text was spoken to Christians. "Christ desires to come into the soul, to root up and cleanse out sin from every part. He knocks by His Word and by His providences.

Dea. Morse led the love feast on the Sabbath. Nearly two hundred testified for Christ as an uttermost Saviour, after which Dr. Levy preached from Lev. 10 : 1–3. "The history of the Israelites teaches how God's greatest gifts may be man's greatest injury. The holy fire on God's altar is often used as a type of the Holy Spirit. There is often a lack of this holy fire in the pulpit, as well as in the pew. Strange fire is offered in preaching, prayer, and in giving praise." It was a blessed sermon A shower came up in the afternoon, but the tabernacle would not hold the people. So when the shower ceased a second meeting was organized at the stand, and for nearly two hours the word of God was proclaimed by Bros. Sprague, Gill, Morse, and Perry, Mrs. Earle and Mrs. Carter. At the same time Dr. D. Clark was preaching in the

Tabernacle. After supper, another impromptu meeting was held near the dining hall; Bros. Gorham, Levy, Davies, Thomas, and others took a part. It was a holy hour, an overflow meeting, full of glory. Rev. J. H. Irvine of East Maine preached, at half-past seven, a most heart-searching sermon, from Gen. 2: 17. "The law of the Bible is, 'Sin not.' We must quit once and forever, or God will not accept us." There was great power in the altar service.

Dr. Dougan Clark preached on Monday, at ten o'clock, upon "Faith," from Heb. 11: 1. "The temple of Christian experience was built upon four pillars. The first two are justification and regeneration. These two are co-instantaneous. The second two are entire sanctification and the baptism of the Holy Ghost. The baptism of the Holy Ghost bears the same relation to entire sanctification that regeneration does to justification."

At half-past two, Rev. G. Hughes preached on being "Filled with all theFulness of God." The fulness of God is the conscious indwelling of the Holy Ghost. The Word was in power.

In the evening, Bro. Gorham gave us one of his marvellous sermons from 2 Cor. 3: 18: "But we all, with open face beholding as in a glass the glory of the Lord, are changed into the same image." The whole service was blessed.

The next morning Dr. Daniel Steele preached ; text, Rom. 14: 17: "The kingdom of God is not meat and drink; but righteousness, and peace, and joy in the Holy Ghost." We have no space to report this admirable sermon. He dwelt mostly upon "righteousness, and peace, and joy in the Holy Ghost."

In the afternoon Rev. John Parker preached on "Heaven," with its many mansions, robes and palms, saints and angels, and the triune God. It was a great blessing to many.

In the evening we had another eloquent sermon from G. A. McLaughlin; text, "Purify your hearts, ye double minded." It produced great searching of heart in many. His preaching is clear and incisive.

Rev. W. H. Daniels preached the next morning, on "Jesus the King." There was a royalty in Christ's nature, and also in His claims. It was a sermon of rare interest and power.

Mrs. Levy conducted the children's meetings, and Mrs. Carter the mothers' meetings, each day, after dinner, and great good was done in each meeting.

Rev. C. J. Fowler preached at half-past two ; text, 1 John 3: 3: "Every man that hath this hope in him purifieth himself, even as he is pure."

1.   The Christian hope is real Christian experience.

2.   This hope is an inspiration to Christian purity.

3.   The degree of Christian purity is that of un-mixedness.

4.   This purity is as universal as the Christian's hope.

Many were blessed by the preaching and in the altar service.

Rev. G. H. Butler preached in the evening a good, clear, definite sermon, from Eph. 5: 25-27. God blessed him and us.

Rev. B. W. Gorham preached the next morning from Rom. 1: 16. We have all kinds of power in the natural world, but the gospel is the power of God unto salvation.

Rev. J. Parker preached in the afternoon, from Job 35: 3, 4. The sermon showed the plan of salvation, in regeneration, adoption, and entire sanctification. He especially set forth the instantaneous and blessed character of "the second blessing."

Bro. Ballentine preached in the evening from, " Let your light so shine." It was a searching sermon. Many came to the altar at the close. It was hard to close the service at ten o'clock.

Bro. Daniels preached the next morning on " The Atonement." Christ is for us, and Christ may be in us. He suffered death for the sinful race. He gives life to the believing penitent.

In the afternoon Bro. McLaughlin gave a description of the two experiences of Jacob. There are two separate experiences for us. It was clear and convincing.

Bro. Fowler, in the afternoon, showed us how Cornelius was saved. He had initial salvation before Peter preached in his house; then he received the Holy Ghost for heart purity. He exhorted ministers and others to put holiness on the main track in their churches. Many pledged to do so.

The early meetings of Saturday were led by Bros. Wood and Joy. Rev. H. N. Brown was the morning preacher; subject, " Growth in Grace." It was a very clear and profitable sermon.

Rev. D. P. Updegraff of Ohio preached in the after-noon. His subject was Isaac and Ishmael. Hagar and Ishmael represented a state of bondage, or legality; regeneration is represented by Isaac and Ishmael in the house together; entire sanctification, by Ishmael cast out.

Bro. Gill preached in the evening with great power. The altar was crowded at the close, and one young man brought up five dollars for Taylor's missions. Men, women, and children were at the altar for conver-sion or entire sanctification. It was a heavenly time.

Rev. A. Hartt led the Sabbath love feast. There were two hundred and forty testimonies, full of light and truth. A great feast of love.

Bro. Updegraff followed with a sermon upon the difference between "the law of sin and death" and "the law of the Spirit of life in Christ Jesus." He is one of the most spiritually minded and sweet-spirited men, and a great favorite with the people. He is full of the gospel of Christ.

Bro. Johnson led a most glorious meeting at half-past one. Many were under conviction and some came and sought Christ.

H. N. Brown followed, with a blessed sermon upon Christ's model Church; text, Cant. 6: 10. The Lord was in the word, and a good altar service followed.

The closing sermon of the camp was in the evening. Short speeches were made by Bros. Joy, Levy, Gill, Gorham, Morse, and Updegraff. It was a very precious and tender hour. Many parted to meet no more. There was a blessed harmony during the whole camp

meeting.   Many were converted or reclaimed or fully
sanctified.   God was glorified, and this old glorious
camp kept up its record as one of the best, if not the
best, camp meeting in all New England.

I ought to have noticed that James H. Earle, editor
of *The Contributor*, of Boston, led a very profitable service on Tuesday morning.   He is a very acceptable and
efficient worker.   On Sunday morning, Dr. Levy baptized the two daughters of J. H. Earle, and also the
two daughters of Mrs. Carter, and John Lanman and
others, in the stream that runs through the camp ground.
It was a lovely service and the sun shone in great
splendor upon the scene.

The Camp Meeting of 1888.

This far-famed meeting opened July 27.   Dea.
Morse, Bros. Bowen, Johnson, and Stone were all at
their posts.   It seemed almost as though the meeting
had been running all the year.   The following ministers were present: McDonald, Levy, Short, Davies,
Gorham, Eastman, Atwater, Crowell, Thomas, Perry,
and Ray.

The first meeting was led by the president, who read
the sixth chapter of Deuteronomy about perfect love,
which was to be made prominent among the Israelites.
So it should be with us.   There was a large attendance
and faith was in lively exercise.

Bro. Thomas led the half-past eight meeting on the
first day.   He dwelt upon his favorite topic, " Meekness,
Gentleness, and Tender Love."   Bro. Short preached the
first sermon, on Jas. 4: 17: " To him that knoweth

to do good, and doeth it not, to him it is sin." Man is a moral being, but cannot do God's will in his natural state. He must be changed by the power of God. For this God has made ample provision in the gospel. The condemnation is because men will not come to Christ for this free and full salvation. Light is come, but men love "darkness rather than light, because their deeds are evil."

Rev. J. M. Hervey of California preached at half-past two, from Heb. 8 : 5. God has given in His Word explicit directions how men are to live that they may obtain eternal life. All they have to do is to follow the plan which God has presented. Rev. J. Gill preached in the evening from 2 Pet. 3 : 18. Several found salvation at the close.

Sunday, E. Davies led the early meeting. Rev. C. L. Eastman led the love feast, which was indeed a feast of love. The testimonies showed that the people had come here to enjoy salvation and to scatter the holy fire.

W. McDonald preached at ten, from Rom. 4: 3: "Abraham believed God." The life of Abraham was a grand illustration of a life of faith. We should all clearly distinguish between " the *gift* of faith," and " the *grace* of faith." All Christians have the grace of faith, but few have the gift of faith. The first is for salvation, the second for extraordinary occasions. The mighty power of faith was then enforced and illustrated. Many were blessed by the sermon.

Rev. John Parker preached to a great crowd at half-past two, from 2 Thess. 2 : 13 and Rom. 6 : 13. Sal-

vation was defined and explained and the processes
stated; and how to obtain it was illustrated. There
was power in the word, and a glorious altar service
followed.

Dr. Levy preached in the evening from Heb. 7 : 25.
The uttermost salvation was set forth in a most attractive manner. Immediate results followed in the altar
service.

On Monday Bishop Taylor preached his remarkable
sermon on the salvation of the heathen; text, Rom. 2 :
12–16. This is the clearest and by far the best statement of the condition of the heathen and their relation
to the gospel, that I ever heard. The heathen like the
rest of the world, will be judged according to the light
they have or might have. All the ways of God are
equal, and all will be left without excuse " in the
day when God shall judge the secrets of men by Jesus
Christ." Dr. Levy cried like a child during this great
sermon. It ought to be spread through all the world.

On Monday afternoon the bishop gave another of his
masterly addresses which show so clearly the majesty
of his simple mind. The people were so stirred that
they gave him at the close about twelve hundred dollars for his mission work. Dr. Daniel Steele delivered
one of his instructive and profitable sermons, describing
the new order of the Sons of God. Dr. Levy preached
three sermons of spiritual worth. One of them was on
Sundaymorning, upon " Keep yourselves in the love of
God."

Bro. McLaughlin preached two excellent sermons, one
from " Whosoever is born of God doth not commit

sin," the other from "But the path of the just is as the shining light."

John Parker preached twice in his peculiar and winning way. H. N. Brown preached from "Contending for the Faith." Bro. F. B. Joy from, "Not by might, nor by power, but by my spirit, saith the Lord." This was a heavenly sermon. The Spirit filled him and applied the word to the people. This was his last sermon at this camp, and was well worthy the man and the occasion. Before the next camp his soul was with God, and his precious wife was a lonely widow, for their hearts were made truly one both by nature and grace. He was well beloved. B. W. Gorham also was on the camp ground for the last time, and was quite feeble, but still full of divine energy. I remember he had charge of the first afternoon meeting before the opening service. I began to sing that glorious hymn, "In the secret of His presence." While we were singing the fire of God fell upon us, till before we got through there was a heavenly conflagration. He was a blessed, holy man, never to be forgotten. His last sermon was on "Blessed are they that do hunger and thirst after righteousness for they shall be filled." His devoted wife was a constant benediction, always ready to wait upon him and to watch with him. He died saying, "Precious Jesus, I am thine! Hallelujah!" at Sea Clift, N.Y., spring, 1889. His last sermon was printed in the *Christian Witness*.

Rev. H. C. McBride and wife aided the camp by their heavenly songs, and by his blessed sermon about "having religion in the heart, and having the heart in

religion"; text, Gen. 26. It was a blessed sermon.
Rev. G. Hughes preached from " The prince of this
world cometh, and hath nothing in me." Though not
well in body, yet the Lord helped him mightily. It
was a glorious camp meeting all the way through.
The leaders of the social meetings did good service, and
all helped; God was glorified, and the people justified
or fully sanctified, or both.

I have only recorded the sermons, but there were
many excellent exhortations and testimonies that
were just as good as the sermons; but we have no
room for them. Indeed, this was a heavenly feast from
six A.M. to ten P.M., when silence was insisted upon
that we might be rested for the next day.

> "How blest the righteous when he dies;
>   When sinks the weary soul to rest!
> How mildly beams the closing eyes;
>   How gently heaves the expiring breast!
>
> " A holy quiet reigns around, —
>   A calm which life nor death destroys;
> And naught disturbs that peace profound,
>   Which his unfettered soul enjoys."

I have just had an interview with Mrs. F. B. Joy,
and learn that her husband died in holy triumph, at
Watertown, Mass., April 6, 1889. Before he died he
had a radiant smile of holy joy on his countenance.
He exclaimed, " Oh the heavenly glory ! Oh the beautiful world ! O Jesus, precious Jesus, so sweet !" To his
granddaughter he said, " Meet me in heaven." To his
wife he said, "Sweet woman, you have been a help-
meet many years, you will go with me to the brink of

the river, won't you?" His last words were "Though he slay me yet will I trust in him."

The glory of God that covered his heavenly face still lingered after his spirit had fled; the undertaker marveled; he had never seen such a face before.

CHAPTER VI.

" The word of God is sure,
And never can remove ;
We shall in heart be pure,
And perfected in love :
Rejoice in hope, rejoice with me ;
We shall from all our sins be free."

DOUGLAS CAMP MEETING.

THIS memorable meeting began July 26. President
McDonald spoke the first evening from Isa. 62. The
same heavenly power was present as last year. Rev.
J. Gill preached the first sermon, text, John 1: 29.
Rev. Mr. Freeman preached in the afternoon from Eph.
5: 25-27; and H. N. Brown preached in the evening
from Matt. 5: 28.

Dea. Morse led the love feast on Sunday. Such was
the power already manifested that ninety-two testified
for Christ. The president preached at half-past ten,
from 1 John 1: 7. Rev. J. A. Wood preached at half-
past two from Matt. 5: 8. Rev. Ross Taylor, son of
Bishop Taylor, preached in the evening, text, 2 Chron.
16: 9. It was a sermon of rare merit, showing that
much of the spirit of the father rested upon the son.
The writer preached the next sermon from Ps. 51:
10. Rev. J. A. Wood was the next to preach;

[59]

text, Heb. 2 : 3. Rev. Ross Taylor led the half past six meeting for testimony and praise.

A number had been converted during the day including a poor drunkard. Bro. Ballentine preached in the evening, text, Rom. 6 : 13, " Yield yourselves unto God, as those that are alive from the dead." This is all we can do, there lies our responsibility. There is no more important word in the Bible than " Yield," " Yield yourselves" " As alive from the dead." As we yield ourselves to him, he delivers us from all sin. Then our members become instruments of righteousness to God. The sermon was closed by a storm that continued all night. This was a very rainy camp meeting, but the holy fire burnt right on through the whole.

Bishop Taylor's son spoke upon the African Missions the next morning and took subscriptions for the *African News.*

Dr. Reddy preached at half past ten, text, Acts. 15 : 8, 9. The gift of the Holy Ghost is a superadded gift to what we received at regeneration. This was so at the Pentecost and also in the text. The Holy Spirit is with all justified Christians. He *dwells* in all that are fully sanctified. The reception of the Holy Ghost brings purity of heart. After regeneration there is an inherited taint in our nature called " Original sin." We need a thorough cleansing.

The seat of sin is not in the body, it is in the carnal mind. The old man must be crucified. The two nature theory is not taught in the Bible. It was a precious sermon. Rev. John Parker followed with one of his heavenly songs; a good altar service followed.

Dea. Loring of Putnam, Conn., led the half-past one meeting, and God was in the midst. A powerful rain fell outside, but salvation was within. Rev. H. N. Brown preached after the storm, upon Christian perfection. It is just as much the command of God to be filled with the Holy Ghost as to be free from stealing. John Parker followed with a song and a testimony telling of the meeting which he and Bro. Hughes held on the steamer the night before, when coming from New York. How they witnessed for Christ before one hundred and fifty passengers. Rev. G. Hughes preached in the evening; text, Acts. 10: 44. The New Testament endowment is not an influence, but the personal Holy Ghost bringing in all His gifts and powers. At the Pentecost the Holy Ghost fell upon them; it purified them; it was a fiery baptism. It burned up sin and filled the soul with God.

The fulness of the Holy Ghost makes a mighty stir in the soul and leads us on to conquer the world.

Rev. C. J. Fowler preached the next morning. Text, 1 John 3: 9. Faith is agreement. Faith in God is agreement with God. Faith is commitment. He that believes commits his way unto God, and waits for the divine direction. This text will test your faith. It will divide almost every congregation. It does not say he that commits sin was never born of God, for spiritual declension is possible; neither does it say, "He that is born of God has no sin," for carnality remains in the hearts of some believers. The text does say, "He that is born of God doth not commit sin." The new birth antagonizes sin. They are partakers of the

Divine nature, and that nature is utterly opposed to sin.
Even the seeking sinner turns instinctively from sin.
He that is born of God is not committing sin (a contin-
uous present). "His seed remaineth in him," and while
that seed remaineth in him, he cannot sin. It is not a
volitional "cannot" but a moral "cannot." He cannot sin without sacrificing his sonship. This is the
lowest state of grace. An act of sin has the same
reflective influence on the soul as a life of sin.
"There is no condemnation to them that are in Christ
Jesus."

This is not the ethics of holiness, but the ethics of
the new birth.

Holiness is far beyond the mere non-committal of
sin. It implies that the old man has been crucified,
and the body of sin destroyed, that henceforth, we
should not commit or serve sin, Rom. 6: 6. It was a
heart-searching sermon.

Dr. Reddy preached at half past two. Text. 1 Thess.
3 : 12, 13. The central thought in the Christian system
is holiness. Christ gave himself for us, to redeem us
from all iniquity, that we may be holy and without blem-
ish, also without spot, or wrinkle, or any such thing.

All Christians are partially holy. Some are perfectly
holy. We are to become "established in unblamable
holiness." There is a mighty growth in holiness after
you are fully sanctified; steady advancement, abound-
ing love. And with this the testing will come. Dr.
Reddy is among the best expounders of Bible Holiness.
His closing appeal was powerful indeed.

Rev. E. O. Mallory, of Lowell, preached at half past

seven. Text. Dan. 11 : 32. "The people that know their God shall be strong to do exploits." This being true, then, how can we know God?

1. By believing His promises ; putting them to the test.

2. By trusting God.

3. By perfect obedience to God.

4. By perfect consecration to God.

All who do so know God, are strengthened to do exploits: to do mighty things in the name of God. Jehoshaphat overcame his mighty foes by just singing, "The beauty of holiness." There are many exploit Christians in the world. Come, let us submit ourselves wholly to God and take a full breath of the Holy Ghost. This was a very welcome and profitable sermon. A number were converted or fully saved at the altar service.

Memorial Service of Bros. B. W. Gorham and F. B. Joy.

These precious men have gone to glory, and the people were delighted to have a memorial service. Bros. Mallory and Stratton led in prayer. Bro. McDonald spoke chiefly of Bro. Gorham, and said he was one of the ablest and most intelligent expositors of holiness, the church had produced.

Bro. Ballentine said: "Bro. Joy was a man of a remarkably gentle, tender, and childlike spirit, and had lived for twenty-five years in the blessed experience of perfect love.

Bro. Wood said: "I was led into perfect love by

Bro. Gorham, and have known and loved him for forty years. He was fifteen years my senior, and preached this doctrine for years when I opposed it and battled him. He would not let me go till I had the fulness. He stirred up men, and led more into the light than any other man. He was a marvellous preacher, both in holiness, and also to sinners. He was a mighty man in prayer. He would pray a campmeeting out of the mud into the third Heaven. He had enemies, for he pushed the truth. He was a successful minister, both as a pastor and as an evangelist."

Dea. Morse said: "I knew both these men so as to love them, and they loved me. I first met Bro. Joy on the train, and we talked about Jesus. I considered him a bulwark of this meeting. I met Bro. Gorham ten years before I got sanctified, and put twenty dollars into his hand to encourage him. Glory to God for these men."

Rev. G. Hughes said: "I am wonderfully impressed by the power of Bro. Gorham's prayers, and sermons, and songs. I took Bro. Joy deeply into my heart. He was a sunshiny man. He was a great big walking piece of sunshine."

Rev. John Parker said: "Bro. Joy was true to his name. Bro. Gorham had great courage. He was a saintly character. He compelled the church to give attention to the doctrine of holiness. He lived for God, and died shouting."

Bro. McDonald said: "This holiness movement began in Boston. Timothy Merritt was the headlight of this movement as a specialty. He established the holiness meeting at New York. Wilbur Fiske was sanctified, and lay five hours under the power of the Holy Ghost, under a sermon preached by Timothy Merritt, at Eastham, Mass. Bro. Gorham came in as an associate, and was one of the grandest."

> " Their toils are past, their work is done,
>   And they are fully blest :
> They fought the fight, the victory won,
>   And entered into rest.
>
> Then let our sorrows cease to flow,
>   God has recalled His own;
> And let our hearts in every woe,
>   Still say, — "Thy will be done."

Rev. L. P. Cushman, who labored in the South, so long and so well, preached at eleven, from, 1 John 1 : 9 Men sin naturally without being taught. You cannot make men better only by purifying their hearts. Let us look at our own sins and confess them. The confession must be as broad as the sin. My wife was sanctified at Round Lake National Camp Meeting. I found it at Hamilton National Meeting. Before this I was,

> "Sometimes up, and sometimes down,
>   Sometimes, I was level on the ground."

The rain broke up the service.

Dr. Levy preached at half past two, from Luke 26 : 33. It was a precious sermon upon the Virgin Mary as an example of entire sanctification.

1. In her perfect humility.
2. In her perfect resignation to the will of God.
3. In her perfect faith.

At the close of the sermon, while dwelling upon the fact that we all may be brought into the closest spiritual relations with Christ, and be thus made vessels of honor, cleansed and made meet for the Master's use, one young lady fell before the altar, under the power of God.   A glorious service followed.

Rev. Bro. Huntress preached in the evening from "I will follow thee, but."   He sought to show the difference between a disciple and a believer.   The one trusts Christ, the other simply believes in Him.   It was a good sermon.   The altar service continued till a late hour.

The meeting at half past eight on Friday morning was a rich season of testimony.   Bro. Wood said, "The Lord help us to keep to the fundamentals, and not run into collaterals.   Mr. Wesley stuck to one point 'Love out of a pure heart.'   Beware of formalism on the one hand and of fanaticism on the other."

At half past ten, Rev. J. Parker preached, text 2 Thess. 2: 13, "God himself being holy could but choose us unto holiness."   It would not be salvation, up to God's ideal, unless it saved us from all sin, root and branch.   Between what we are by nature and what he would have us be, is the realm of grace.   This involves the dethronement of the old nature, the elimination of your mixed experience.   Faith is impossible without this abandonment to God.   You may have an inheritance in the Holy Ghost, and every hour a consciousness of His indwelling.   And the inheritance of liberty and joy and victory.   Bro. Wood led the altar service.

Rev. G. A. McLaughlin preached at half-past two, text,

Matt. 5 : 5, "Blessed are the meek, for they shall inherit
the earth." "Christ gives the characteristics of those
that belong to the kingdom of heaven. It is a spiritual
and supernatural kingdom. It is Jesus in you." It
was an excellent sermon. Rev. G. N. Ballentine
preached in the evening, from The Songs of Solomon
It set forth the attitude of the soul toward Jesus, and
also of Christ to the soul. Many sought for purity at
the close.

Rev. W. D. Woodward led the early meeting on
Saturday. F. L. Sprague led the meeting at half past
eight, and Rev. S. L. Brown preached from John 14 : 15,
16. He showed the condition on which we may receive
the Comforter, that there must be implicit obedience.
This reception is for the Christian, for he comes as a
Comforter, and cannot come to the sinner in that way.

Bro. I. T. Johnson led the half-past one meeting, and
the power of God fell upon the people so that they
shouted and wept before the Lord, in the old-fashioned
way. Bro. Wood preached at half past two, from " This
is the the will of God even your perfection." He
showed the Scripturalness, the moderation, and reason-
ableness of entire sanctification.

Rev. A. Hartt preached in the evening from Heb. 12:
1, 2. The sin spoken of here is inbred sin, which is
manifested in pride, impatience, ambition, cowardice,
anger, etc. The only remedy is looking unto Jesus.
A blessed altar service followed. Thus was ended the
most rainy week of this Camp.

The Sabbath was a lovely day. Thousands came to
camp, and the order was good. Dea. Morse led the

love feast. Bro. McDonald preached on "Christian Perfection" to an attentive crowd, in his usually calm and effective manner.

Bro. Wood preached to a still larger crowd at half past two. It was short and sharp and was followed by a profitable altar service till nearly supper time.

I find I have failed to record the sermon that I preached at this last camp meeting. Text "Create in me a clean heart." Ps. 51: 10, topic, "Inbred sin: its cause and cure." Inbred sin is the sinful tendency of our moral nature. Always to be distinguished from actual transgressions. One is the mother, the others are the offspring. The latter must be pardoned but the other must be cleansed. We are responsible for our depravity when we fail to come to God for the cleansing. Responsible for all the harm that it leads us to do, and for all the good we might do if we were fully saved. So we must be wholly sanctified or we cannot be justified. The Bible teaches this. Many have obtained it in all ages. Who will have a clean heart created in them now? J. A. Wood led the altar service. The sermon has been published in "The Christian Witness." Rev. J. Gill preached the closing sermon of the camp meeting, from "Ye cannot serve two masters." It was plain and pungent, and many rushed to the altar and found salvation. There was a precious closing service. The mercies of God were remembered, and the people parted with a fixed purpose to follow the Lord fully the rest of their lives.

CHAPTER VII.

"Jesus, the crowning grace impart;
  Bless me with purity of heart,
    That now beholding Thee,
  I soon may view Thy open face,
  On all Thy glorious beauties gaze,
    And God forever see."

The Great Camp Meeting of 1890.

This camp meeting may be said to have begun on the train from Boston, for four sisters told their experience to each other till : —

"Their souls were all aflame,
  With the love of Jesus' name."

There was a spiritual conflagration when they burst out singing : —

"I have anchored my soul in the haven of rest,
  I'll sail the wide seas no more.
The tempest may rage o'er the wild stormy deep;
  In Jesus I am safe evermore."

Indeed, it seemed as though they had been at camp meeting, when they were only on their way there. We met Rev J. A. Wood, at Waterford, in good health and full of faith and of the Holy Ghost. He is a glorious man of God.

The camp meeting really began July 18, with impromptu meetings, which were held in different tents during the first day. In the evening President Mc-

Donald presided. The doxology was sung twice, after a season of silent prayer. Rev. J. A. Wood led the host at the throne of grace, in a triumphant prayer. Many sublime passages of scripture were quoted all over the tabernacle; then testimonies followed. Bro. Wood said: " It is my supreme delight to do the will of God. This is about the dearest spot on earth to me. It is worth a trip across the continent to mingle with the saints on this ground."

A sister said: " We talk about Douglas camp meeting six months after we go home, and then begin to get ready for the next meeting."

Rev. J. A. Wood had charge of the half-past eight meeting on Saturday. He said: " Seek to be right in your hearts, so that all the springs of your being will be in harmony with God. Then Satan will find nothing in you." A sister said: " This is a hallowed spot to my soul." " This is our Thanksgiving," said another. Abbie Mills said: " The mountains and the hills break forth before me into singing." Bro. Read, from Stoneham, said: " Here God called me by name. Here God spoke perfect peace to my soul. I always go home with a thankful heart. It is a Pentecost to my soul. God saves me all the time. I trust myself less and less." A sister said: " I never heard of holiness till last May; I was fully sanctified in a holiness convention, in Norwich, Conn." A sister: " This is not death; this is eternal life. I had heart failure, could hardly breathe; God healed me, and here I am."

Sister Storms said: " I have been sanctified eight years. I would not exchange what I have received for the city of Boston. I would live on a crust, drink cold water, and sleep on the ground, for the privilege of attending this meeting."

A sister from Norwich said : " I have Jesus, and all my wants are supplied. Bro. Gorham led me into this fulness. God is with me all the time."

A sister: " I knew Bro. Wood many years ago, when they said hard things about him. I said, his face shines with glory. I stood still and God has led me on."

Brother Covley, from Norwich, said : " I had a great soul hunger, and cried mightily to God, and was wholly sanctified before I knew what to call it. I am full, but I can hold more. I want more."

Sister Ballantine said: " Let *Christ* keep you, and not the blessing. I went down in my room all alone. I was going to have Jesus. He came and saved me fully."

Dr. W. Reddy preached the first sermon from Col. 2 : 9, 10. " In him dwelleth all the fulness of the God-head bodily." There is a being *in* Christ, and a being *complete* in Him.

To be in Christ we must accept Him as our Saviour. " In Christ " denotes a vital union with Him. But what means this completeness in Christ ? Every spirit-ual desire is satisfied. The soul that accepts this perfect Christ is rendered complete in Him. Christ is the great reservoir, the Church is the main pipe, and there are many branches running into our hearts. The gospel is a complete system. To be in Christ is the criterion of orthodoxy. This system involves all our behaviour. It is a complete system of morals. A true

Christian will be courteous, and not be wanting in the suavity, and gentleness of the gospel.

The completeness is predicated of the individual Christian. He is complete in Christ. Christ is the head " to present you holy, and unblamable, and unreprovable in His sight." Being complete in Christ takes in all our needs in morals and religion. In Him are all the treasures of wisdom and knowledge. He gives us the key and tells us to walk in and help ourselves. This was a blessed sermon and service.

Rev. A. Hartt led the half-past one meeting, which was given up to prayer and testimony. Rev. J. S. Johnson told a long experience, till the rain finished the afternoon.

Rev. E. Davies preached on Saturday evening, from 1 Thess. 3 ; 13. " To the end He may establish your hearts, unblamable in holiness before God, even our Father; *at*, or *unto* the coming of our Lord Jesus Christ." This refers to a work of grace that we may experience now, and in which we may live until Christ comes to call us home. The Greek word rendered "at," in this passage is rendered " unto," in 1 Thess. 5 : 23, when He prays that we may be sanctified wholly, and preserved blameless unto the coming of our Lord Jesus Christ. The same doctrine is taught in 1 John 3 : 20, 21 ; Thess. 2 : 17; 1 Cor. 1 : 8. It is also implied in Matt. 5 : 48; also Col. 4 : 12, and Phil. 3 : 15, and Col. 1 : 9–11, and Eph. 4 : 1, and Eph. 3 : 14–21.

We may not attain the perfection of unfallen angels, or of unfallen man ; neither can we be saved from infirmities, and errors of judgment, and these may lead to errors of practice, so that we shall constantly need the blood of Christ. But we may be sanctified wholly, and preserved blameless, and live in unblamable holiness all the days of our lives. Like Enoch we may walk with God and be constantly ready for heaven. We may be enabled to discharge the duties of life, and endure the trials of life, while : —

> " Like Moses bush we mount the higher,
> And flourish unconsumed in fire."

And, as it was said of Jesse Lee, that " the tide of Salvation ran in him so high, that there was but little left of him to die." A blessed altar service followed. This sermon was preceded by a song and testimony service of great spiritual power, led by Dr. E. M. Levy. The tide of Salvation was rising.

The early Sabbath morning meeting was, indeed, precious and profitable. Sister Boice led it, and made special reference to " the fellowship of Christ's sufferings " into which we were called to enter.

The love feast was hallowed, and the testimonies were fully on the line of full salvation. Pres. McDonald led the services. J. A. Wood testified that he did not believe there was such a company of fully sanctified souls on the continent, as were on this ground. Then New England was the strongest centre for the holiness movement of any part of the nation. That we ought to be good, who had such privileges.

After the love feast Dr. Levy preached one of his remarkably strong, clear, and scriptural sermons. He is one of the most sweet-spirited men that we have in the holiness movement. His sermons are all well prepared, and delivered in the Holy Ghost, and are always, made a blessing. His text was, 2. Thes. 2 : 13. "We are bound to give thanks always to God for you, brethren, beloved of the Lord, because, God hath from the beginning chosen you to salvation, through sanctification of the Spirit, and beleif of the truth."

This is a great text, and this is a great doctrine that we come to expound and enforce. This experience is the great want of the age. Our God is waiting for the church to bring this doctrine and experience to the front, where it belongs. "Be ye holy, for I the Lord your God am holy." This sanctification is the work of God, and is received by faith. Faith cuts a channel from each heart, to the great fountain of blessedness. Sanctification is the object of our calling. It is complete redemption from the curse, pollution, and power of sin. Christians are not only consecrated, but are made holy. Sanctification is by God the Father, Christ the Son, and God the Holy Ghost. There must be a death of self, yet this fulness may be received in a moment.

This sermon was a great spiritual feast. The altar service was glorious indeed. The Holy Spirit was manifested in great power. Quite a number came forward for entire sanctification and received it.

I. T. Johnson led a powerful meeting at half past one. Deacon Morse, E. Davies, Deacon Lovering, J. S. Johnson, and Mrs. Storms addressed the meeting. Many came forward for pardon or purity. A slight shower scattered the people, and Brother Johnson followed them to the Tabernacle, and continued his meeting. Some of the same workers went with him. After the rain ceased, Dr. Reddy preached one of his blessed soul-inspiring sermons, to the edification of the people. He is one of the ablest ministers of our day, and manifests a lovely, sanctified temper, which commends him to all. His text was, " These men are the servants of the most high God, which show unto us the way of salvation." He dwelt upon the plan of salvation, and how to obtain it, and the difference between present and eternal salvation, also between universal and special salvation, and also between partial and entire sanctification.

Rev. J. A. Wood preached a most blessed heart-searching sermon, in the evening, on "Spiritual poverty," "Blessed are the poor in spirit for theirs is the kingdom of heaven." This sermon ought to be printed in letters of gold.

1. Spiritual poverty includes a sense of our unworthiness, and comparative worthlessness in the sight of God. We are utterly destitute of goodness in ourselves. " In me (that is in my flesh), dwelleth no good thing."

2. It includes also, a penetrating sense of the guilt of our past sins, how we provoked God to anger, and deserved to be damned,when God had mercy upon us, and saved us. It is good to see the hole of the pit from which we were digged.

3. It includes also a sense of our proclivities toward sin, and the hellward tendencies of our regenerated hearts, before we were wholly sanctified, and

the long interior warfare. When the heart is fully cleansed, your proclivities are set right, and inclined to be good, then you have religion made easy.

4. Spiritual poverty shows us our utter dependence upon God, and this help is only received by faith. We are shut up to believe or be damned.

1. Why are the poor in spirit blessed? Not so much in a sense of joy, but in a sense of their relation to God, and to their position before God. God is near to them that are of a contrite spirit.

2. Poverty of spirit removes the great obstacle of pride out of the way of our salvation. It involves the death of self. How many draw back? They will not die, therefore they do not have the resurrection life.

3. We are blessed in spiritual poverty, because it shows us the exceeding sinfulness of sin.

4. The saints of old had seasons of humiliation before God. So must we. Then we may be able to say with Professor Boardman, " My soul is with God."

There was a great going down in the altar service, and a wonderful lifting up afterwards. It was by far the best service of the camp, up to that time, and produced eternal results. One man lay on the ground, having lost his strength, but came to, saying "Glory!" Rev. A. Hartt said he had reached a point far beyond shouting. He had the stillness of God in his soul. The multitude were gloriously blessed.

Dr. Reddy led the half past eight meeting on Monday, there were many testimonies of the blessings received on the Sabbath. The tide was rising.

Rev. G. W. Coon preached on Monday morning, a very blessed sermon upon Christian fellowship.

1. The fellowship of the saints, whereby they were partakers of the divine nature.

2. Opposition to this fellowship.

Satan is a real devil, and seeks to break through this saintly fellowship, and make schisms in the body of Christ, even among holiness people.

3. But God is faithful to sustain us in this fellowship. He sustained Job and Daniel, and the three Hebrew Children in the fiery furnace, so that the smell of fire was not upon them.

It was a precious sermon, just in season. A blessed altar service followed.

In the afternoon, Rev. F. A. Everett preached from "Put on charity as the bond of perfectness." He showed that in this chapter there were seven characteristics of all true Christians, that we should put on.

1. "Bowels of mercies." We should have a compassionate heart, like Jesus, for all that were in trouble.

2. "Put on kindness." Denying ourselves for the good of others.

3. "Humbleness of mind."

4. Meekness, gentleness, softness of temper. Temper is good like steel, but steel must be tempered. Moses was the meekest man, and God vindicated him before his enemies.

5. We should be long-suffering. Suffer as long as there is anything to suffer.

6. Forbearing one another. Imputing good motives to others.

7. Forgiving one another, as God for Christ's sake forgave us. Christ never gave us any occasion for

sinning against him, but we may have given occasion to our fellows to sin against us.

These are the characteristics of all true Christians. Now notice what God requires of them. "Above all these, they are to put on the bond of love." This bond will bind all the other graces together, and make them all complete.

Rev. J. A. Wood followed with a glorious exhortation, and a heavenly altar service.

Rev. J. C. Reece, of Portsmouth, R. I., preached in the evening, one of the sermons that can never be forgotten. He was one of the "Friends," but was filled with the Holy Ghost, and carried the camp by storm. Text, Col. 2. 9–10. "For in Him dwelleth all the fulness of the Godhead, bodily, and ye are complete in Him."

There is a great restlessness in mankind. Man was built for God, but sin has banished God from all the chambers of his soul. Christ is the centre of my text, and also of the Christian system.

1. In Christ there is fulness of life. He came that we might have life, and have it more abundantly. Christ destroyed the power of death, and delivers us from every fear. We obtain life in regeneration, and the abundant life in entire sanctification. The fulness of life comes only by death. The old man must be destroyed. It is hard to die, but glorious to have a resurrection.

There is a fulness of love, and a fulness of power, and a fulness of joy. It is well to learn that all power is in Christ. Therefore there is none in us,

This fulness is the great want of the Church. We have machinery enough in the Church, but there is no fire in the wheels. One church said they did not need a revival, for all their pews were let. If you are great on Methodism, you are light on salvation. It is the same with other denominations.

You should make your heavy trials into chariots, and get in and ride. Some people pray for patience, and the Lord sends them some heavy trials, and they are groaning under the wheels, the first thing.

This was a heavenly sermon, and many shouted for joy. The altar service was blessed.

CHILDREN'S MEETINGS

Were held daily during the camp meeting, led by Mrs. Dr. Levy and Miss Rose Williams, and great good was done day by day. Many were converted.

We were glad to see at this camp meeting Rev. T. L. Poulson, D.D. He is one of the ablest ministers of our church, and has been pastor in some of the large churches in Baltimore.

T. J. Mathewson testifies that he came to the camp meeting of 1887, a wretched backslider, having backslidden from entire sanctification. The Spirit said to him distinctly, "Now, or never." He confessed his condition, and went forward and found the fulness, and has been kept ever since, and been used for the divine glory in pointing others to this full salvation. He is an earnest worker.

Tuesday, H. H. Perry led the six o'clock, and Rev. C. L. Eastman the half-past eight social meetings.

Rev. W. McDonald preached at half past ten, text Acts 18: 24, 28. Apollos was well instructed in the way of the Lord. He had a fervent spirit. He was an eloquent man and a teacher of God's truth. Aquila and Priscilla were tent-makers like St. Paul, who wrought with them. Aquila and Priscilla knew the way of the Lord more perfectly. They had the spirit of discernment; they knew the difference between the letter and the spirit of the gospel, also between being mighty in the Scriptures and wanting in the Holy Ghost. They did not refuse to hear Apollos preach, but took him to their home, expounded to him the way of the Lord more perfectly. This is what the holiness people should do if their minister is not clear in the doctrine and experience of holiness. Apollos was open to conviction, and profited by this private instruction.

This was a plain hand-to-hand sermon touching on many practical and useful matters by which preachers and people profited. A good altar service followed. Dea. Kies led the half past one service and read "Lord, who shall abide in Thy tabernacle, who shall dwell in Thy holy hill?" Rev. J. Ballentine preached one of his convincing sermons at half past two, text, Matt. 20: 23, "But it shall be given to him for whom it is prepared of my Father." The sermon was in power to many hearts, and many flocked to the altar at the close, to obtain heart purity.

Rev. E. O. Mallory of Lowell, Mass., preached in the evening, text, Ps. 40: 3. Many were blessed under the word and in the altar services.

The six o'clock prayer meeting on Wednesday was

led by Mrs. Macfarlane. The half past eight service
was led by S. L. Brown. There were many prayers and
testimonies after Bro. Brown had read Eph. 6: 10.
" Finally, my brethren, be strong in the Lord and in
the power of His might. Put on the whole armor of
God, that ye may be able to stand against the wiles of
the devil. Praying always with all prayer and supplication in the spirit, and watching there unto with all
supplication for all saints." It was a profitable hour.

H. N. Brown preached at half-past ten, Ps. 50: 2.
" Out of Zion, the perfection of beauty, God hath
shined." All the attributes of God are in eternal opposition to darkness. Light is the emblem of God in the
soul. Christ's mission is to dispel the darkness. There
is the light of nature, and the light of divine revelation.
The light of the Christian Church, and the direct illumin-
ation of the Holy Ghost. The Church is the perfection
of beauty when Christ is enthroned in each heart. He
closed with a careful analysis of the character of Noah,
Daniel, and Job, as illustrating the subject. This was
really three sermons in one, and each of them excellent.

I. T. Johnson led the half past one meeting, aided by
Brothers Davidson and Perry.

Bishop Taylor preached at half-past two, from Rom.
2: 14, 15. This experience of the law written in the
hearts of the heathen, would be a good experience,
even for us. How could they get into such an experi-
rience. St. Paul says it was made known to him by
revelation. What they knew of God was manifested
through the medium of the material universe. " For
the invisible things of Him from the creation of the

world are clearly seen, being understood by the things that are made, even His eternal power and Godhead: so that they are without excuse." This is the primary school of our God which has been open day and night since the creation, without even an hour's vacation. "Day unto day uttereth speech, and night unto night showeth knowledge." The written revelation is God's high school. "The law of the Lord is perfect converting the soul." The light of the Holy Spirit shines through both these revelations, so that all men are without excuse. The heathen are depraved, but they are also redeemed. We should send them the gospel because they need it, and God commands us, and, also because we cannot be saved ourselves if we disobey God in this matter.

He closed with his own experience. He was converted when a boy, and fully sanctified afterward, and had enjoyed this great blessing for forty-four years *without a break.*

The bishop was weak from hard labor, and could not be heard in the distance. A blessed altar service followed.

Rev. Ross Taylor, the bishop's son preached a glorious sermon in the evening. Text, Lev. 12: 34, 35. Subject: Present personal preparation for the coming of the Lord. The way of salvation was made plain, and his own experience furnished the illustrations. Many were saved at the close.

Thursday, at six A.M., Rev. F. W. Henck, led the service. The half-past eight meeting was led by Bro. Wood who is so full of the Spirit and so apt in his teachings that all his services are profitable.

At half-past ten, C. J. Fowler, preached from 1. Cor. 3 chapter. Christian experience is spiritual life. This is a fruitbearing life. The Christian has all the fruits of the Spirit. He has also the opposites. So that pride is mixed with humility, and fear with love. The Corinthians were spiritual on one side and carnal on the other, and this is the state of multitudes now. Entire sanctification received by faith will fill the whole soul and make it meet for service and sacrifice on earth and for a home in heaven.

It was a clear, logical, and effective sermon.

Sale of the Douglas Camp Ground.

Deacon Morse had felt for a some time that he ought to transfer his property in this camp ground into the hands of a company that could hold it forever for the promotion of holiness. So it was sold to the Douglas Camp Meeting Association, which was organized at Douglas, in July, 1890.

These grounds cost eighteen thousand dollars and were sold for six thousand dollars. Deacon Morse and his immediate friends took one hundred of the shares; so there was only five thousand dollars to raise to pay for the real estate and personal property, but the shareholders thought it best to raise four thousand dollars more to build a Tabernacle and make other necessary improvements.

The half-past one meeting on Thursday was occupied in stating these facts to the people, and in taking subscriptions for shares, four thousand seven hundred dollars were subscribed that day, and the balance is coming.

The deed and the charter are to specify that these grounds are to be held forever for holiness. The executive committee of the association were appointed to transact the business and to make the improvements.

At half-past two Bishop Taylor gave a deeply interesting address concerning his own work in Africa and concerning the Africans. He shows that he has had three hundred converts in his thirty-five new mission stations in Africa; and that his mission steamer for the lower Congo river, will be afloat in a few weeks.

Over four hundred dollars were subscribed for his mission.

In the evening, J. A. Wood edified the people with an excellent sermon in perfect love, Matt. 5: 48. "Be ye therefore perfect as your Father in heaven is perfect." This is both permissive and mandatory. You *may* be perfect, for the gospel provides for it. And ye *shall* be perfect, for God requires it.

It is not absolute perfection, or angelic, but Christian perfection, which admits of many imperfections. It includes perfect consecration, perfect submission, and perfect faith and love. This brings with it an increase of light and obligation. This perfection may increase unto the perfect day.

It was a glorious sermon. Blessed altar service followed. The tide of salvation is still rising.

Words of wisdom are often falling from the lips of Bro. Wood. In exhortation he said: —

"There are many duties, but God gives us power to do them all, in the bond of perfect love. This heart full of love will flow all through a man's activities, and regulate the whole. Get the heart right, and it will be second nature for you to be religious. When the heart is right, the principles and the practices will be right. The substance of the whole is to love the Lord your God with all the heart."

CHAPTER VIII.

"Me with that restless thirst inspire,
That sacred, infinite desire,
And feast my hungry heart.
  Less than thyself cannot suffice;
  My soul for all thy fulness cries —
For all thou hast and art."

DOUGLAS CAMP MEETING IN 1890. (CONTINUED.)

FRIDAY it rained, and we were all glad, for there was
a great necessity for it. Miss Mary Woodbury led the
early meeting. At half past eight there were small meetings in the tents. At half past nine Rev. Westmore Smith,
a missionary from Hayti, gave us a thrilling account of
his mission work for fifteen years in the West Indies.
The people gave him $84.00. Rev. E. M. Pike preached
at half past ten, text John 17: 9; " I pray for them."
He also prays for us. He prayed that His disciples
may be kept and his prayer was answered. They had
been chosen out of the world, yet they needed clean
hearts. So Christ prayed that they may be sanctified.
And they were sanctified at the Pentecost. We all
need the same pentecostal power.

At three P. M. Rev. A. McLean preached. Text, Heb.
13: 20, 21. God, in His great salvation, has amply provided for every need of His creatures. God has promised to mold to perfection the soul that is wholly

JAMES B. BOWEN.

given up to Him. He has promised to make their wills one with his. We need to be connected with the centre of God's power, like a piece of machinery that has no will of its own. The people were greatly blessed in hearing the sermon, and in the altar service that followed. At half past seven Bro. Ballentine preached from " Our Father." The redemption scheme of salvation was born in the thought of God. This blood cleansing originated in the heart of God. If we could contemplate those words " Our Father" until we were filled with the fulness of their meaning we should find that Jesus came to save us from all sin. It reveals to us the Father. The gospel provides that our actual transgressions should be pardoned, and our inbred sin cleansed, for we are redeemed from all iniquity. We are to be crucified with Christ.

Saturday at half past ten Rev. J. Gill preached from Phil. 2: 14, 15. " Do all things without murmurings and disputings that ye may be blameless and harmless ; the sons of God without rebuke," etc. This text shows us a dark line of environment called " the world " and ourselves as lights illuminating the darkness. It is a sad fact that the world is drifting away from the church. I sometimes think that the holiness people will have to change their tactics and go in bands and preach to the Sabbath breakers the religion of the Lord Jesus. The world is fast drifting away from us, and we must bestir ourselves and let our light shine. If we do not light up this darkness who will do it ? I believe that a salvation of the world is to be accomplished by a sanctified church. There would

be no difficulty in bringing about a revolution if the
church would only get saturated through and through
with holiness; then we could send out heavenly rays to
light up this darkness. It was a good sermon and well
received.

Dr. E. M. Levy preached at half past two, text, Gen.
41: 55. Joseph was a type of Christ. He was the
beloved son of the father; so Jesus is the beloved Son
of God. "Hear ye him." Joseph was gifted with
knowledge; he interpreted dreams. In Christ dwelt
all the wisdom of God. Joseph, like Jesus, was
tempted, and yet maintained his purity. Joseph was
sold by his brethren. Jesus was sold by Judas. You
should go to Jesus for pardon; for restoration from
backsliding; for a clean heart; for deliverance from
the power of the devil. Go to him as your Brother,
your rich Brother, your Mediator. Many went to
Jesus after the sermon. God was there.

At half past seven Rev. Mr. Riggs, of Vermont,
preached a heavenly sermon, which greatly moved the
people; text, Matt. 5 : 13. There was a blessed altar service. Many were saved. The love feast at Douglas, July
27th, was full of glory. Deacon Morse was in charge.
In opening he said, " The old-time religion was no
better than that of the present time. There never were
so many good people on the earth as now. Sectari-
anism is vanishing. The people of God are more than
ever united in one. I went to a Holiness Convention
at New Bedford years ago and found full salvation,
and have maintained it ever since. ' Behold, what
manner of love the Father hath bestowed upon us

that we should be called the children of God. Beloved, now are we the sons of God, and it doth not yet appear what we shall be. But we know that when he shall appear we shall be like Him for we shall see Him as he is. And every man that hath this hope in him purifieth himself even as He is pure. Little children, let no man deceive you: he that doeth righteousness is righteous, even as He is righteous' (1 John 3 : 1, 3, 7). We have no power in ourselves to keep God's commandments, but when we are all the Lord's, we run in the way of God's commandments. We may be strengthened with might by his Spirit in the inner man. So that there is no excuse on account of our infirmities. You get into God all over, and then this planet is not large enough for your feet to walk on. Spiritual childhood is the humility of the Holy Ghost. God's love is as unfathomable as the Atlantic Ocean, and is as broad as the universe." Then, turning to the ministers upon the platform, he said, " None of you know the depth or the height of the love of God."

He then led in one of his most fervent prayers, in which he thanked God for all the good ever done on this camp ground, and now, as he was about to transfer it to other hands, he prayed that God would bring out the fruitage of spiritual good through this meeting to the end of time ; that he would save our families. God's promises and powers are infinite.

There was a general shout among the saints while this man of God prayed. There is such a heavenly simplicity about him and such a fervency of soul that we all delight to hear him speak or pray. Indeed he is so filled with the Spirit at times that he leaps for joy and bounds with delight. He opens the Bible and reads the great promises of God with perfect faith. I have had many answers to his prayers when I have been in Revival work, and have sent him requests for prayers. Rev. E. M. Levy said: "I find I have not testified on these grounds this year. There is a great difference between preaching on holiness, and testifying to the experience of holiness. I used to preach on holiness before I had the experience. This has been the best year in my life. I have had the best revival of my life. I am fully saved, and expect to be fully saved unto the end. I expect to see my Lord. I am looking for Him. I believe He is coming. I would rather see Jesus coming in the clouds than have all the world." Singing,

"Glory to the Lamb!"

The following testimonies were given and many more that I could not record: "Thank God for the power that He puts in our hearts to love one another. When filled with the Comforter we are able to live without sin; I am more and more settled with God. My heart is fixed. I have been in the land of Beulah a long time. I am possessing more and more of the good land. Through the acceptance of the truth I am walking in the light, saved to the uttermost. Bless the Lord!" "Never felt so small in all my life. I am under the blood, and through His power I am saved to the uttermost! I have learned not to trust in men but in God! The Lord saves me all the time! I know that our God is a sun and shield. Holiness is the greatest thing on earth. The blood of Christ is all my plea!" Mrs. Pettis said, "I am learning lessons every day. I am sitting at the feet of Jesus. I praise him for his blood shed on Calvary. I am sanctified and satisfied. I rejoice that God is love."

> "O love, thou bottomless abyss!
> My sins are swallowed up in thee."

"I do bless God for what He has done for me in this meeting."

"I praise God for a salvation, that is all complete in Him."

"Jesus, my Saviour, is all things to me; He saves me from sin."

Mrs. Gill said: "I belong to God, soul, body, and spirit; I am every whit whole."

Miss Colter said: "I overcame by the blood of the Lamb."

"These words abide in my heart, and I shall live forever."

"When I was down low in sin, Jesus took me in."

"Christ is my life, my hope, my all."

"This is the best moment of all my life."

Singing by Rev. A. Hartt: —

> "I have anchored my soul in the haven of rest,
>   I'll sail the wild seas no more,
>   The tempest may rage o'er the wild, stormy deep,
>   In Jesus I am saved evermore."

Brother Avery, of Boston: "I am all the Lord's, and I propose to do more for God than ever."

"I never felt so sweetly saved as now,"

" I am one of the little ones that we have heard about."

" How Jesus has filled my soul while listening to these testimonies."

" I was saved here a year ago, God has kept me in the trying hour."

" Praise the Lord for full and free salvation."

A child's testimony. " I love Jesus, and know that Jesus saves me."

About two hundred and fifty testified, and the glory of God covered the camp. At the close I sat by the side of Rev. Mrs. Gorham, and inquired as to the death of her husband. She said : " Mr. Gorham led in family worship two days before he died, and sat up all the day on Wednesday. He told me he expected to die soon. His mind was very clear. The day before he died he broke out in rapture, saying ' Precious Jesus, Thou art mine, I am Thine, all Thine, Thine forever. Praise the Lord ! Glory to God ! Hallelujah !' Before midnight he was unconscious, and died the next day in holy triumph, and great peace. His last word was ' Jesus.' "

About three thousand people were present to hear Rev. W. McDonald preach, at the close of the love feast. The Lord mightily helped him to preach from 1 Thess. 5 : 24. " Faithful is He that calleth you who also will do it." Like all other true Christians, the Thessalonians were sanctified when they were converted, but they were not wholly sanctified. Entire sanctification not only keeps us from sinning, for justification does that, but it also extracts the root, and seed of sin from our soul. It purifies every part of our being, bringing us under the

entire control of the law of God. Hundreds were
blessed under the word.

Rev. A. B. Riggs, of Vermont, offered the closing
prayer, and the Holy Ghost fell upon the people. One
woman cried out mightily. The crowd was so great
that a company of zealous women held a spiritual service
for an hour near the head of the auditorium. Miss
Hattie Currier, of Stoneham, was the chief speaker, and
much good was done. Immediately after dinner, I
began a service in front of the dining hall; I sang,

> "Standing on the promises of Christ, my King,
> Through eternal ages let His praises ring,
> Glory in the highest, I will shout and sing,
> Standing on the promises of God."

After speaking awhile, we formed a circle of prayer.
Many were under conviction, and many wept while
John Norberry, Evangelist, sang the beautiful hymn
called " The Golden Landing."

> Chorus: " While on Pisgah's mount I'm standing,
> Looking toward the vernal shore :
> There I seem to see them banding,
> Just beside the golden landing,
> Waiting to receive me o'er,
> Precious ones that went before."

This young minister is full of faith, and of the Holy
Ghost, and has been very successful in winning souls,
and seemed to me like Thomas Harrison, No. 2. The
Lord bless him forever!

A Catholic woman and a young woman came forward
and knelt on the ground, and gave themselves to Christ.

There was great rejoicing in the heart of the Catholic woman's husband.

Mrs. E. M. Levy had charge of about one hundred and fifty children, and forty of them gave their hearts to God. She is a successful worker among children. At the same time, Rev. I. T. Johnson conducted a large and successful service in front of the preacher's stand. Many were seeking God. No doubt some of them found the Saviour.

Rev. J. A. Wood preached at half past two, from " God is love." There was such a crowd of people, and so many were talking, that it was hard work to be heard. But God helped him till he conquered. " God's love is manifested on every side, All human love is a manifestation of God's love in us. It is God incarnated in the soul. To love God with all the heart, and our neighbor as ourselves, is the whole duty of man."

There was so much power among the people that the altar service was continued till supper time, and many were saved. One woman hurt the cause very much by her loud and continued shouting, or screaming. It seemed to harden the sinners. Dea. Morse stood in front of the stand, weeping and beseeching sinners to come to Christ.

After supper, George E. Tilley, Evangelist, from Jamaica, N. Y., led a blessed service in the dining hall for the benefit of the caterer, W. B. Stone and family, and the waiters, who had worked so hard to feed the bodies of the people. It was a good service, and was well received.

Dr. E. M. Levy preached with great power in the evening, on the second coming of Christ. The multitude including the children, felt that they must get ready to meet the Lord. Many was saved at the close. Bless the Lord for that great day of God! We trust that one hundred were saved during the day, and multitudes blessed. Hallelujah! Amen!

I was so utterly weary that I did not leave the ground till nearly five o'clock on Monday. I wanted to write up the services, and rest a little. I went to the station several times and sang a good-by to hundreds. It was a touching, tender time. After dinner I held a service in front of the stand, and was edified and delighted to hear the testimony of Moses Charbono, a converted French Catholic, who was converted at Putnam, in his own house, while reading the word of God. One Catholic woman threw hot water upon him and tried to abuse him. In a few days her husband died. He went to the store and sent her five dollars' worth of provisions. She was ashamed and asked his forgiveness, and turned to be his true friend. He is an overseer in the mill and can control the Catholic laborers. He treats them well, and they return the compliment. This dear brother stands all alone in Willimantic, among the French Catholics. But he commands respect. He was at the first camp meeting held on these grounds, and is a monument of redeeming grace. He walked eight miles to be present at this camp, and came just in time to attend this impromptu service. By turning it into a class meeting I found a poor woman, dressed in mourning, that could not forgive God for taking away her mother. She began to weep. We had a heavenly season of prayer, and she was saved, Glory to God !

CAMP MEETING ECHOES.

As the thousands of dear people are scattering to their homes and churches, I seem to hear the echoes of their voices : " What a feast of fat things we have had at Douglas ! " " What heavenly sermons ! " " What glowing testimonies ! " " What lovely singing ! " " What sweet communion of saints ! " " What love feasts ! " " What days of sunshine ! " " What harvest moonlight nights ! " " What refreshing showers ! " " What health-giving breezes, laden with the sweet balm of the pine trees ! " " How good the Lord has been in saving us from all harm of body and soul ! " "Surely Douglas is the next place to heaven, yea, it seems like heaven itself ! " Rev. W. D. Woodward exclaims, " Douglas Camp Meeting is the Saratoga Springs of the soul. A delightful summer retreat. This is the true meeting place. It is a peaceful lake of itself, reflecting the rays of the Sun of Righteousness. Had I the skill of the Bible word-painter, I could not portray the Spiritual beauties of this charming camp. The testimonies at Douglas are worth going many miles to hear They are a tonic to faith." Dr. Steele, in a soft and expressive voice, says, " If Jesus should suddenly appear to summon me to his throne in heaven, my soul would be in full accord with all that is going on there ; so much alike are the two places."

And thus our book must end. But Douglas, in its

hallowed memories, its mighty influences upon the destinies of thousands, and its triumphs for Jesus, will never end. Eternity alone can tell the story and count up the results.

The past is already secure. But what of the future? When God's dear servant who established Douglas, and the men and women who have sustained it by their prayers, and tears, and sermons, and shouts, have all passed into the joy of their Lord, other thousands will pitch their tents on this old camping ground, unfurl the banner of holiness, and push the battle of Full Salvation. "Hallelujah! The Lord God, Omnipotent, reigneth!"

ERRATA.

Contents, Chapter I. — For " Dea. Finn," read " Dea. Fenn "; for " P. P. Botham," read " T. P. Botham "; for " Rhodes Allen," read " Rhodes G. Allen."

Page 2. — For " Rhoades Allen," read " Rhodes G. Allen."

Page 3. — Two of Dea. Morse's children were born in Providence, R.I.

Page 4 (First line). — For " forty years," read " twenty-eight years."

Page 5. — For " Stillman Morse," read " Stillman F. Morse."

Page 8 (Fourth line). — For " 1872," read " 1871."

Page 34. — For " J. G. Covley," read " J. G. Cooley."

Page 61. — For " Dea. Loring," read " Dea. Lovering."

Page 71. — For " Bro. Covley," read " Bro. Cooley."

AN ILLUSTRATED HAND BOOK ON AFRICA.

GIVING AN ACCOUNT OF ITS PEOPLE, ITS CLIMATE, ITS RESOURCES, ITS DISCOVERIES, RIVERS, LAKES, AND SOME OF ITS MISSIONS. PRICE, TWENTY-FIVE CENTS.

In cloth, with steel portrait of Bishop Taylor, Price 50 cents.

Rev. Daniel Steele, D. D., writes: "I have read your ILLUSTRATED HAND BOOK ON AFRICA with great interest. Not many people have time to read Stanley's large volumes, and a still smaller number can afford to own them. Your Hand Book, scattered widely among Christian people, will awaken our interest in the great enterprise of the evangelization of the dark continent. I hope you will be called upon for a hundred thousand copies."

"Our enterprising and indefatigable co-laborer, Rev. E. Davies, has published an ILLUSTRATED HAND BOOK ON AFRICA. We have read it several times, studied the newly made map, looked at the striking pictures, and it is surprising to see the amount of valuable information he has gathered so rapidly together." And again, "Not one person interested in Bishop Taylor's work ought to be without this Hand Book. It contains ninety large pages of excellent reading, ten illustrations, and a map of the New Congo State." Rev. E. I. D. Pepper, in *Christian Standard*.

"Those who have not access to larger works will find this very useful, as giving a good deal of information in a brief space touching Africa, its rivers, lakes, animals, inhabitants, idolatries, and products." *Christian Standard*, Cincinnati.

"Rev. E. Davies, as a compiler of books, exhibits a degree of energy and activity quite on a par with his chosen profession of an evangelist at large, in the harvest field, where he has met with a large and substantial measure of success. For Bishop Taylor and his missions, Bro. Davies has evinced uncommon interest; this led him to prepare and publish a popular life sketch of the great missionary. Now he has written and published an ILLUSTRATED HAND BOOK ON AFRICA. The appearance of such a publication just at this juncture is timely, not only for the specific information it contains for those who may join their fortunes with Bishop Taylor, but for the general public, who are without access to the sources of such historical and geographical facts as are grouped in this convenient form." Dr. A. Wallace in *Ocean Grove Record*.

HOLINESS BOOK CONCERN, READING, MASS.

TESTIMONIALS

ON

The Life of Rev. John Weslev by Rev. E. Davies, 261 pages, 12 mo., five illustrations. Fifty cents, paper; seventy-five cents, cloth.

"Mr. Davies has disposed of his material to good advantage, and produced a most readable book. He furnishes a good outline of the early life, collegiate career, spiritual experience, evangelistic labors of John Wesley, and of the organization which perpetuates his name and work."—*The Wesleyan, Halifax.*

"There is unquestionably a place for this book, and we doubt not it will be well received."—*North Western Christian Advocate.*

"It is compiled from the latest biographies, and makes a very entertaining and profitable volume, giving a good outline of his early life, his college days, religious experience, evangelistic labors, the founding of his societies, his doctrines, extended ministry, and the closing incidents of his eventful life. It will be read with interest and profit."—*Zion's Herald.*

"The author has succeeded in giving us a well-written and interesting volume."—*The Free Methodist.*

"We have just finished reading Rev. E. Davies' 'Life ot Wesley.' It is glorious, reading of God's wonderful dealings with his servant. The power of God came down as I finished reading the book, and I shouted and praised the Lord."—Capt. R. Kelso Carter.

"The greatness of the character of John Wesley, and the depth of his consecration, have overflowed all denominational lines. This volume deals with the leading facts of his life. It is good for the closet and the study."—*The Contributor.*

This book is illustrated, and gives a large amount of very interesting matter concerning the life of this man of God, which should be read by all church members, of whateve denomination.

Holiness Book Concern,

READING, MASS.

CONTENTS

LIST OF ILLUSTRATIONS

PORTRAITS

8

FOREWORD

No report of the Kansas City Convention can adequately express the enthusiasm of the meetings, or their practical character. The following pages, however, will give some idea of what took place during those convention days. The registration, approximately 13,000, represents a respectable number, and the attendance was all that could be desired. At no previous convention have the young people buckled down more earnestly to work. The forenoon audiences were excellent, and in the evenings the great auditorium was well filled. The overwhelming conviction to an observer that looked upon the activities of these young people have been that Christian Endeavor is very much alive.

This was more of a youth convention than conventions in the past —not that more young people attended it, but that more took part in it. The oratorical contests were a revelation of the mental and spiritual potentialities of our societies.

Perhaps the greatest figure of the convention was Mrs. Francis E. Clark, wife of the beloved founder of Christian Endeavor. Her brief speeches were gems of modest good sense, and the thousands that met her will never forget the experience.

Again, those that attended the meeting at which Schumann-Heink sang will hold the memory dear throughout the years. They will not soon forget seeing the great diva standing at the top of the choir steps above the platform, while the audience sang the song, "God Be with You Till We Meet Again." It was as if the great singer were taking an affectionate farewell of public life.

Best of all, the young people who attended the convention caught new visions and went back home to live better lives and do better work for Christ and the Church.

It is our prayer that this report will keep fresh in memory those days of vision and inspiration and high fellowship.

ROBERT P. ANDERSON.

OFFICERS OF THE INTERNATIONAL SOCIETY OF CHRISTIAN ENDEAVOR, 1929-1931

DANIEL A. POLING, D. D., LL. D.,
President

HOWARD B. GROSE, D. D.,
Vice-President

WILLIAM HIRAM FOULKES, D. D., LL. D.,
Vice-President

EDWARD P. GATES,
General Secretary

ALVIN J. SHARTLE,
Treasurer and Field Secretary

STANLEY B. VANDERSALL,
Christian Vocations Superintendent

CLARENCE C. HAMILTON
Publication Manager

ROBERT P. ANDERSON,
Editorial Secretary

IRA LANDRITH, D. D., LL. D.,
Citizenship Superintendent

CARLTON M. SHERWOOD,
Extension Secretary

CARROLL M. WRIGHT,
Travel and Recreation Superintendent

PAUL C. BROWN,
Pacific Coast Secretary

HAROLD SINGER,
Mid-West Secretary

W. ROY BREG,
Southern Secretary

S. C. RAMSDEN,
Army and Navy Superintendent

FREDERICK A. WALLIS,
Social Service and Prison Work Superintendent

CHARLES F. EVANS,
Manager Western Office

State Christian Endeavor Field Secretaries

CALIFORNIA, Howard Brown, Los Angeles.

IDAHO, Mrs. J. Q. Hook, Boise.

ILLINOIS, Frank P. Wilson, Chicago.

INDIANA, Miss Elizabeth Cooper, Indianapolis.

IOWA, Evertt Robie, Des Moines.

KANSAS, Harold Lovitt, Topeka.

MASSACHUSETTS, NEW HAMPSHIRE, CONNECTICUT and MAINE, Russell J. Blair, Boston.

MARYLAND, WEST VIRGINIA and DELAWARE, F. C. Dixon, Baltimore.

MICHIGAN, Ernest S. Marks, Detroit.

MISSOURI, Alfred C. Crouch, Kansas City.

NEBRASKA, Marion Simms, Jr., Broken Bow.

NEW JERSEY, Frederick L. Mintel, Rahway.

NEW YORK, Willard E. Rice, Buffalo.

OHIO, Herman Klahr, Columbus.

OKLAHOMA, Paul Clark, Oklahoma City.

OREGON, Ross Guiley, Eugene.

PENNSYLVANIA, Warren G. Hoopes, West Grove.

TEXAS, E. F. Huppertz, Dallas.

VERMONT, Mrs. Rex Fullam, Montpelier.

WASHINGTON, Miss Louella Dyer, Seattle.

WISCONSIN, Clifford Earle, Milwaukee.

TRUSTEES AND COMMITTEES

Life Trustees

OFFICERS OF THE INTERNATIONAL SOCIETY OF CHRISTIAN ENDEAVOR

Left to right, back row: R. P. Anderson, Paul C. Brown, Harold Singer, W. Roy Breg, Stanley B. Vandersall. Front row: Clarence C. Hamilton, Carlton M. Sherwood, Daniel A Poling, E. P. Gates, and A. J. Shartle. Carroll M. Wright is missing

14

CHAPTER I

GETTING THE BUSINESS STARTED

Important Business Meetings—Reports of the Officers of
the International Society of Christian Endeavor

Wednesday Morning, July 3

Dr. Daniel A. Poling was in the chair promptly at ten o'clock, Wednesday morning, July 3, for the annual meeting of the International Society of Christian Endeavor, when a goodly crowd of trustees and members of the International Society greeted him.

Dr. W. A. Mactaggart of Toronto, offered prayer, and Dr. Poling made a brief report of achievement in the past, and outlined earnest hopes for Christian Endeavor in days to come.

The treasurer's report, presented by the treasurer, Mr. A. J. Shartle, was decidedly encouraging. Gradually, if slowly, a fund is being built up for the carrying on and spread of Christian Endeavor work in all the world. This fund is established through the generosity of individual Endeavorers, and through money and property left by will to the organization. The largest of these gifts is from the late Mr. and Mrs. Charles O'H. Craigie, who left to the International Society of Christian Endeavor real estate on Long Island which will yield a goodly sum when it can be sold. It was emphasized that the money given to the International Society is primarily an investment in youth.

Trustees' Meeting

Much of the business of the International Society was at this point postponed till a later date, and the gathering was organized as a meeting of the board of trustees of the society.

Dr. Poling asked those present each to rise and introduce himself or herself, which made a happy and witty opening, an informal reception which clearly showed the comprehensive and inclusive character of our organization—all one in Christ Jesus.

Feelingly Dr. Poling referred to the death, within a few days, of Dr. William R. Patterson of New York, a lifelong associate in the movement. Briefly and tenderly Dr. William Hiram Foulkes offered prayer especially for the bereft wife and daughter of our beloved brother.

15

E. P. Gates Has the Floor

Mr. Gates, general secretary of the International Society of Christian Endeavor, was in fine fettle when he rose to make his report to the trustees. As a matter of interest, as Dr. Poling remarked, this was the largest meeting of trustees that he had ever seen at an International Convention. The speech in full appears at the close of this chapter.

And Dr. Landrith

Dr. Ira Landrith reported wittily that he had no report, and then proceeded to outline work and travel that constitute a remarkable record. He has crossed the continent twice and spoken, with great encouragement, in twenty-seven States. There was perhaps more wisdom than is apparent at first sight in his closing remark that "the greatest weakness of Christian Endeavor is its universal popularity."

Then Followed Sherwood

Carlton M. Sherwood is extension secretary of the International Society of Christian Endeavor. He has visited and addressed Christian Endeavor and citizenship meetings in thirty-eight States in the Union. His judgment as to the value and present-day force of Christian Endeavor he gave in the following paragraph:

"In my judgment, no Christian challenge in this generation has so swept the life of the youth of all the churches and of Christian movements as has the Crusade with Christ, which came from our own Cleveland International Convention of 1927. This comprehensive program for youth evangelism, Christian citizenship, and world peace has captured the imagination of the youth of the churches in an unique way. Modern leaders of the church, as well as young people themselves, have increasingly indicated their confidence in Christian Endeavor, both as a dynamic evangelistic force and as a movement awake to the vital modern problems that need consideration and action by the youthful constituency of the churches."

The Editor Reports

The editor of THE CHRISTIAN ENDEAVOR WORLD, who is also editorial secretary of the International Society of Christian Endeavor, made a report of work done, with part of which, at least, our readers are familiar, since much of his work appears in these pages.

Clarence C. Hamilton

as publication-manager, told of the service the department is rendering by issuing books, pamphlets, and leaflets dealing with various aspects of Christian Endeavor. One interesting feature is the fact that no fewer than 126,500 copies of "Hymns for

Christian Youth'' have been sold, sufficient, surely to prove that the book is appreciated. More use might be made of the publishing department by Endeavorers on the field than is now the case. It must not, however, be forgotten that every sale made by the department is a definite service to the cause.

Stanley B. Vandersall

who heads up the vocations department of the International Society of Christian Endeavor, presented the following concise description of the work he is trying to do through his department.

To bring to the attention of all young people the proper consideration of the principles involved in choosing a life-work; to study, analyze, and make available for common use particular information concerning any and all gainful occupations; to present to all young people the Christian viewpoint in the choice of a vocation; to answer questions and provide vocational counsel to individuals or groups; to encourage the use of every possible means of personal evaluation and character diagnosis in order that a wise choice may be made; to present the claims of full-time Christian service in a clear and attractive manner; to discover, call out, and enroll those who voluntarily respond as recruits for such full-time service; to disseminate detailed information concerning particular places and tasks in full-time Christian service; to advise the recruits as to the steps necessary to be taken to carry out their expressed intention; to relate them to the proper religious agencies, principally denominational, looking to their placement in service.

In all of this work the department has maintained a close relationship to the J. C. Penney Foundation, which is primarily interested in vocational guidance. The department has gained many contacts through the radio work of Dr. Poling on the subject of vocations; and since through the financial co-operation of the J. C. Penney Foundation, this department in the International Society can function without asking for financial return from those helped it becomes a very strong part of our service.

Clarence C. Hamilton's

report on THE CHRISTIAN ENDEAVOR WORLD told of the improvements that have been made in the paper typographically and as to contents. He reported that eight young people had won Free Trips to Kansas City, four of them also to Yellowstone. ''Free Trips to Berlin'' August, 1930, was announced as the slogan of the new CHRISTIAN ENDEAVOR WORLD subscription campaign to begin October 1, 1929.

Paul C. Brown

Pacific-Coast secretary, who has just returned from a visit to Hawaii, received a hearty welcome. He brought the greetings of Endeavorers in Hawaii, and described some of the complex conditions there. He told of his success in reorganizing the union on the island of Oahu, where Honolulu is situated. On the list of officers of this union are not only some American names, but also names of five different races, and several mixtures of races. In the recent annual meeting of the Hawaiian Evangelical Association Christian Endeavor was definitely placed on the program. The leaders of this organization promised new and happy cooperation in young people's work. This journey of Mr. Brown is the only visit to Hawaii made by any of the present officers of the International Society.

Dr. W. A. Mactaggart

a leader in the United Church of Canada and a great-hearted friend of Christian Endeavor, spoke of the outlook in Canada, an outlook that showed a world of opportunity.

W. Roy Breg

Southern secretary, told of encouraging features in the South, especially the indorsement of Christian Endeavor by the General Assembly of the Presbyterian Church, South. The number of Christian Endeavor societies in this denomination in 1916 was 1,410, and the present number is 2,284, a steady and wonderful growth.

Contacts have been made with many denominational leaders in the South, and the service of the International Society is being placed at their disposal. These contacts have developed splendid co-operation.

Finances

Dr. William Hiram Foulkes, vice-president, and chairman of the finance committee, drew a heartening picture of the

HOWARD L. BROWN
Field-Secretary, California

RUSSELL J. BLAIR
Field-Secretary, Connecticut, Maine, Massachusetts, and New Hampshire

future; but presented another picture of the present, pointing out that the income of the International Society is not sufficient to meet the needs of the work to-day. The task immediately before us is to do our best through ordinary channels to increase our financial support, and to live within our income. Surely we dare not let all our beautiful visions collapse because we have not money to give them life.

YOUTH IN AN AIRPLANE AGE

Christian Endeavor Prosperity—A New Day in Co-operation —The Challenge to Service—More Forward Steps— 4,562 New Societies—Three Great Needs

Address of Edward P. Gates, General Secretary of the International Society of Christian Endeavor

Young people are better to-day than ever before, and they have to be, because it is harder to be good to-day than it was a generation ago. Thirty years ago father gave son a bicycle as a graduation present. Now the magazines are advertising, "Give that boy of yours an airplane when he graduates." It takes more moral stamina to live in an airplane age than in a bicycle age.

There is, however, more need to-day than ever before for the character-building service which movements such as Christian Endeavor can render to young people. And there is reason for rejoicing that the experience of the past two years gives the lie to those misguided observers in the halls of Congress and elsewhere who have recently been proclaiming that the present generation of youth is hopelessly bad and that young people in general are chiefly interested in pocket-flasks and petting-parties.

This convention itself is evidence. While not the largest gathering in Christian Endeavor history, the out-of-the-city attendance is larger in proportion to the Christian Endeavor population within a five-hundred-mile radius than at any previous convention. Our conventions do not specialize in entertainment features. Young people have come to Kansas City by thousands, not for recreation and entertainment, but to talk and study together about ways of doing better work in their own communities and churches.

Christian Endeavor Prosperity

The prosperity of the Christian Endeavor movement and of other Christian organizations for young people is evidence. There are more Christian Endeavor societies in more churches, in more nations of the world to-day than ever before. Christian Endeavor is distinctly a Christian movement. It believes in the acceptance of Jesus Christ as a personal Saviour. It emphasizes the importance of outspoken Christian testimony, practical Christian service, and unwavering loyalty to the church. It upholds high ideals of Christian living for young people. It is an encouraging fact that millions of young people in all countries of the world continue to respond to a challenge of this kind.

A third ground for encouragement is the increasing spirit of co-operation among all Christian youth groups. While their elders are talking church union, Christian young people everywhere are practicing it. Nationally the Crusade with Christ proposed by President

Poling at the International Christian Endeavor Convention in Cleveland two years ago has enlisted the co-operation of practically every Christian youth group in North America and many organizations in foreign lands. The Crusade has focused the attention of millions of young people upon the great questions of world peace, Christian citizenship, and evangelism; and inevitably in thousands of communities it has brought the young people of the different churches closer together than ever before in united effort for things worth while.

The Day of Co-operation

This convention is a striking evidence of this growing feeling of Christian fellowship. Members of denominational young people's societies, the Boy Scouts, the Young Men's Christian Association, the Young Women's Christian Association, and every other Christian agency in Kansas City, have worked together to make this meeting possible.

Christian Endeavor rejoices in the success of all of these agencies. There is to-day no competition in the field of young people's work. Denominational and interdenominational leaders are working together as never before to do unitedly those things which need to be done.

This growing tendency toward co-operation is manifesting itself within the Christian Endeavor organization in an increased number of union or federated societies in smaller communities. In hundreds of communities where the churches have not found it possible to unite, the young people have got together in one Christian Endeavor society, and are working out in a practical way the problems of Christian fellowship.

A vital contribution to this spirit of fellowship is being made by the Christian Endeavor union organization. There are now approximately fourteen hundred city, county, and district Christian Endeavor unions, each including from four or five to three hundred Christian Endeavor societies. These unions are officered by more than fourteen thousand young people. They give to the societies in the individual churches the inspiration of fellowship with young people of other denominations and churches, the opportunity to share in co-operative community enterprises, and practical help in doing the work of the local organization.

A fourth reason for faith in youth is the evidence that these young people are eager to make their lives count in some kind of worth-while service. Two years ago, through the generosity of the J. C. Penney Foundation, the International Society of Christian Endeavor was enabled to create a department of Christian Vocations. To this department have come literally thousands of requests from young people for advice in the choice of a life-work, information about educational opportunities, and kindred subjects. Among the best-attended meetings at conventions and conferences have been those relating to this matter of vocations. The demands for help have far exceeded the present resources of the department. Under the direction of Superintendent Vandersall a national organization of trained volunteers is being developed, which will some day make it possible to give personal Christian counsel to all young people desiring it.

A fifth reason for encouragement is the fact that young people are putting religion into their play as well as into their work. Present-day young people are interested in clean recreation. They are hungry for wholesome fun and worth-while good times. If young people go to the bad now and then, it is often because we fail to give them a chance to go to the good.

The establishment three years ago by the International Society of a Department of Recreation met with an instant response. The monthly recreation service of the department is now reprinted by nearly a score of church papers, and is distributed through State and city union bulletins to probably several thousands of societies. No service offered by the International Society has met with a more enthusiastic welcome.

The events of these two years have further proved that young people are interested in world problems. They believe in prohibition, and want to have a part in encouraging observance of law. Christian Endeavor can point with pride to its citizenship activities and to its activities in behalf of world peace and international friendship.

Forward Steps in Christian Endeavor

As a matter of record and as causes for rejoicing there should be listed here the following additional forward steps of the International Society during the past two years.

The acceptance of the generous gift of THE CHRISTIAN ENDEAVOR WORLD from its former owners and its continued publication as the official organ of the movement under the editorial direction of Rev. R. P. Anderson.

The creation of the office of mid-West secretary and the election of Mr. Harold Singer to this important position. Mr. Singer's service to the seventeen States in his territory has been of inestimable value.

The change in the organization of our Southern work, which has made this field directly a department of the International Society. W. Roy Breg in his first year of service as Southern secretary has made gratifying progress in emphasizing co-operation with denominational leaders and strengthening State and union organizations.

The fruitful campaign for Christian Endeavor in Hawaii conducted by our splendid Pacific-Coast secretary, Paul C. Brown, and made financially possible by that great friend of Christian Endeavor, Mr. Theodore Richards.

The extension of the influence of Dr. Poling's Radio Youth Conferences which have reached literally millions of young people throughout the country.

The campaign for prohibition and Christian citizenship, in which President Poling, Extension-Secretary Sherwood, and Citizenship-Superintendent Landrith have rendered, and are rendering so conspicuously, efficient service.

The pre-Easter evangelistic emphasis in both 1928 and 1929, through which hundreds of societies were enlisted in efforts for personal soul-winning.

The development of a program for world peace, including the organization of study-classes in racial and international problems, the creation of International Correspondence Clubs, and the preparation of material for world-friendship activities and discussions and debates on international questions.

Thousands of New Societies

The regular activities of the International Society have been contined. 4,562 new Christian Endeavor societies have been reported during the two years, most of them organized with material supplied free of charge by our offices. 10,623 Comrades of the Quiet Hour and 1,772 members of the Tenth Legion have been enrolled. Thousands of personal letters have been written in response to requests for help from the field. Our introduction service continues to bring young people moving from one community to another in touch with friendly churches in the towns to which they go. Not less than two-thirds of the time of the officers of the International Society is spent in field-service in conventions, institutes, conferences, and local church meetings. The International Society seeks to exercise no authority over any Christian Endeavorer or society, but it is seeking to serve to the best of its ability.

For the future three needs are particularly apparent:

1. More young people. If the activities of Christian Endeavor are good for four million young people, they should be good for many more. Not for the sake of adding more members, but for the sake of sharing its blessings, every Christian Endeavor society should seek to serve the largest possible number of young people in its community.

2. More adult sympathy. Young people need more confidence and less criticism. They are not saints. They are normal human beings facing every-day problems. They would be helped immeasurably if in every church there could be enlisted a group of those adults who have formerly served in the young people's society to give them encouragement, counsel and support.

3. More financial support from adults for Christian youth movements. This need applies not only to Christian Endeavor, but to other youth organizations as well. If the unlimited possibilities of Christian youth are to be released for the betterment of the world, money must come not from the young people, but from consecrated men and women of means. We give thanks for those who by their gifts have already manifested their faith in present-day young people. For a comparatively few dollars invested now this world could be literally turned upside down for Jesus Christ.

MRS. J. Q. HOOK
Field-Secretary, Idaho

REV. FRANK P. WILSON
Field-Secretary, Illinois

CHAPTER II

HOURS OF INSPIRATION

The Opening Meeting—A Triumphant Key-Note—Honors
to Prize Winners and States—Mrs. Clark Presents a
Chain of Freedom—Superb Service in Song

Wednesday Evening, July 3

Long before half past seven, the opening hour for the first
great inspirational meeting of the convention, the main auditorium was filled with singing groups of Endeavorers.

The auditorium is one of those mammoth structures that have
become necessary in this day of immense gatherings. The main
floor covers a huge stretch; around it, on each side of the platform, are rows of boxes, and elevated above them, all around the
hall, is the first balcony; while above that again a second balcony
seats an audience that would fill a cathedral.

Of course there are the usual decorations, all sorts of flags
hanging from the ceiling and draped around the balconies. A
pretty sight! One big sign hung in full vision reads, "Milwaukee, 1933," for Milwaukee is thus early on the war-path to win
the convention of that year, the first convention in the second
half-century in the life of Christian Endeavor.

The delegates sit in groups, each around a placard with the
name of the State on it.

It is a colorful scene, with red predominant; red blouses, red
scarfs, red caps, and so forth.

There is plenty of noise, what with yells and singing. In this
contest of song Missouri, a host in the gallery, led by trumpeters,
naturally wins the victory, although other groups will not down.

The Gavel Falls

The gavel in the hand of Dr. Daniel A. Poling, president of
the International Society of Christian Endeavor, falls; and in
the silence that follows he declares the thirty-second International Convention of Christian Endeavor formally opened.

But the choir chairs, banked behind the speakers' platform,
are still empty. Yet not for long. From the sides file in the
girls of the choir all dressed alike in white and exceedingly be-

coming vestments. The men, forming the central group of the
choir, are similarly vested in black. The leader is John R. Jones,
a Welshman, who has trained this group of five hundred voices
to perfection. They have the honor of "singing in" the convention with a finely rendered stanza of "Onward Christian Soldiers." This was followed by another selection, "Open Up the
Portals." It is all sung from memory, sung with the verve and
feeling that stir us and move us to worship as we listen. It is
as if the portals were thrown open wide and the King of glory
enters to place His hand on every meeting.

Mr. Foster Takes Charge

Mr. Jones did a beautiful thing when he handed his director's
wand to Percy Foster, veteran song-leader and favorite of Christian Endeavor conventions throughout the length and breadth of
our good land. He led the great audience in "Crown Him Lord
of All" and "Praise God From Whom All Blessings Flow.' It is
a stirring sight, this great audience of American youth. They as
well as the choir can sing as they demonstrate in the echoing
stanza, "Blest Be the Tie That Binds," and the equally ringing
verse, "My Country 'Tis of Thee." Yes, they are patriots!
America-lovers! Not from this group will come the anarchic
lawbreakers who are making the name America a stench in the
earth! With hands uplifted they sing it in a song that is an in-
vocation, "Great God, Our King!"

This was only the introduction to the song service, which
was led by Mr. Foster in his inimitable style. He can sing himself, of course; but he has the greater and rarer gift of getting
others to sing, and to sing willingly. He never scolds and never
finds fault, yet he holds an audience in the hollow of his hand.

It is not easy for pianist accompanists to follow his meteoric
changes, but Mrs. Shaw and Mrs. W. E. Manion rose to every
emergency, and splendidly interpreted Mr. Foster's mood.

The Youth of America at the Heart of America

On decorations scattered throughout the city—for flags wave
in honor of our convention—are printed the words "Welcome,
the Youth of America to the Heart of America." This, in a
word, is the thought behind the address of welcome delivered
with eloquence and verve by Mayor Albert I. Beach, a typical
Missourian, full of fire and energy.

"It is a very great pleasure," he said, "to me, representing
the people of Kansas City, to bring to you their most hearty welcome. Kansas City is delighted to be host to Christian Endeavor.
We have had no greater honor than that which is ours to-day,
to be hosts of the fine young men and women of our land. . . .
You represent the church, the greatest organization in the civil-
ized world. Without the churches of Jesus Christ there would be

no moral code to control men and nations in their relations with one another. . . . I want to say that both the outer and the inner doors of Kansas City are wide open to this Christian Endeavor gathering.''

After prayer by Dr. Abram E. Cory, Dr. Poling introduced Vice-President William Hiram Foulkes to preside over this opening session and to reply to the hearty welcome voiced by Mayor Beach.

"Honor to Whom Honor Is Due"

Briefly, of course, recognition was made under the leadership of E. P. Gates to States that have done especially good work in the past year.

Checks were given by C. C. Hamilton to winners in THE CHRISTIAN ENDEAVOR WORLD subscription campaign, and the winners of free trips to Yellowstone Park and to Kansas City were presented. Honor banners were given to representatives of States that had exceeded thir quotas in support of the International Society of Christian Endeavor, and their goals in financial and registration campaigns.

Oklahoma's High Honor

Oklahoma won first place in one of the warmest pre-registration contests that we have ever experienced in connection with International Christian Endeavor Conventions. This contest was launched by the International Society of Christian Endeavor in the fall of 1928. Registration quotas were opened at high noon, November 1, by all States in the Union. The long look ahead of the leaders of the Oklahoma Christian Endeavor Union in anticipation of this contest caused them to have more than enough registrations to reach their quota at the opening of the quota envelopes, thus placing them ahead of the rest of the States. In recognition of this splendid service Oklahoma was the honor State at the great International Convention held in Kansas City, July 3-8, and received Banner Number 1, led the great parade, and occupied front seats at the convention auditorium. The accompanying picture represents only a part of the delegation from Oklahoma in attendance at the convention.

Closely following Oklahoma in reaching its quota came South Dakota, which won Banner Number 2; and on its heels came Utah with Banner Number 3; then came the District of Columbia, Idaho, California, and Colorado in the order named.

The other honor States in order are as follows: Arkansas, Louisiana, Connecticut, Oregon, Pennsylvania, Delaware, Arizona, Wisconsin, Missouri, Kansas, Indiana, New Mexico, Vermont, North Dakota, and New Jersey.

Besides these special honors a printed list of honor societies— that is, societies that have especially distinguished themselves in their work during the past year—was available.

The Light of the Cross

A wonderful effect was produced by the exquisite singing by the convention chorus of the beautiful Psalm, "Send Out Thy Light and Thy Truth; Let Them Lead Me; Let Them Bring Me Unto Thy Holy Hill." The rendering was superb, and every heart was moved when, at the close, in a dimly lighted house, an electrically lighted cross behind the platform flashed upon the audience.

President Hoover's Greeting

Dr. Foulkes read the following telegram from President Hoover.

The White House,

Washington.

July 2, 1929.

Daniel A. Poling
President International Society
of Christian Endeavor
Baltimore Hotel
Kansas City, Missouri

My dear Dr. Poling:

Please convey to the members of the International Christian Endeavor Convention my cordial greetings and my deep appreciation of their cooperative spirit in working toward the furtherance of obedience to law and of world peace, for the one is vital to the perpetuation of our free institutions of government and the other is vital to the happiness and prosperity of all mankind.   Yours faithfully

Herbert Hoover

A Moving Moment

Every International Convention has its high, moving moments, and one of these came at this point.

Dr. Poling called to the front Mrs. Francis E. Clark, wife of the founder of Christian Endeavor. He called her the best-loved Endeavorer in the world, loved not only for her husband's sake, but for her own sake and for her devotion to the cause of Christian Endeavor.

By this time the audience was on its feet giving to Mrs. Clark a great ovation. Mrs. Clark had a message to deliver. On his sixtieth birthday the Endeavorers of every State in the Union presented to Dr. Clark a golden chain of forty-eight links with the name of a State on each link. Mrs. Clark wished to present this chain of office, as it were, to Dr. Poling as president of the International Society of Christian Endeavor.

MRS. FRANCIS E. CLARK
Wife of the Founder of Christian Endeavor

Mrs. Clark to Dr. Poling—Presentation of the President's Chain

Dr. Poling, I am glad to present to you this chain as a memorial of him who wore it for so many years. Ever since the day when he laid his hands upon you in blessing as you were installed president of the World's Christian Endeavor Union you have been as a dear son to us, and I can think of no one to whom Mr. Clarke would so gladly have me pass on this chain as to you.

I hope you will wear it in loving memory of him as a trust and as a reminder of the high spiritual aims with which the first Christian Endeavor society was organized. I am sure that you will try to keep the standard just as high.

I hope that you will wear this chain so long as you are president of the International Society of Christian Endeavor; and if the day should come, many years hence, I hope, when you shall be so old and "full of years" that you feel you must lay the burden down, then I trust that you will pass on the chain, with its memories and its trust, to your successor.

This chain has traveled in many parts of the world, and has been gazed upon with earnest interest by Endeavorers in many lands, because of what it stands for. Mr. Clark greatly prized it because it was given to him on his sixtieth birthday as a love-token by Endeavorers in every State of our own country and every Province of Canada, and I am sure it will carry to you also the affection and warm regard of all the original givers.

May this chain ever remind the wearer and those who look upon it of our promise, "Trusting in the Lord Jesus Christ for strength, I promise Him that I will strive to do whatever He would like to have me do." God bless you, dear Dan Poling.

Dr. Poling accepted the chain with a sense of new consecration to the great task to which, trusting in Christ for strength, he has set his hand. As Mrs. Clark handed him the chain, he kissed her in token of that deep affection he has always felt for her, and as a seal of his promise to be true to the highest ideals of Christian Endeavor.

More About the Chain

Many of those at the Kansas City Convention inquired what kind of chain it was that Mrs. Clark presented to Dr. Poling. This chain was presented to Dr. Clark, the gift of Endeavorers

ELIZABETH COOPER
Field-Secretary, Indiana

EVERTT ROBIE
Field-Secretary, Iowa

all over the United States, on his sixtieth birthday. There are forty-eight links in it, and on each link is engraved the name of one of the States. In giving it to Dr. Poling, Mrs. Clark hoped that it would become a president's chain, and be handed from president to president of the International Society.

The case in which the chain is kept was furnished by the New York Christian Endeavor Union. It is an expensive, hand-made leather case lettered in gold, the inscription indicating that the chain is the gift of Mrs. Francis E. Clark, and that it will pass from the hands of one president of the International Society of Christian Endeavor to another. In other words, it is the president's chain and not the possession of any individual.

The presidential or keynote address by Dr. Daniel A. Poling found ready response in all hearts. The title was

THE TRINITY OF TRIUMPH

Problems of Progress—Crusading with Christ—The Trinity of Triumph—Christian Endeavor and Organic Union— Citizenship and World Peace—A Ringing Challenge, "All for One, One for All"

By Daniel A. Poling,
President of the International Society of Christian Endeavor

The Thirty-second International Convention of the Christian Endeavor movement opens under auspicious circumstances. The report of our general secretary, Mr. E. P. Gates, will reveal progress, definite and in some respects quite remarkable, along all lines and in every department. Our correspondence from overseas indicates that the work in America but reflects the state of Christian Endeavor abroad. The next World's Convention is to be held in Berlin one year from this month. We shall then be rapidly approaching our fiftieth anniversary, our golden jubilee. One year later, in our year of jubilee, two notable international gatherings are in prospect, one, the International Convention on this continent; and the other, a similar convention in Australia. To the second of these the young people of Australasia have invited a gathering which will reveal and emphasize the scope of our movement's ministry in the Southern Pacific.

From our general secretary, Mr. E. P. Gates, has come the suggestion that during the next two years we enroll one million former active Endeavorers, men and women who have known the fellowship and training that are our common heritage, and who, though no longer serving with us in the active ranks, are now identified with the home, social, religious and public life of their communities and States. I offer this suggestion as a definite recommendation. Let this enrolment be entirely separate from any financial appeal and from every other campaign. Let is stand as a living memorial to Christian Endeavor. Let those enrolled become the big brothers and sisters of all Endeavorers.

The gift of Charles O'Hara Craigie and his wife, both of whom passed from the church militant to the church triumphant during the year, has enabled us to think in terms of a yet larger service. Certainly Christian Endeavor has for nearly half a century demonstrated the divine principle that Christian agencies live largely by living unselfishly, and that they receive unto themselves in proportion as they give of themselves. Jesus Christ came that "they might have life, and that they might have it more abundantly." For organizations as for individuals the life abundant is the life of sacrificial service. Francis E. Clark, our founder, was a living demonstration of this truth in which the Christian Endeavor movement has gone forward in all lands.

Problems of Progress

The problems we face—and there are problems—are problems of progress. If we are as true to the principles of this movement as were those we follow, the program of Christian Endeavor has an expanding future. Her genius in adaptability as well as in direct service commends her now as perhaps never before to the individual church. We believe that her response to both denominational leadership and denominational control, with the world-wide Christian fellowship and the united Christian service which are her peculiar glory, have brought her to the kingdom for such a time as this.

I would make particular reference, not only to my associates in the Boston headquarters, but to those of our number who are the executive and field leaders of the State unions. Under these devoted men and women new and greater achievements have been recorded. Particularly significant and happy have been the relationships of these secretaries with the officers of the great denominational youth groups. I have had personal satisfaction and joy in these associations.

But even more praiseworthy and significant than the accomplishments of our full-time, salaried executives is the ever-enlarging ministry of the young people themselves. Without remuneration they give their time, ability, and enthusiasm to make Christian Endeavor what for young men and young women we believe it distinctively is, "the greatest youth movement of the world."

In my own church the individual societies have played an ever-growing part in the parish ministry of Christ's kingdom. Without the slightest friction they have carried forward a common cause side by side with the church school and the organized clubs and classes. I would not consider favorably a pastoral responsibility in down-town New York without the aid of Christian Endeavor. Expressionally it is at once the simplest, the most efficient, and the most constant instrument the pastor has available for the direction and leadership of youth. Again and again I find young people confirming the testimony of Mr. Roger W. Babson, who said: "All that I have and all that I am I owe to a little Christian Endeavor society in Gloucester, Mass. After joining the church at fourteen years of age I became interested in the Christian Endeavor movement. This gave me an opportunity for expression in a religious way which held me until I went to college. It truly saved my soul."

Crusade with Christ

At the Cleveland International Convention two years ago Christian Endeavor gave to the youth of the whole church the Crusade with Christ. It is estimated that more than ten million young persons in more than forty associated groups are now united in this great enterprise. The Crusade with Christ has already done something to lift "Like a mighty army moves the church of God" out of the realm of poetic fancy.

During the recent Lenten period more than ten thousand Easter sunrise services were conducted by young people under the Crusade auspices. A National Loyalty Sunday was observed, and the enthusiasm of young people was concentrated upon a national election so as to raise the Constitution and the law above partisan politics.

The Crusade with Christ has materially affected the attitude of adults toward young people. Here we have made just a beginning, but a real beginning. We hold that youth are as intrinsically fine as they have ever been, and that the Christian challenge is not only their hope of salvation, but their way to larger living. In the Crusade with Christ this challenge is delivered with directness and power.

Fifteen men and women, serving without remuneration, have comprised the general committee of the Crusade. The total expense incurred has been pitiably small, but they have materially affected the atmosphere surrounding denominational relationships and the attitude of young men and young women toward the world-wide ministry of Jesus Christ.

What of the future? We present the Crusade with Christ to-night as the imperative of the hour and as the challenge for the next two years. In its program we find the sufficient answer to the question of both the individual Endeavorer and the organization.

Trinity of Triumph

Evangelism, citizenship, and peace; this is the trinity of triumph. Personalized in the words of Mr. Fred W. Ramsey, they bring home to the heart of each of us the driving dynamic, "Myself, my country, and my world." Again evangelism is first this profound, this timeless challenge to personal religion and for personal rightness, this clear call to personal devotion and personal allegiance. One man can change a community; one woman can revolutionize a city; but it must be a new man and a new woman. The new world, with its Christianized social order, waits forever on these. Here lies the supreme business of Christian Endeavor, for here is the fundamental reason for Christianity itself. To lead young people to Jesus Christ, to strengthen and train them in the Christian life, to relate them definitely to the services of Christ and His cause—thus we express the fundamental business of our society, which is Christian first, pre-eminently, and always!

For the Jerusalem Message

During the next two years it shall be our purpose to co-operate with all communions associated in the Christian Endeavor movement in order that Christian missions may feel a new tide of life flowing from Christian youth. Our conventions shall carry an even stronger evangelical emphasis. The time has come again when the student generation should be brought more definitely face to face with the world's need, the need that cannot be met at any station short of Calvary.

This International Convention is at one with the Jerusalem message. The work of the missionary may have changed. His place in the life of the peoples to whom he goes may be different now from what it was a generation ago, but the vital business of the missionary has not changed. While ancient civilizations are in the travail pains of a new birth and while indigenous churches rise through social convulsions, the missionary is needed as never before, needed to counsel and to inspire, as well as to teach and direct.

From Christian Endeavor thousands of young persons have gone to the missionary field at home and abroad. To-night let us join our lives to the greater missionary task ahead. Let this be at the heart of our passion and program for evangelism.

To make our missionary purpose definite and the plan practical, we propose a special covenant declaration. We shall ask this convention to give the declaration its first public indorsement.

Crusade Unique

A unique feature of the Crusade with Christ is this: that each church, each denomination or communion, may make the Crusade peculiarly its own. There are no restrictions as to organizational procedure. The Crusade with Christ is at once the crusade of the particular organization while its unity is a unity of spirit in a common cause. Christian Endeavor has only the profound joy of its origin and of a place with all others in its plan.

Christian Endeavor and Organic Union

As to organic unity, Christian Endeavor calls the youth of the whole church to support the commissions on union that have been authorized by practically every denomination and communion. Our movement is in itself a commission for unity, spiritual unity first, that unity which must precede and accompany any organic plan. Christian Endeavor is also a vital factor in bringing about those physical contacts and organizational relationships that open and prepare the way for organic union.

But it is in our own field, the field of fellowship and co-operation, that we shall continue to operate. Our functional life is not without and apart from the church; it is within the churches in which our societies are established and to which we belong. Christian Endeavor is not a young people's church. Christian Endeavor is part of the church. Christian Endeavor is a youth agency of the church, loyal to the church and responsible to the church. It is for this reason that Christian Endeavor does not have a special commission on church union. It is for this reason that we serve the great principle and ideal of union at the call and under the leadership of our denominations. Such a gathering as this is the outward and visible expression of the spirit that in God's own time shall bring to pass the fulfilment of Christ's prayer that His children should be one. To this glorious consummation youth will bring increasingly the enthuiasm and faith that dispute with schism and that are impatient with delay.

Citizenship

We present at this convention the beginning of a new citizenship library. "Ye shall know the truth, and the truth shall make you free" is the basis of every great educational enterprise of the Christian church. We shall strive to discharge our trust more effectually in the future than we ever have discharged it in the past.

Fundamentally the Christian Endeavor Society is in its citizenship emphasis a Christian-citizenship group.

While I shall allow the convention itself to unfold the details of our program, I do particularly call your attention to the fact that we have a responsibility for law-observance and law-enforcement all our own. We dare not lightly regard the implications of our slogan of eighteen years ago, "A Saloonless Nation by 1920." By our private practice and public testimony we must challenge lawlessness. We must throw our whole influence behind the government and in support of the Constitution and law. The words "observance" and "enforcement" have for us a special significance. The invitation of the President of the United States does not fall upon deaf ears to-night. We shall call you to personal, definite commitment.

"Evangelism, citizenship, and peace"—aye, and let me remind you that not only in evangelism, but in citizenship and in the campaign for world peace, the missionary program of Christian Endeavor finds its expression. I think of the message of Christian missions as strengthening us for each of these vital tasks, and the spirit, the veritable miracle of missions, as binding the tasks into one.

World Peace

With us world peace can never be an empty phrase. We do not forget that it was our beloved founder, Francis E. Clark, who at the New York International Convention in 1921 launched the Christian Endeavor crusade for a warless world. Our field is the world. Our associates are of all nations and all tongues. Our program for more than two generations has carried us, in the flesh as in the spirit, to the ends of the earth. We shall never escape the horror that brought Christian Endeavorers face to face upon the field of battle in bloody throes of war. To-night our vow to have a part in ending war comprehends at once the passion of a personal Christian testimony and the fervor of a fellowship that has made of the world a Christian Endeavor community. We are of one faith, one tongue, one objective, and we have a single high command. "For Christ and the Church" is more than a motto. It is a program for service and the expression of personal dedication.

But, aside from all else that we may do through our individual societies and our unisons, by means of study-courses and the conferences and conventions that are to be held in half a hundred countries in all quarters of the globe, let us to-night launch a campaign that shall be a veritable crusade, a crusade more significant than any that ever swept forward towards the sepulchre of Christ, a crusade to bring the young people of the world first to think peace and then so to practice peace that nations shall learn war no more forever.

We Launch a World Movement

Let us to-night launch a world-wide movement to make prompt and effective use of that most promising instrument for peace, peace among all peoples, that most promising instrument yet devised by human statesmanship. Let us request the executive committee of the International Society of Christian Endeavor to bring our action to the attention of all national Christian Endeavor unions. Let us set in motion a program that shall call to a common purpose and plan Christian Endeavorers of every land, of every race, and of every tongue. The providential instrument of this advance is the Pact of Paris, which we to-night rechristen the Pact of Peace.

This pact has changed completely the psychology and the basis of the crusade for a warless world. Now youth campaigns for peace as a crusade of national honor. Our banners in North America are not the flags of "pacifism"; they are the flags of our countries, the Union Jack, the Stars and Stripes, and the banner of Mexico. Yesterday we strove against age-old traditions to overcome precedents and to change law. Now we strive to vindicate national honor, to make law effective, and that our countries shall not be found either in failure or in falsehood. Surely God is in this matter.

Every national Christian Endeavor organization, particularly every national society in the countries of the sixty sovereign powers ratifying the Pact, may unite with us, as we unite with them, in this new war to end war.

"All for One, One for All"

Christian Endeavor formally accepts the Pact of Peace. We take it in full earnest. To it we give our indorsement. With it we pledge our personal—aye, and our Christian Endeavor—honor. It is our individual and collective declaration of faith. It is equally our platform of principle and our field of action. It renounces armed conflict as a means for settling all differences between the high contracting nations. By it we are authoritatively committed to the proposition that henceforth all questions between nations, all disagreements, shall be settled by conference and arbitration; that there shall never come again any dispute that shall not be submitted to a proper tribunal for peaceful adjudication. The Pact outlaws war forever. It is British. It is German. It is French. It is American. It is Christian Endeavor.

Finally, from this Pact of Peace and as the next step toward organizing the machinery of peace, let us move forward to the World Court. Let us enter here without delay. To-night I call you to a threefold covenant which is at once a personal vow and a world program.

The Trinity of Triumph

After Dr. Poling's eloquent appeal crusade covenant-cards were distributed with the following challenge to young people. The three pledges on the card printed below were signed singly by practically every person in the audience. In signing the crusade-for-peace promise right hands were lifted and the people repeated the pledge, "I will see this thing through."

I PLEDGE

1. *My Crusade for Evangelism.*

   Believing that the supreme need of the hour is pledged allegiance to the ideals of Jesus, I promise Him, trusting in His strength, that I will co-operate with my pastor in whatever ways he may suggest to lead others to accept Jesus Christ as Saviour, Master, Friend, and Great Companion.

   Name...................................

2. *My Crusade for Citizenship.*

   With President Hoover, I believe that "prohibition is an experiment noble in purpose," that it was enacted for the "protection of the American home"; and with him I "wish it to succeed." To support the President and the Constitution, to strengthen public health and public morals, and to advance my own well-being and the well-being of others, I pledge myself to abstain from all alcoholic liquor as a beverage and to give my utmost endeavor for the enforcement and complete success of prohibition.

   Name...................................

3. *My Crusade for Peace.*

   I accept the Pact of Peace as a covenant of personal and national honor. I pledge myself to abide by its principle and to work for its complete fulfilment.

   Name...................................

   Address..................................

So, with prayer and song one of our great meetings was brought to a close.

CHAPTER III

EVANGELISM AND WORLD FRIENDSHIP

A Challenge to Good Will
Thursday Morning, July 4

To fill or nearly fill the main floor and more than half the gallery of the huge convention auditorium for a forenoon public meeting immediately following a two-hour conference period is a splendid testimony to the interest of the young people. This was done Thursday forenoon.

The first action in the meeting was the reading of the following letter to President Hoover:

"PRESIDENT HERBERT HOOVER,
  "THE WHITE HOUSE,
    "WASHINGTON, D. C.

"The delegates in attendance on the Thirty-second International Christian Endeavor Convention received your message with appreciation and enthusiasm. They send you the assurance of their affectionate regard, and pledge their loyalty in the following words:

" 'With President Hoover I believe that "prohibition is an experiment noble in purpose," that it was enacted for the "protection of the American home;" and with him I "wish it to succeed."

" 'To support the President and the Constitution, to strengthen public health and public morals, and to advance my own well-being and the well-being of others, I pledge myself to abstain from all alcoholic liquor as a beverage and to give my utmost endeavor for the enforcement and complete success of prohibition.

" 'I accept the Pact of Peace as a covenant of personal and national honor. I pledge myself to abide by its principle and to work for its complete fulfilment.'

                                        "DANIEL A. POLING,
                                                  President."

The meeting took the form of a class in evangelism, using the International Society's book, "Acquainting Youth with Christ." Dr. F. G. Coffin, editor of *The Herald of Gospel Liberty*, was the speaker. We give an abstract of his speech.

YOUTH'S GREATEST TASK

By Dr. F. G. Coffin,

Editor of The Herald of Gospel Liberty

"The committee which planned this program is wise in pushing to the forefront of this convention a theme which, in its broadest significance, will determine the whole future of the church. Every movement of the church in the past which has been considered worthy of the attention of the historian has been made in an evangelistic atmosphere. Every backward step taken may be indexed by the absence of such atmosphere.

"Evangelism is a broad term. When employed in behalf of one it is called 'personal evangelism.' When it is community wide it has been designated as a 'special effort,' 'revival meeting,' 'Kingdom-enlistment' period, etc. It becomes home missions when country wide, and foreign missions when the world is included. When it is accomplished by teaching it is denominated 'Christian Education.' When realized through gifts it is called 'benevolence.' If the printed page or periodical is the medium it is called 'Christian publications' or 'silent evangelism. It may be accomplished by near natural processes under ideal conditions as when a child grows up into righteousness; or it may be reformatory, as when the wreckage of a life is redeemed as far as such redemption is possible.

"An evangelistic program gives to youth a worthy task. A task-less young Christian passes into an early spiritual decline. The church cannot make itself an end of its own existence. Its own life is kept from stagnation and decline in reaching out to others. The religious life needs its thrills and adventures for its own sake. Nothing supplies these so perfectly as active and successful evangelism. What is inside the church must be pushed out into the world or what is out in the world will be pushed into the church.

"Evangelism is the church's highest strategy. It sends youth out for youth. Youth is the responsive age. Receptivity of good impressions has been found to be greatest from nine to nineteen and the climaxes of response at thirteen and sixteen. The period before twenty determines the religious life for most people. The majority of people who have remained non-Christian up to thirty years of age will continue so throughout life.

"Much has been done for this generation of youth, therefore much obligation to the future is upon it. In no way can this obligation be discharged except to others. The most useful Christian religion is that which serves Christ by helping others. Men may be aided by theories, rules and moral codes, but they will be helped most by personalities which they can understand, feel with, and respond to.

"The evangelistic impulse is the gift of conversion. It is a primary prompting of the Christian heart. The saved soul immediately becomes a soul-saving agent. When this is not the case development has been arrested and the Christian life is sub-normal.

"Operating a program of evangelism answers the craving of the young. Youth is the beginner of new things and the explorer of new ways. Like that young pastor—now of sainted memory—Dr. Francis E. Clark, youth desires to find the best ways and the largest service. If this passion to evangelize men can come to effective program in this convention, Christian Endeavor will be entering the largest usefulness of its life."

World Friendship

"Young People and World Friendship" was the theme of the following stirring address by Harry Holmes, Field-Secretary, World Alliance for International Friendship through the Churches. He drew three word pictures, the first about ten thousand young people gathered in the ancient city of London. As they marched to their meeting, one of the banners carried this sentence: "All the world is one family."

The other picture was taken from Europe. It was that of a great meeting of youth called an international camp-fire, when each one of many nationalities placed a fagot on the fire. The first to bring his fagot was a youth from India; and, as he laid his fagot in place, he said: "As light begets light, so friendship begets friendship. We, the young men of fifty-six countries, *will be friends.*"

The third picture was that of a meeting of Englishmen and Americans. One man at this meeting said, "Herein lies the tragedy of the race, not that men are ignorant, for who is wise? not that men are poor, for who has enough? the tragedy is that men are strangers." Our world was made for friendship. It is but a small place, and we cannot be happy in a small place unless we are friends.

Mr. Holmes thrilled his audience as he described this shrinking world and the need of friendship if peace is to be achieved. The very heart of the kingdom of God is not service, great as it is, but *friendship.* "Ye are my friends if ye do whatsoever I command you."

"Making Discoveries"

Another of those unexpected and delightful episodes that come up in our meetings was entitled "Making Discoveries," and was introduced by Frederick L. Mintel, executive secretary of the New Jersey union.

The discoveries related to THE CHRISTIAN ENDEAVOR WORLD, each of a number of field-secretaries presenting a "discovery" he or she had made in the paper. Each gave a brief message, bright, witty, snappy, telling of good things found week by week; and each urged the worth-while character of our international organ.

PROBLEMS ON THE AIR

Dr. Poling's Radio Broadcast

Dr. Poling's radio conference, which was "put on the air" at noon Thursday and succeeding days, proved a popular feature as question and answer always are. Young people, too, are full of interrogations, and they are sure to get from Dr. Poling sympathetic understanding and answers. Different Endeavorers presided at these meetings, reading the questions that Dr. Poling answered. Each day Dr. Poling prefaced the question period with a short address. A large number of the questions will be found in another chapter.

A COLORFUL PARADE

Groups Vie with One Another in Costumes and in Original Ideas

The Kansas sun was kind on Thursday afternoon, July 4, for the Christian Endeavor parade, always an interesting event at an International Convention. The sky was partly clouded, and a gentle breeze helped to mitigate the summer heat, a fact which was decidedly good for the marchers.

Nearly an hour before the parade started the streets along the route were lined with spectators. A reviewing-stand was erected on one of the main streets, and here Dr. Poling, Mrs. Clark, and many International Society trustees and officers veiwed the marchers as they passed.

Waves of Color

Now they come, headed by a contingent of motor police. Behind them, but in front of the procession, comes an American Legion band with three Boy Scouts carrying United States flags.

Then a row of dignitaries—Percy Foster, A. J. Shartle, Homer Rodeheaver, Frank Getty and Harry Holmes. And then

Oklahoma

winner of the highest honors, and therefore first in the parade. Imagine a host of girls, finest of youth, dressed in white and carrying white umbrellas with the Christian Endeavor monogram on them. Happy? Yes, singing! And quite rightly proud!

South Dakota next with an "Extra Special" honor banner. The delegates are in yellow and red, and a large sign informs us that they are from "the friendly State." They look friendly, too.

Utah marches, carrying red-and-white parasols and wearing pretty red-and-white sashes. A red-coated band with a magnetic leader is next in the procession.

Six Crusaders from *Wisconsin* are next in line, and then comes the *District of Columbia* with many copies of "Uncle Sam" garbed in white. There are Negroes in this section, and one little fellow carries a placard inscribed, "This is your nation; evangelize it." The paraders have kazoos, and use them lustily. A pretty sight, too.

There are a few from *Idaho* and a very respectable delegation from sunny *California*. They are dressed in red capes and wear yellow caps, and the front rank carries a gilded gate with a key across the top of it ready to unlock it. California is inviting the convention of 1931 to the Golden Gate.

CALIFORNIA CAPTURED THE 1931 INTERNATIONAL CONVENTION
"The Golden Anniversary in the Golden State by the Golden Gate"

39

Colorado has a fine group wearing red-and-white sashes.

The *Arkansas* delegation wears black bands or sashes, and carries black-and-white umbrellas. The outside marchers hold black lines that inclose the delegation. They make a pretty picture.

But here is *Connecticut*, a fine crowd, wearing pretty blue-and-white sashes; and they, like many other delegations, are happily singing.

Oregon is a long way off, but a small group of delegates is evidence of interest.

A Pennsylvania Host

Pennsylvania! How magnificent a sight! This huge delegation is dressed as Quakers, the girls in long, slate-colored dresses with white collars and bands, and the boys wearing regular Quaker hats. One in front is carrying a Bible. They made an impressive picture as they passed.

Delaware and *Maryland* march together. They make a goodly showing, are clad in red-and-white garments, and play upon kazoos as they march.

Arizona is next, and tells us by means of a placard that she "leads in copper." A youth follows, trundling a wheelbarrow carrying some copper ore and some implements of mining.

Here comes a group from *Milwaukee*, who tell us that they want the convention in 1933.

It is now *Missouri's* turn. First comes a handsome Missouri mule led by a girl and two young men. Follows the Salvation Army band wth a group of marchers and Girl Scouts behind.

A Brilliant Stunt

An unusual stunt has been prepared. The great *Missouri* delegation, a vertiable host, carries purple balloons; and, as the marchers reach the grand stand, they release the balloons, which ride the air like liberated birds. There seem to be hundreds of them. Up they go, higher and higher, filling the space above the street and rising until they become mere specks against the sky. Admirable!

Missouri is fertile in ideas! Next comes a float with a man tending a revolving dynamo. A placard reads, "The Power behind Missouri."

Kansas, just across the river, won herself great credit. First comes a band of boys and girls in white, and then an army with yellow predominant in dress. They carry the prettiest sunflowers as parasols. Another group have broad yellow ribbons dependent from their necks, producing the effect of living sunflowers. A truckful of smiling girls inform us by placard that "Kansas grows the finest young people in the world." And we believe it.

Indiana marchers wear beautiful purple capes. This fine delegation is led by Miss Elizabeth Cooper, field-secretary, who

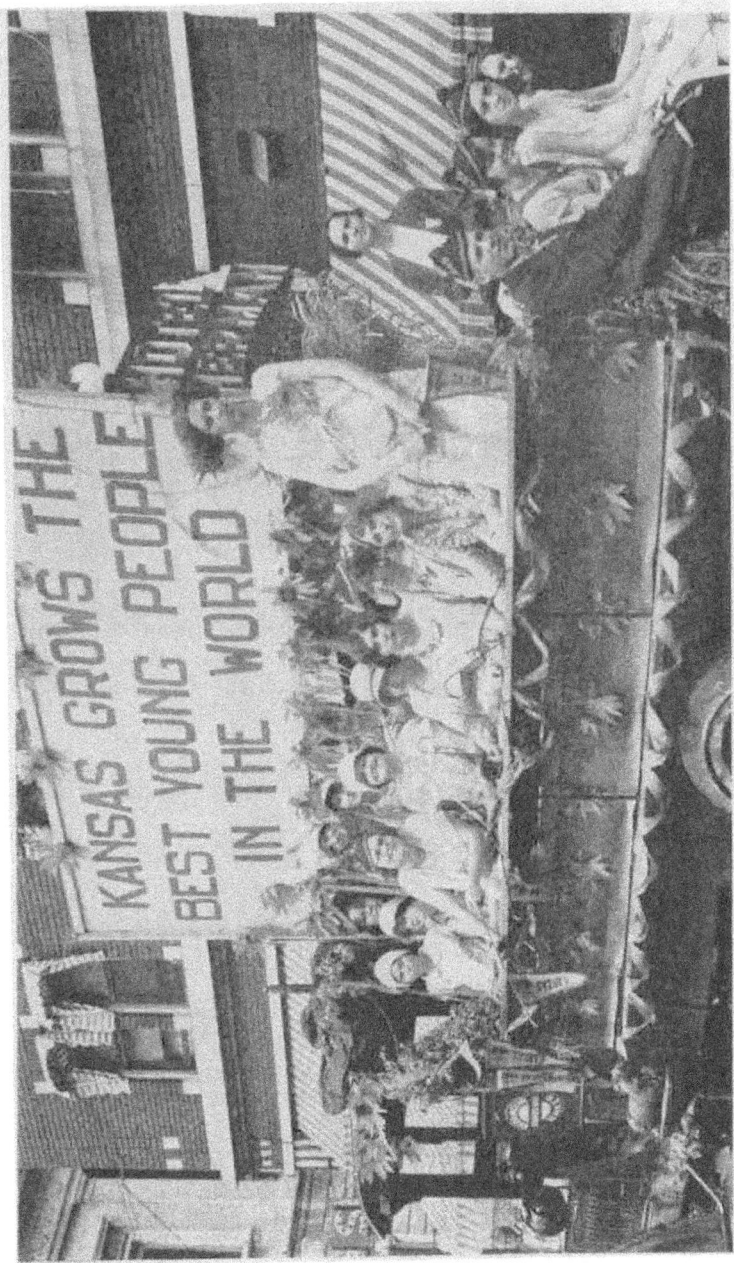

KANSAS IN THE PARADE

marches in front carrying an imitation torch suggestive of Liberty leading on the hosts of youth. In the front rank are three girls, one carrying scales (justice), one a living dove (that sits quietly on her hand), and one a Bible. Most impressive.

More Color

New Mexico delegates are dressed in part as cowboys and in part in Spanish costume. An Indian beating a tom-tom dances in the procession.

North Dakota is garbed in striking black capes, and is followed by a host from *New Jersey* in yellow capes trimmed with black.

What a host is this from *Illinois!* White and red predominate. Pennants are waving, and two trumpeters make joyful music.

Iowa, in red and white, is decidedly impressive. The crowd carry imitation cornstalks ending in a yellow tasselled head, and they attract attention as they raise these stalks when they sing, "Iowa; that's where the tall corn grows."

Massachusetts has a delegation dressed as Puritans, John Alden over again, the men carrying guns to make the picture real!

Field-Secretary Klahr leads the splendid *Ohio* delegation whose members wear rainbow-colored head-decorations.

Nebraska is headed by a trumpeter, and the entire delegation passes at salute, the right arm extended from the shoulder.

Texas—and one is surprised at the size of the crowd—carries white umbrellas, and red pennants are flying in the breeze. As the delegates pass the grand stand, they "make whoopee" sure enough by giving, we believe, the rebel yell.

Michigan is headed by a crusader in mail on a white horse. Knights walk on each side carrying shields, making a striking picture.

The delegation from the State of *Washington* is small; but a great man, George Washington, leads the van.

Then *New York* in purple capes with red lining, the red showing as the cape is thrown over the shoulder. They march in the form of a cross, holding red and blue lines.

Minnesota has a single but gallant line, and then comes *Dixie* in solid ranks. As they pass the grand stand, the lines break with wonderful precision, and the delegation takes the form of a cross. After passing, the delegates re-form in solid ranks. It took some practice to do this so well.

As a demonstration of Christian friendship the Epworth Leagues and Baptist Young People's Unions of Kansas City were in the parade and made an excedingly fine showing. One of the groups had a beautifully arranged float with a group of girls facing a "queen" on a chair.

MICHIGAN CRUSADERS WITH SHIELDS

MILWAUKEE WANTS THE CONVENTION IN 1933

INDIANA'S SPLENDID GROUP IN THE PARADE

43

Clever Ideas

Kansas City, Mo., Christian Endeavor union followed, a mighty host wearing red capes with a large white cross on them. One amusing and striking feature was inscribed, "The Clarks going to their first convention." It was an ancient chaise such as was used a century ago, battered and weather-beaten, and drawn by two horses. A battered, time-worn trunk was fastened on behind, and thick iron bars formed the window-panes, which were destitute of glass.

Then came individual societies; a crusader on a gray horse; a society carrying a silver cup won in some competition; more Puritan-garbed young people; a float with Pilgrims armed with guns; the Italian Institute society with a float presenting the idea of world friendship, children carrying flags of the nations; a float presenting the resurrection scene; a float with the inscription "Christian Endeavor Forever;" a banner with "The Only Road With a Foundation—Christian Endeavor;" a grass-covered float with Uncle Sam on it; a float with Endeavorers facing the cross; a float with a globe on top and the inscription "World Peace To-morrow;" and finally a float with a huge globe emphasizing the missionary needs of mankind.

By long odds this was one of the most colorful and striking Christian Endeavor parades we have ever seen. The ranks were close together, and the young people marched briskly; yet it took one hour and twenty minutes to pass the grand stand.

It was a parade of *youth.* No one that saw it could turn away unmoved. So long as America has such young people—and she has them by the million—the country is safe. It was a parade that made us thank God and take courage, a parade that disproved the slanders so freely broadcast about youth.

PRIZES AND ORATORY

After a ringing, reverberating song service led by Homer Rodeheaver Thursday evening, Mr. Fred W. Ramsey, general secretary of the Y. M. C. A., uplifted a simple prayer that included most sympathetically and thoughtfully leaders, speakers, singers, delegates, every one.

And O how Professor Jones's big choir did ring out their choruses! And how "Rody" sang into all hearts and mouths new songs from the collection he praised so highly!

Prizes for the Street Parade

In that setting, floor and balconies alive with youth, color, expectation, a herald in courtly robe sounded the bugle-call for the awarding of the prizes for the street-parade, four gold and silver cups and two flags, which were presented by Colonel Barrett to the winners: the first to the Iowa delegation; the second, a handsome flag, to Pennsylvania; the third, a cup, to Kansas, which the speaker said grew the finest youth in America; fourth was another flag with a standard, to Indiana, whose full delegation responded with a song, as had others. California, "land of fruit and flowers," won a beautiful loving-cup, and sang a favorite "sunny-California" song. A silver loving-cup went to "that great wind-swept State," New Mexico. Dr. Poling voiced great appreciation of Kansas City's splendid showing in the parade.

Oratorical Contest

Paul C. Brown, Pacific-Coast secretary, had charge of the oratorical contest. The four contestants who had won in nation-wide State elimination contests were of the stuff most of the great audience was made of, from seventeen to nineteen years old; and keen was the interest as James Lohman of Ohio, Arnold Evans of Utah, Gwendolyn Gaskill of Michigan, and Paul Rhoten of Nebraska, spoke on "Christian Endeavor and Christian Citizenship."

This national oratorical contest was broadcast over a wide "hook-up."

A great treat awaited the audience in the final address of the evening, by Justice Florence Allen of the Supreme Court of Ohio, one of the leading lawyers of national fame. In opening, she spoke feelingly of her early membership in the Christian Endeavor society of the Congregational church of her home town. It was a high peak of interest, this witnessing of the intellectual and legal giantess who had made her first forensic efforts in a little Christian Endeavor meeting, as the girl contestant in the previous oratorical contest is still doing.

Justice Allen made a clear and masterly analysis of the structure of our government, showing how the Declaration of Independence as to the equality of all men had been, as Lincoln allowed, in relation to the black slave, a "hard nut to crack," but was intended as a future theoretical safeguard, which more and more is becoming a practical reality.

Justice Allen told the young people that, in spite of repeated emphasis on the complexity of modern life, the boys and girls of to-day will be asked to face no new moral questions.

She believed that if George Washington were living to-day he would shake his head, and say, "We are going at too fast a pace."

The serious questions we face are those which we ask of our own souls. The supreme, vital thing to-day is not the wealth of America, or the culture of America, but the soul of America.

She got a round of applause when she declared, "There is no such thing as a 'mild' violation of law." She denied that prohibition created disrespect for law. "Prohibition inherited disrespect for law. Some men have assumed to choose and pick the laws they will observe. The wonder is not that prohibition has not succeeded better, but that it has succeeded at all.''

Justice Allen, after thirty years' experience in politics, expressed a belief that partisan politics must be broadened so that Republicans and Democrats will say to officials they have elected, ''We did not elect you as Republicans or Democrats, but to enforce all the laws.''

Only so can the soul of America be preserved and developed. The thing that is wrong in private life must be stamped as wrong in public life by Christian citizenship.

Some Resolutions

Resolutions on prohibition and citizenship were presented by the committee and approved by the audience. These and other resolutions will be found in a chapter on ''Resolutions.''

TO EVERY ONE HIS TASK

By C. C. Hamilton,
Publication, Manager, International Society of Christian Endeavor

A Chinese laundry tag issued some years ago carried a line which read, "What we say we do we do do." That sentence contains one "say" and three "do's." Likewise, the major portion of the time of Christian Endeavor has been given to doing rather than to simply talking about doing. That first and most important part of our Christian Endeavor pledge, "Trusting in the Lord Jesus Christ for strength, I promise Him that I will strive to do," is the very heart of Christian Endeavor. Learn to do by doing is axiomatic with the Christian Endeavor movement.

The activity of Christian Endeavor is secured through a system of committee work. To every one his task. In a well-organized society every member will be placed upon some committee. Each member's duty to the society is thus made definite. The purpose of committee work is two-fold—for training and for service. Service of first importance is rendered to young people and to the Christian church. Grateful pastors by the thousands will testify in regard to the definite lines of helpful service performed in their churches, aiding, co-operating with, and extending the work of the minister. However, as the committees function and this service is performed, certain beneficial developments occur in the life of the individual engaged in the activity.

Self-Expression is provided by committee work. There is no hard and fast way to do the work. There is no regular routine to follow. The daily flood of mail that reaches our desk indicates that the young people perform their work in a variety of ways that is simply amazing.

Fellowship is developed by committees, as those interested in certain activities are drawn together for their planning and work. Any organization that is really *doing* anything, automatically shuts out those that can not be interested in what it is doing. Christian Endeavor is not exclusive any more than a Bible study class or a women's missionary society are exclusive that do not include all the women of the church. On the other hand, young people of like minds and worthy motives are recruited from the Sunday school, the church, and the community, and voluntarily associate themselves together in the society.

The more intimate contact of the committees develops in a member both the desire and the ability for intimate friendship that will make for his own and others' happiness throughout life.

Initiative is developed by committee work, for the reason that there is no required program—no fixed procedure. The challenge is always to survey conditions among the young people in the churches and community, and then formulate a program to meet the need. The church of to-morrow, manned by leaders who have thus developed, will be enterprising and aggressive always.

Leadership ability is one of the products of the committee system. Perhaps one of the most permanently helpful things learned in committee is how to work with others for the accomplishment of a definite task, without friction. That "without friction" is important. Ask the pastor who has had trouble with some members of his choir, his Ladies' Aid, or some other group. The minister of a great New England church which I visited recently told me of his happiness in serving a smooth-running church, and explained it by saying, "Every officer of the church and Sunday school, and every Sunday school teacher, with one exception, is a product of Christian Endeavor. They have had training and experience in the give and take of happy co-operative effort." Many other results of committee activity could and should be listed, but time will not permit.

Christian Endeavor Unions

Just as soon as the second Christian Endeavor society is formed in a community the thought of fellowship between them naturally arises. They have the same plans, the same purposes, the same pledge, the same ideals, the same service objectives. They can hardly resist the natural attraction that brings them together. So local Christian Endeavor unions are formed, with the object of stimulating interest in the societies, increasing the number of societies, developing mutual acquaintance of the members, making more effective the service to the churches and the community, and in every way enlarging the service of the Endeavorers in Kingdom enterprises.

The general public quite naturally seems better acquainted with the work of a Christian Endeavor union as represented by its large mass meetings and rallies and by its conventions, rather than by the numerous lines of activity promoted by its committees. The inspirational value of large gatherings of young people can not be overestimated. They give a definite stimulus and uplift to all who attend. Dozens, hundreds, or thousands of young people, as the case may be, uniting their voices in prayer and in the songs of Zion, provide experiences that influence life for all time. Then, too, these public gatherings serve notice on the public and re-sell the idea that young people in large numbers are to-day definitely interested in the program of the church and in the welfare of their fellows.

However, the Union committee activities represent the larger service of a Christian Endeavor union. Perhaps the majority of Christian Endeavor societies are organized by a group of friendly, interested, young people representing the union lookout committee. Increased numbers of Intermediate societies and Junior societies in a community can usually be traced to the activities of union workers. President Poling years ago made the statement that an efficient union makes almost impossible the death of one of its members. Said Dr. Poling: "For a society with sinking spells it is an almost never-failing oxygen tank." Many weak, struggling societies are furnished leaders for months at a time until their own leadership can be developed. It is usually members of the lookout committee who find openings for new societies, discover a church, or make contact with a group of young people who are without a Christian Endeavor society.

Inter-society visitation is promoted which results in a more intimate fellowship and a very happy exchange of ideas, plans, and methods that is mutually helpful. Membership campaigns are frequently promoted simultaneously in all the societies, resulting in a greatly increased membership and a wider influence among the young people of the community.

The local union initiates educational campaigns among the societies, resulting in the organization of mission-study classes, Expert Endeavor classes, classes in Christian citizenship, stewardship, teacher-training, personal work, Bible study, etc. Much of this work is organized and promoted in the individual society, but summer conferences and winter institutes are promoted by many unions directly under their own supervision and leadership. These serve in large measure as normal classes, sending back to the individual societies trained leaders capable of promoting similar efforts in their own groups.

The old-fashioned so-called monthly or quarterly "rally" is no longer representative, and a generally used plan is to have the early part of the evening given over to sectional conferences where definitely practical, and workable plans are given for every department of society work. This educational period is then followed by a brief inspirational service, perhaps including an address.

Union work for the churches represents a large part of a union's activities. Numbered among these efforts are help-our-church campaigns, a religious census, go-to-church Sunday, mid-week prayer-meeting campaigns, tithing crusades, and evangelistic campaigns. Mention could be made of some most successful evangelistic efforts, which were initiated and largely promoted by Christian Endeavor leadership. Almost unbelievable results have been attained in certain unions in the promotion of Bible reading and missionary-reading contests. Citizenship campaigns and reform movements innumerable have had Christian Endeavor union direction. Helpful ministries in homes for aged women, orphanages, jails, penitentiaries, hospitals, etc., are included in the program of every active Christian Endeavor union.

The fellowship of the local society eagerly adapts itself to the wider fellowships of the local union. It is a significant fact that among local-union leaders denominational barriers are completely broken down. Acquaintances of years sometimes discover that they do not know the denominational affiliation of their associates. Some time ago we visited Washington, D. C., and a great Christian Endeavor rally was held in the Calvary Baptist Church. A roll-call was taken of the States represented and it was found that more than half the States in the Union were represented. It was then discovered that more than a score of denominations were represented. However, at the close of the rally a fellowship circle was formed around that great auditorium, and under the expert leadership of that old-time friend of Christian Endeavor, Percy Foster, hands were clasped and all joined in singing "Blest Be the Tie That Binds." Bright-faced, happy youth from all over the country, young people representing more than a score of denominations, in a friendship circle almost under the shadow of the Nation's capitol, singing "Blest Be the Tie That Binds" is significant to them and to the organized church life of America.

Widening Horizons

However, again following a natural inclination, the local Christian Endeavor union widens its activities to include the county and a county union is formed: or perhaps a portion of a county, or in some cases a number of counties, and a district union is formed. Through these agencies the union functions, perhaps not as intensively as a local union, but nevertheless with splendid results. Flying squadrons tour the territory, carrying inspiration, help, and encouragement, informing the societies of the latest developments in the program and the general objectives of the movement. Unquestionably the greatest asset of Christian Endeavor is the splendidly sacrificial and enthusiastic volunteer leadership of the Christian Endeavor union. Its vital importance can not be over-emphasized.

During the years of our early experience in city-union and county-union leadership we studied carefully the writings of Dr. F. E. Clark, the beloved founder of Christian Endeavor. During those days we ran across a statement to the effect that Christian Endeavor waxes or wanes as the Christian Endeavor union flourishes or languishes. Even though engaged in union work at the time, we did not fully understand the importance of that statement. During the years we were serving as field-secretary of the Ohio Christian Endeavor union the value of that statement was not fully understood. However, as later we toured up and down this whole country, night after night perhaps for many months at a time, coming in contact with a different Christian Endeavor union in a different city, we came to a full appreciation of the wisdom of that observation. Truthfully, the crux of the whole matter is in the Christian Endeavor union, and most certainly the thermometer of Christian Endeavor influence and service rises and falls with that of the Christian Endeavor union.

Then follows in order the State or Provincial Christian Endeavor union, probably with its employed field-secretary. The State union furnishes direction and guidance for the organized work represented throughout its territory. Tirelessly day after day the field-secretary tours the State, encouraging and helping the leaders in one of the most inspiring "big-brother" relations that can be found in any line of organized effort in the Christian church. Perhaps the most brilliant of the State union activities is the annual State convention, bringing together the young people from all parts of the State into an inspiring, uplifting, educational, challenging fellowship which sends them back to their homes, their societies, their churches, and their communities with strengthened purposes and new vision.

The International Society of Christian Endeavor, with its biennial convention, perhaps bears to the States in large degree the same relation that the States bear their county unions. The International Society of Christian Endeavor is primarily an organization for the assembling of plans and methods, and for the dissemination of ideas. Democratic always, it has maintained its intimate relations with the youth it serves. Its policy, its procedure, its program are representative of the mind, the heart, and the purpose of youth as this is learned by the intimate contact continually maintained with boys and girls, young men and young women, in the organization throughout the country. Exerting no authority and desiring none, the International Society of Christian Endeavor continues to be simply a vehicle for the organized expression of Christian Endeavor.

The World's Christian Endeavor Union, embracing all the national Christian Endeavor unions throughout the world is simply an extension of the idea, plan, and purpose represented by the International Society. Advice, co-operation, sympathetic interest, and encouragement are given Christian Endeavor everywhere, and in many countries the work is almost entirely financed by the World's Christian Endeavor Union. However, the democracy of Christian Endeavor is maintained even here, for in no instance does the World's Christian Endeavor Union dominate or control, seeking only to exert its influence for the development and strengthening of the work.

Thus from the work of the individual society, with its definite help, to the organized work of the Kingdom and its beneficial influence on the individual, we have carried forward the thought of the fellowship of Christian Endeavor from the individual society into the local union with its community interests and its splendid interdenominational fellowship. We have widened that fellowship to include the State, and then our perspective has included the United States, Mexico and Canada in the International Society of Christian Endeavor. And now we find Christian Endeavorers joining the fellowship of the World's Christian Endeavor Union, representing Christian Endeavor from every country where the name of Christ has been sounded, for Christian Endeavor is found among virtually all the peoples of the earth.

Perhaps the most spectacular and significant demonstration of the fellowship promoted by the World's Christian Endeavor Union was witnessed in the last World's Convention in London in 1926. A roll-call of nations was held and thirty-two countries responded. Dr. Clark stood on the platform and received the representatives as they brought their national emblems one by one to the platform. Finally all these national emblems were grouped around a large illuminated Christian Endeavor monogram at the back of the platform. These national emblems, clustered in friendly fashion about the monogram, represented in a striking and significant way the intimate fellowship formed through Christian Endeavor, and visualized for all the peoples of the earth the intermingling of the nations under the banner of Christian Endeavor.

We are grateful to God for the glorious past of this world organization. We appreciate the large place Christian Endeavor occupies to-day in the church of Christ throughout the world. We look forward with unbounded enthusiasm and confidence to a greatly increased number of societies and unions, an enlarged and more effective program, and a still more glorious service during the years ahead under the able leadership of that beloved friend of the Christian youth of the world, and the President of the World's Christian Endeavor Union, Dr. Daniel A. Poling.

THE SOUL OF AMERICA

By Justice Florence E. Allen
Of the Supreme Court of Ohio

I would like to think that somewhere in this audience there are some delegates from the Congregational Church in which I was baptized and in which I first became a member of the Christian Endeavor society, where I played the piano sometimes, and sometimes raised my quivering voice. I am glad indeed to have been a part of this great movement and I am glad, too, to see many thousands of young people here, from Kentucky, from Iowa, from Pennsylvania, and all these other States.

The Declaration of Independence is the blood descendant of the Magna Charter and all the English-speaking nations, along with all the other nations of the world, inherit the truths of the Declaration. How astounding that Declaration was! What it meant to history can only be understood when you look back through the pages of history and see that in those days the generally accepted theory of government was that the government is an entity detached from the citizens who composed the state and is in no way responsible to them; furthermore, that the government, mind you, does not have to do right; that the government is a sovereignty unlimited by any moral consideration.

They took that doctrine directly from the old doctrine of the divine right of kings. They used to say "A king can do no wrong," and so, when in the slow march of history the kings had their powers clipped they began to say "The state can do no wrong," and when our forefathers protested to George III against paying taxes without representation they said in effect, "You are doing wrong," and his ministers replied in effect, "Why you belong to him; you are his subjects; you are his chattels; the state can do no wrong to its subjects." The astounding thing about the Revolution was not simply that we decided to fight for our freedom and won; the amazing thing was that we repudiated that old conception that the state can do no wrong, and we wrote a new doctrine that the state *shall* do no wrong.

America's Aim

Our forefathers and foremothers said that no matter what the system was in the old world, here we were to establish a nation in which the government should be directly responsible to the citizens who constitute the state. Also, they declared that no matter what the rule might be in the old world, here the purpose of government should be an ethical purpose, to maintain right and justice.

Sometimes we forget how important it is to declare a standard. Abraham Lincoln pointed out that our forefathers erected this standard in the Declaration of Independence. You remember in the great Lincoln-Douglas debates, how Stephen Douglas, the great orator who played upon his audience just as a musician plays upon his musical instrument, was compelled to argue his way around the Declaration of Independence. Of course, if he once admitted that all men are created equal and endowed with inalienable rights, he had to concede that the institution of chattel slavery had to go, and so Douglas argued that when our forefathers wrote the Declaration they were not talking about every kind of man. He said they were just talking about Englishmen and that what they meant was that Englishmen in America should have the rights of Englishmen in England; but that when they said all men are created equal and endowed with inalienable rights they did not mean Germans, Frenchmen, colored men, or any other kind of people.

Lincoln cut through that argument with unanswerable logic. I am not going to tell you all he said because it is quite a long passage, but he asked: "Why did our forefathers say then in the Declaration of Independence that *all* men were created equal?" Abraham Lincoln understood and taught that in the Declaration of Independence a new page was opened in human history and that for the first time at the founding of any nation, we dedicated our community life to the proposition that all men in this country were going to be given even handed justice.

Material Power

You and I live in a new and swift-moving time. Perhaps the most astounding incident which illustrates our power over mechanical forces happened recently in New York City when one of the great New York papers desired to get in touch with one of its staff who lived in New Jersey. This man in New Jersey was a radio operator who had been very successful in keeping in touch with the Byrd expedition at the South Pole. He could always get Byrd on the radio even when others failed, but because of the interference in the midst of the city he had asked permission to remove the radio to his home. On this particular evening he was at his home in New Jersey. A very urgent crisis arose in the editorial office and they desired to communicate with their radio operator in New Jersey, but when they tried the telephone there was no response, and by and by the chief operator reported that evidently the operator in New Jersey had left the receiver off the hook of the telephone. Then, because the matter was so urgent it occurred to some bright person in New York to suggest that they radio Byrd's camp at the South Pole and ask the operator at Byrd's camp to radio back to New Jersey and request the radio operator there to please hang up the receiver on his telephone so that New York could talk to him. That thing actually took place and New York City communicated with New Jersey via the South Pole.

But No New Moral Standards

But surely we are quite well aware that no new standards of human conduct have come out of these marvelous devices; no new principles of living have been invented along with the radio and the airplane and the submarine; we ask the same old questions that have been asked of the men and women in all ages, from the beginning down to the present, namely, whether we have done justice and loved mercy and walked humbly with God.

It makes no difference how much wealth you have amassed; the only question which faces you is, "What have you done with yourself?" and that question remains regardless of the questions which confront America. It is always to be emphasized, "What are we making of our souls?"

But how about the soul of America; that fine, free, generous, wonderful soul, which found its first expression in the Declaration of Independence? What shall you and I make of the soul of America?

I like to think my friends, that the soul of America is expressed in our pledge, in our support of law enforcement; in our support of the abolition of war; in our support of the great forward look to those things which in time to come will be the glory of this country.

Law Enforcement

And now I want to say just one word with regard to the problem of law enforcement, and I speak here as a lawyer and a judge; as one who under the law is compelled to deal with liberty and life and death and the great questions of crime in a community of over eight million people. *There is no such thing as a light violation of law.* You and I may pick out the traffic law to disregard. You and I may drive our Ford, or Chevrolet, or whatever it is, past the red light when the policeman isn't looking. The bootlegger picks the prohibition law to disobey, and the gangster makes very light of the law against murder, and so my friends when you once concede the right of the individual to decide which law he will obey, you concede the right of the gangster to sweep the streets of our great cities with machine guns.

And one word about prohibition. Prohibition did not create disrespect for law; prohibition inherited disrespect for law; and that disrespect for law has been created for decades by men and women who thought so little of their country that they deliberately swore false oaths in their tax returns rather than pay their share of the fairly assessed tax value: deliberately created by men and women who believed that it was their right not to share in the burden of the country when they did not wish to; deliberately created by large groups of people who here and there sought a way to evade law.

For decades disrespect for law has been mirrored in our mounting criminal statistics, and when I look at the situation I wonder not why prohibition has done so badly, but why it has done so well.

Criminals in High Places

Now, in this year of our Lord 1929, as we look at America we have to ask ourselves whether or not the soul of America has been expressed in government. Where, in one great State, a former governor has been held guilty of a felony; where, in another great State, a governor has been held guilty of misappropriation of government funds, in keeping back huge sums of interest on large deposits of State money in State banks; where, in other States, officers in high places are impeached upon very serious charges; where council after council in great cities is shown to have been tainted with bribery; where the entire election board is removed in one metropolitan town; and seventeen indictments for election frauds are returned in another important place; when we could go through a list of things that have happened in the last twenty years in the United States both in State and national government, can we say to ourselves that the soul of America has been rightly mirrored in politics?

Who Owns the Office?

Why has it not been rightly mirrored? For two reasons.

We must abolish the theory that the public official owns the office. The king used to own his office; he inherited it from his father just as I might inherit a little piece of land from my father. In these days we seem to be reverting to the conception that the office belongs to the officer; that it is not only his meal-ticket but something that he can use for his own particular gang or crowd. Of course, there are thousands and hundreds of thousands of men, and, I am proud to say, very many women, who stand out like shining lights for integrity in the face of this old-world conception that crowds back upon us, that the office doesn't belong to you and me who pay the taxes and elect the officers, but that it belongs to the man who has the job.

There is another theory that comes back upon us. Washington, Hamilton, Jefferson, and Lincoln, and all the great statesman, declared that the same moral standard should apply in public as in private life, but now the conception leaps upon us that the thing which is wrong in private life is not wrong at all in public life if you can get away with it. While it is wrong for me to steal $100 from you it would not be wrong to steal $100 from the State of Ohio if one can get away with it. That's the conception which begins to be mirrored in the governments of the States, and here and there in the government of the nation, and never until the Christian men and women, the men and women who want decency and honor and justice from the government demand that we go back to these old standards can we bring the soul of America to the high spiritual point to which it was meant to go.

And now I am going to tell you what to me is the most American story in the world.

It's about Benjamin Franklin. You remember how during the Revolution they sent Ben Franklin to France to get the men and money we needed to end the fight. When he arrived they didn't think much of him, but by and by, with his shrewdness and his judgment and eloquence, they changed their minds. Once he was invited to attend a great dinner at the palace, and was even asked to deliver a speech. When the night came the palace was thronged with ladies and gentlemen in golden lace and jewels and they sat down to a magnificent repast. After they had eaten, one of them said of Great Britain that it was like the sun, because it shed light and warmth on the whole world. Then the French Minister of State spoke. He said if Great Britain was like the sun, France was like the moon which sheds beauty and poetry and romance on the whole world. Everybody thought that nothing more could be said, because after you talked about the sun and moon there was nothing left. Then shrewd Ben Franklin remarked that if Great Britain was like the sun and France like the moon, America was like Joshua, who said to the sun and the moon, "Stand still." And when he said that he spoke better than he knew. America did say to the old systems of the world, "Stand still."

But you cannot write liberty into a charter like the Declaration of Independence and send it ready made to the next generation. We have to write liberty in our own hearts and send it out from our own lives. Never until you and I understand our ownership of government, our responsibility in government, and the ethical purpose of government shall we be able even in this country to establish the institutions of liberty and justice that were meant to be established and to this task every man and woman, boy and girl is called. It is not an impossible task surely for us who believe in the ethics and philosophy and religion of Christ; not an impossible task for, "They who wait upon the Lord shall renew their strength; they shall mount up with wings as eagles; they shall run and not be weary; they shall walk and not faint."

*Notes not corrected by Justice Allen.

Honors in Oratory

Jack Huppertz of Texas, chairman of the committee of judges on the oratorical contest, announced that honorable mention had been awarded to Paul Rhoten of Nebraska, and first place to Gwendolyn Gaskill of Michigan.

It was a climax to a splendid program that sent home thousands of happy Endeavorers resolved to seek to raise themselves to higher levels of living.

HAROLD F. LOVITT
Field-Secretary, Kansas

F. C. DIXON
*Field-Secretary, Maryland,
West Virginia and Delaware*

CHAPTER IV

YOUTH AND ITS OPPORTUNITY

How to Invest in Youth—Tell to Youth the Gospel Story—
Our Army and Navy Superintendent—
Friday Morning, July 5

With the sound of a bugle-call the forenoon session on Friday, July 5, opened. Homer Rodeheaver, with two splendid solos, and with his capable and sympathetic leading of the music, literally sang the large audience in the convention hall into responsive and receptive spirit.

Row upon row of eager youth turned expectant faces toward the platform as A. J. Shartle, treasurer of the International Society of Christian Endeavor, rose to speak on ''Enduring Investments.'' One of the standing sources of astonishment in this convention, as in others, is the way in which *all* conferences and meetings are attended. This morning, for instance, Mr. Shartle's conference was crowded out of two halls; and the third hall where they *had* to stay was altogether too small to accommodate the crowd. So the audience in this forenoon meeting we are describing reminds one of the evening meetings in our largest conventions.. There is no doubt about the interest of these young people in religion. One has but to attend such a convention as this to be convinced that the heart of youth is sound and that Christian Endeavor is still a vital and dynamic force!

Big Crowds

Mr. Shartle began by pointing out that the greatest asset is a great crowd of people, but the greatest asset in a crowd is a consecrated man with a consecrated dollar. He emphasized the thought that youth itself is the greatest asset of our nation; and those who give their means to lead youth into the higher life are making the greatest of all investments, an investment in youth. He went one better than the hilarious tellers of Scotch stories by declaring that the man who had made the largest gift to the International Society was a Scotchman, Charles O'H. Craigie of New York.

How to Invest in Youth

Mr. Shartle described the annuity plan of giving to Christian Endeavor, by which the giver receives a fair rate of interest on the amount given as long as he lives, the gift, however, on his death becoming the property of the International Society. He clearly described various ways in which people may give to Christian Endeavorers and in time build up a fund to be used to spread the work of Christian Endeavor all over the world. This is the finest investment in youth.

One Minute about Books

A one-minute talk by Clarence C. Hamilton (an extended minute) was devoted to telling the audience about some books on Christian Endeavor work that are fresh from the press.

The second forenoon class on evangelism was on

CAPITALIZING ACQUAINTANCESHIPS

By Dr. F. G. Coffin,

Editor, Herald of Gospel Liberty

An evangelistic program in any group is mostly a matter of making a place for it. If it is written large in the Christian Endeavor program and everybody works for it, it will succeed.

Success is assured if conditions are met. Nothing which may be entered in the church schedule can yield greater results in the educational, benevolent, social, and missionary objectives of the church than the practice of evangelism. We have held "socials to save," but actual saving makes the most perfect sociability. It enlists everybody. The Kingdom of God will be victorious in that day when laymen rediscover their function in the evangelistic program and discharge it.

Results will not come without plans. We work too much by indirection and impulse instead of going directly to the task and continuing until success has been reached. Preparation, consecration, intelligent industry, and presistence make success certain. The gospel is light and will diffuse according to the opportunity given it. The light is not us but we make its penetration possible by giving it a chance to shine into dark corners. Christian efforts succeed under a statesmanlike program which assembles and directs the best of every kind. Capricious impulses offer no more assurance of success here than elsewhere. Evangelism is not the exploitation of friends to make an institution succeed. It is "one loving spirit setting another on fire" for its own best welfare. This is the "great venture of faith" with few hazards and many assurances.

In this task Christian Endeavorers should first get acquainted with themselves. They should measure their preparedness for the task, take temperatures on their own spiritual health, overcome their group weaknesses of non-co-operation and self-centered purposes, and make the big things in the mission of the society the dominating things of their programs. We may lose the real way in a multitude of incidentals. Begin by relocating emphasis on really important things.

Then there should be acquaintance with other youths. Despite all queries it is an honor really to know the youth of to-day. They are worthy, except in small minorities. What they are should be capitalized into what they may become. They are frank, daring, earnest, get-at-able, and in pursuit of the things that are real. They are disgusted with meaningless haggling in religion. They want a Christianity that makes all things in life Christian, and are only slightly interested in its doctrinal or denominational antecedents. In such a state of mind drift is easy and many are as sheep needing a shepherd.

Then we should make thorough acquaintance with the evangelism of Christ. Forget any sensationalism that formerly may have attached itself to evangelistic propaganda. Forget likewise the exclusively emotional appeals, narrow interpretations, and questionable methods which have accompanied some campaigns. Evangelism is first reading the heart of Christ aright and then "publishing the Good News." The world is news-bent on politics, finances, sports, and scandals. The Gospel is the best of all good news for the needs of the world—better than the news which would announce to the world an unfailing cancer cure—and he is a gladdening messenger who bears it.

An Army Chaplain Speaks

Dr. Abram E. Cory introduced Chaplain S. C. Ramsden of Fort Sam Houston, Texas, who is superintendent for the International Society of Army and Navy Christian Endeavor.

Mr. Ramsden briefly described the various fields of service for Christian Endeavor in the army and the navy. There are only about 125 chaplains in the army and about 75 in the navy, a number inadequate to the need. It is not necessary to live on the seaboard or near an army post in order to help, through Christian Endeavor, the men of the army and the sea. He urged that societies organize an army and navy department, not, however, as part of the "prison" department, placing soldiers and sailors in the same class as prisoners, which would be an insult to the uniform of the United States.

Chaplain Ramsden invited the Endeavorers to attend an army and navy conference to hear the work explained in detail.

A Musical Interlude

Mr. Porterfield, a member of the Missouri delegation, delighted the audience with piano selections, proving himself a master of the art.

WORLD PEACE AND WORLD MISSIONS

"Are We as Bad as They Say?" a College Girl's View

Peace Orations—Dr. Cory's Appeal for Missions

The Friday-evening, July 5, session opened with the reading of three resolutions, one on loyalty to the church, one on international Golden Rule Sunday, and one on the missionary task in relation to the Christian Endeavor movement.

In response to a letter from Director Schurmann of the German Christian Endeavor Union, it was voted to send a letter of greeting to our German friends, and also greetings to former General Secretary William Shaw and to Amos R. Wells, for many years editor of THE CHRISTIAN ENDEAVOR WORLD.

Percy Foster had charge of the opening song service, which means that the *people* sang with enthusiasm. Never in fact, have we had at any convention such a team of song-leaders as we have at this convention: John R. Jones, the Welshman, Percy Foster of Washington, veteran, and Homer Rodeheaver, who gained deserved fame as song-leader in Billy Sunday's and other evangelistic campaigns. And we may add that no convention ever sang more melodiously than this. Thank God, there is one thing for which we do not blame youth—their fresh and beautiful voices.

A Splendid Choir

Another thing must be said; namely, that we have one of the most wonderful choirs we have ever had at any international convention; and the members of the choir deserve the highest praise for their untiring faithfulness.

A College Girl Answers Critics

"Are We as Bad as They Think We Are?" is the question Virginia Tuxill, a young college graduate, and a "modern girl," sought to answer. Naturally she believes in modern girls, but not blindly. She knows that there are various types of girls, and the majority are sound at heart. It is the minority that makes most noise.

What do "they" say about us? They say that we smoke, that we drink, and that we pet. They say that we aim only at speed, and are irreverent and irreligious. The trouble is that many who bring these indictments simply do not know us as we know ourselves, and it is no wonder that some girls resent being misunderstood by their elders.

The speech was one of the most thoughtful we have ever heard from the lips of youth. We shall not attempt to condense it. It has been printed in full in THE CHRISTIAN ENDEAVOR WORLD. It a frank and fair statement of the attitude of thoughtful girls to-day, and is worth pondering.

A Burst of Oratory

On Thursday evening three boys and one girl were the contestants in the national oratorical contest. Friday evening this was reversed, and three fine-looking high-school girls and one boy entered the oratorical lists. One is amazed at the self-control of these young people, their poise, and their assurance, not to speak of their eloquence. The theme of the orations was, "Christian Endeavor and World Peace." The contestants were Mildred Lindblom, Washington, D. C.; Elsie Meyer, Spokane, Wash.; Rolia Nuckles, Kansas City, Mo.; and Elizabeth Taylor, Texas.

The winning orations appear in another chapter.

The Oklahoma Mocking-Bird

An interlude was some very interesting and beautiful whistling by Miss Esther McRuer, the "Oklahoma Mocking-Bird." And well she deserves the name, for her whistling—dare we say it?—seems to excel that of the birds, as it certainly does in its breadth of understanding and in the range of its choice. Miss McRuer astonished and charmed us all, and received a great ovation.

Two Awards

Two awards, silver loving-cups, were made; one for the largest registration went to St. Paul's Church, and one for the largest percentage in registrations went to the Independence Boulevard Christian Church, both of Kansas City.

A Missionary Voice

Dr. Abram E. Cory of Kinston, N. C., is a leader, not only among the Disciples of Christ, but in the religious world at large. He is a great soul and a preacher that sweeps his audience forward on the tide of his eloquence. His speech was one of the high-water marks of the convention, the theme being

WORLD EVANGELISM THROUGH THE MISSIONARY ENTERPRISE

By Rev. Abram E. Cory, D. D.

The future of the church depends on whether it is national or world-wide in its outlook and outreach. When Christianity digs in, it dies. When it reaches out, it lives and thrives.

Jesus reversed the order of the heart of man. From the earliest days man had said, "Go and get." Now Christ said, "Go and give," reversing every instinct of the human heart; and that is new in the history of the world.

We have heard of a new apologetic for missions. The old arguments that some of us heard thirty years ago were based upon the particular. When I first went to China as a missionary, I answered the call on the basis of the particular. They said there were temples full of idols, and I was to go and destroy the idols. They said there was slavery in the dark places of the earth, and I was to go and preach liberty. They said there was disease, and worse than disease, and I was to try to mitigate those conditions. I have lived to see slavery ended because of the missionary enterprise. I have seen the temples almost emptied, and I have seen vile disease yield under the hands of missionary doctors. The particular sin that we do not have in our own land was the basis of the appeal to go to the mission field then.

Now, what is the appeal to-day? The appeal to-day is education. We are to go and teach. We are to go and lift these backward races to a higher moral and spiritual level. The problems of Kansas City and New York and Boston to-day are the problems of all great cities around the world, and we cannot raise the cultural level of cities at the end of the earth until we first raise our own.

I want to put into your minds this definition. The world missionary enterprise is calling for a common Christianity; for the solution of problems the world around, and I want to bring to you the essence of that great missionary conference held some months ago in Jerusalem, which studied the missionary problem. They said there that the first great problem of evangelism, the first great obstacle in its way is the presence of unsettled moral conditions everywhere. The morals of the world are moving and unstable. The Christians of India and China are asking what kind of Christians we are in America. I have been reading a book recently published by that great Indian Christian, Sundar Singh, and he says, "I went to America and everywhere I found Christians without Christ." I wonder if that is true of us. Could he bring that indictment against us? And again he says, "Send not alone educational missionaries but send us life, for only life—Christian life—will save India," and I wish to declare with all the force I possess that a law-breaking America can never save the world.

In the first great conference of the Christian church held in Jerusalem in the days of the Apostles and described in the 15th chapter of Acts, the question of the church was the race question. Strangely enough, in the 20th century it is still the great question that rocks the church to its foundations. It came up again and again in the Jerusalem conference held but a few months ago. The fact is we look too much upon the races and too little upon the individual man. One Japanese said, "I am not asking you to recognize my race, but I do ask, 'Am I a man?'"

Back in the year 1913 I visited William Jennings Bryan in Washington, D. C., when he was Secretary of State. As I entered his office I met the Ambassador from Japan going out. You may remember that relations between America and Japan were badly strained at that time. When I entered Mr. Bryan's presence he asked me if I had seen the Japanese Ambassador leaving, and I said I had. He told me that the Ambassador took with him a letter which he hoped would avert the threatening crisis. "When we were discussing matters," said Mr. Bryan, "the Ambassador asked, 'Is that the last word that is to be said?' and with my arm across his shoulder," said Mr. Bryan, I replied, "There is no last word between friends." So, let us say to the nations to-night, there is no last word between friends.

In the old days we were shocked when we heard of mothers dropping their little babies into the Ganges, and that was bad enough. When I was in China, modern industry had not come to the country but now great factories have been built and China is becoming industrialized and people are feeding their children not into the Ganges but into the maw of industry, and forcing little tots to work long and cruel hours, and that I maintain is something far worse than the loss of a few children through the superstition of their mothers.

We say that the temples of the world are empty. Well, I am sorry that they are empty, for if the temples were filled with worshippers it would be easier to preach to the people, for they would have some sense of religion, but empty temples mean full streets. People may be giving up their religion, but when they are doing that they are not accepting Christianity; they are turning to atheism. We need to-day as never before, as the Jerusalem Conference pointed out, the spirit of prayer, the spirit of consecration, the spirit of sacrifice, the spirit of service, the spirit of fearless witnessing to the supreme needs of life. In all history there never has been such an opportunity for a crusade with Christ as there is to-day. What a challenge to the church to go forward in this hour.

In 1913 the church was giving something like twenty cents a head for world-wide evangelism and the church to-day is giving just about the same amount of money. In 1913 it was worth two and one-half times as much as it is worth now, so that we are giving less than ten cents a head to the great task of world redemption. Giving to missions is going down, but the church is not getting slack in spending money for buildings at home. Any church that builds for itself and forgets the world has many Christians in it without Christ. Are we allowing ourselves to grow pagan? To what church do we belong,—a getting or a giving church? Is it a church that is digging in or a church that is reaching out in service to mankind.

I call you to world service. Think not of the buildings at home, think of this—if I cure the need and improve human life in Kansas City and do not cure it in Shanghai, I am still in danger. Saving the individual man for God is the only solution of the problem of the world.

The Oratorical Awards

Finally, the winners in the evening's oratorical contest were announced. The first prize went to Rolla Nuckles of Kansas City, Mo., and the second to Mildred Lindblom of Washington, D. C.

It must be said that many were glad they were not judges, so excellent were all the orations.

ERNEST S. MARKS
Field-Secretary, Michigan

ALFRED C. CROUCH
Field-Secretary, Missouri

CHAPTER V

EVANGELISM AND ENDEAVOR
Saturday Morning, July 6

After Percy Foster's inspiring song service Saturday morning, Mr. Grimes, chairman of the committee on resolutions, presented resolutions on the use of tobacco and on the plan for enrolling a million former Endeavorers, both of which were adopted.

San Francisco, Cal., Wins the 1931 Convention— "The Golden Jubilee Convention in the Golden State by the Golden Gate"

President Poling announced the decision of the trustees that the 1931 convention should go to San Francisco.

On this announcement the California delegation, in their orange caps, marched down the aisle to the front, and sang California songs. The Iowa delegation formed in the aisle to march as escort to the Californians in their triumphal procession to their seats.

A Class in Evangelism

The convention class in evangelism was then led by Bishop L. W. Kyles, who announced as his theme "The Great Challenge to Evangelism."

He quoted Roger Babson as saying, "The only development that can keep this world alive is a revival of religion." This challenge, the speaker said, demands faith in God and His word.

We need to recover the faith of the apostles.

The "New Evangelism" will be welcomed if it means better methods, but at the heart of it there must be the old evangelism. It calls for church unity, such as is expressed in the Federal Council of Churches, the United Church of Canada, and proposals for other similar unions. Robert E. Speer urges unity on foreign fields to conserve resources, prevent competitions, and present an undivided Christ to the natives.

Christian Endeavor was cited as a practical embodiment of Christian unity.

Missions are adventures, calling for heroism, to which youth has ever responded, as it has responded in war, and won all wars.

The church of Christ is the grandest adventure history has ever known, the adventuring of Luther, Knox, Henry Martyn, and all the heroes and martyrs of all the ages.

The bishop's climax was a high light of presentation, a picture of the splendid accomplishment that the consecration of youth can lay at the feet of Christ, the crowning of God's program with Christ's triumph over all.

A Voice from Canada

Canada wafted the next inspiring breath, through Rev. W. A. Mactaggart, pastor of St. Columbia United Church, Toronto, who was authorized by vote to carry to the widow of Russell Hewetson a message of sympathy.

The message was

CHRISTIAN ENDEAVOR AND THE CHURCH
By Rev. W. A. Mactaggart

There is only one word that adequately expresses the relation that has ever existed between Christian Endeavor and the church. That word is *Loyalty*. Christian Endeavor was born within the church. It was organized to meet the special needs of the youth of the church, and for almost half a hundred years it has never swerved from that ideal.

Her motto has well expressed her motive. "For Christ and the Church," Endeavorers everywhere in their solemn pledge, "Trusting in the Lord Jesus Christ for strength," do "promise Him to do whatever He would like to have them do." Christian Endeavor will be ever loyal to Jesus Christ as she sees and understands Him. If that day shall ever come when Christian Endeavor ceases to render to the church the loyalty that is her due, it will not be the fault of Christian Endeavor, but of the church herself in failing to present to the youth of each generation such a true and holy conception of the church as shall command their homage and their love.

Loyalty like mercy must not be strained, like love it cannot be forced. How do we seek to develop loyalty in these relationships —to the State, for instance? There come to my country each year thousands of new Canadians. What do we do to secure their loyalty, for as we desire a United Canada and a United Empire, it is of the utmost importance that every citizen should be a loyal citizen.

We sometimes, for instance, present him with an Oath of Allegiance. If he desires to live in Canada and enjoy full Canadian citizenship, he must take that oath of loyalty to King and country. But if he has just arrived from Central Europe, what does he know of Canada?

But we do not often bother men with citizenship unless they first ask for it. Far better and far more effective is it to surround every new citizen with such a spirit of loyal fervor for King and country that it becomes contagious, and that he who came with suspicions and mistrust in his mind comes to love and to respect that which he once feared and hated.

But this is not enough. Each new citizen must be informed of the history of his adopted land. He must come to see in the unfolding of those ideas of equality and liberty and justice for all, that which finds a ready response in every honest human heart. Once the heart of the new citizen beats in loyalty and in love, all other expedients become superfluous.

As in the State so in the church. If we are to love the church
and be loyal to it, we must know what the church really is. No
signing of a Christian Endeavor pledge,—and I believe in the pledge
with all my heart,—no high *esprit de corps* in our local society can
ever take the place of clear thinking and sound teaching as to what
the church of Jesus Christ really is.

To some the church is a voluntary society of certain persons
who think alike on certain theological questions. The chief purpose
of such a church is to perpetuate itself and that often at the expense
of some other church in the same community. The day has long
passed when we can expect the loyalty of youth to any such sectarian
institution. Our colleges can never be filled to-day by any appeal
to save Presbyterians, or Methodists, or Congregationalists. We must
have a far higher appeal than that.

To others the church is a sort of machine for the accomplishment
of good works. There are many noble organizations like the Y. M.
C. A., the Y. W. C. A., or even Christian Endeavor itself that were
organized by noble men like our founder, Dr. Clark. But the church
is not in any such class. If it were we could well think that the
day might come when the loyalty of one generation might wane, to be
taken up by the youth of another generation.

The church is not a human institution. The church is a divine
creation; more than that, the church is God's greatest and highest
gift to man.

We are indebted to the scientists for tabulating the various
stages of the great acts of Almighty God in the onward march of
history and revelation. [Dr. Mactaggart traced God's creation from
the mineral kingdom, through the vegetable kingdom and the ani-
mal kingdom to manhood, to Christ.]

In the fullness of time a new man appeared—a new order, as
much higher than man as man was higher than the beast of the
field. That new man was Christ Jesus, the son of the Living God.
In Christ Jesus dwelt all the fullness of the Godhead.

At Cæsarea Phillipi, Jesus gathered his disciples. "Whom do men
say that I am?" Peter said, "Thou are the Christ, the son of the
living God." Jesus answered: "Thou art Peter and on this rock will
I build my church."

A new creation, another new order, new yet not new, but one
and the same—one by one Jesus caught up with Himself broken
fragments of humanity; one by one men and women have been knit
to Him as Peter was in that great confession. This is the new order.
This is the divine creation! The church!

Christian Endeavorers! Think who you are. The church, the
body of Christ. How can one part of the body be disloyal to the
other parts of the body. It is unnatural. It is abnormal.

My hand is part of my body. It will act quickly, even involun-
tarily, to protect or serve my body. But if you tie a tight cord around
my arm and leave it long enough, the blood circulation will cease.
By and bye the whole arm will cease to function. It is no longer
any use to the body. Indeed, it were better amputated, for if it ceases
to function, it not only renders no service but it becomes a menace.
If I am not very careful the bad blood in that arm will get to my
heart and from the heart to all other parts of the body and poison
the whole body. If thy arm offend cut it off. But far better than
that cut the string that is cutting off the circulation.

Fellow Endeavorers, think of who you are and whom you represent. When you think of that little church back home, be it a great
church in a great city, or a little frame dwelling in a prairie town,
that church is the local representative of the church of God in that
community. Your loyalty there is not loyalty to a minister, or loyalty

to the officials, but loyalty to Christ, and through Christ to all your brothers and sisters in a world-wide fellowship.

"He'll Go with Me All the Way," we sing. Yes, we can trust Him. But can he trust you? Did you ever think of the chances the Master took when he went away and left the work of the Kingdom to His church.

Let us yield to Him our hearts. Then we are one with Him. Let us allow nothing to interfere with the free course of his spirit in our lives. Then we shall bear fruit. Let us make a complete surrender to Him; then His Kingdom will come and His will be done on earth as it is in heaven.

The next address was on

HOW TO MAKE THE MOST OF THIS CONVENTION
By Rev. Harry Thomas Stock

You will leave this city with great purposes firmly fixed in your minds. You will resolve that Christ will have a larger place in your lives than selfish pleasure. You will determine that the church is more important than the movies. You will determine to take your lessons in citizenship from the Bible and the Constitution rather than from bootleggers and criminals. You, as a patriot, will take the government at its word when it condemned and renounced war as a policy, and you will determine to march with Jesus and not with Mars and his outlawed sword-rattlers.

But will you make good? How long will your resolutions stand against the laughter and denunciation of the crowd? The hardest problem in life is that of being true to our highest intentions. Young and old are "jumpy"—we go off with a bang like a firecracker and then our resolutions are done. The times demand young people who actually mean what they say when they sing, "I Would Be True." Only the help of God can keep us steady, courageous, and effective.

A second suggestion is that you keep your thinking caps on when you get home. Plan your program for the year, in the light of your local needs and of what you have learned here. Be wise as serpents, but harmless as doves. Reform your society, but don't tear down the house while you're doing it. Be like a wise physician who analyzes your ills, prescribes a cure, but hopes to heal you gradually. A mustard plaster may be a useful remedy, but it doesn't help a toothache to put it on your back. Strong medicine taken in small doses will cure—taken in large doses will kill. Be a fearless crusader against things as they are, but remember that common sense is still a virtue.

Now, a word to the adults. You want to be of all possible assistance to the young people. Often you can help the most by seeming to help the least. Young people do not want, or need, bosses. Their great need is for sympathetic friends who have self-restraint and character and tact. If you are privileged to be one of their appointed counselors, give advice sparingly. If you are not one of their chosen counselors, be even more cautious. Your greatest opportunity is that of coaching behind the scenes, and you can be useful here only as you have been accepted by the young people as one of them. Take them all of the good things that have come from this convention, share these things in the same spirit of comradeship as you offer them your Christian personality.

Poster Awards

Mr. Frank Gentry of the Kansas City Convention Committee presented the awards to winners in the poster contest. The first prize was a gold wrist-watch, won by D. Vincent Redding of Philadelphia. Mr. H. Van Hatton of Chicago won the second prize, a fountain pen. The third prize, to Thomas Patterson, Pittsburg, Penn., was a fine autographed set of Dr. Poling's books.

Dr. Poling turned the tables on the "awarder" by pinning on him a handsome flower.

A Closing Touch

The Mexican president of the New Mexico union, dressed in picturesque Indian garb with feathered head-dress, brought the greetings of New Mexico Endeavorers, and sang in a fine tenor voice one of their Spanish songs. Mr. Victor Durand, Jr., is the first native president of the New Mexico union.

The final number was "How Firm a Foundation," played with spirit by the Memphis, Tenn., Christian Endeavor orchestra.

THE CONVENTION BANQUET

The height of fellowship bloom flowered on Saturday night at the overtopping banquet of all the banquets, at which between 1,500 and 2,000 touched elbows, and sang, and vied with each other in State yells and laughter and encores.

Who could make such an audience hear, and hold its attention for five seconds?

Carlton M. Sherwood, presiding, did in spite of "Louder! louder!" as he rose to introduce "a speaker who needs no introduction."

"Don't try," some one called. "Let him shoot!"

And Rody's trombone let loose liquid gold, and every other sound hushed.

Another who "needed no introduction" was the "Oklahoma Mocking-Bird," Miss Esther McRuer, who trilled and warbled and lilted until eyes went aslant to discover a feathered mimicker.

The spaces between chews and talks were chinked with California's jubilant outbursts of

"California, California,
        Rah! Rah!"

and Texas's rejoinder:

"We're going to San Francisco, 1931,"

and now and then a cowboy form of "Amen," a yell from Oklahomans.

Appeared "Rody" as a sleight-of-hand juggler. Frankly showing empty hands and sleeves, he conjured from nowhere, out of nothing, handkerchiefs, red, white, and blue, out of which he spirited the Stars and Stripes; and, as he cleverly concealed the mystery, he drew practical lessons on conduct and living that teachers and preachers might add to their repertoire of effective talks to boys.

Mr. Sherwood introduced several familiar standbys of Christian Endeavor, first, beloved Percy Foster, for forty-seven years an Endeavorer, who announced the discovery that it takes the use of sixty-four muscles to frown, and only fourteen to smile; then, as John T. Sproull, the veteran New Jersey Endeavorer, suggested, "When you can have a funeral for $50.57, why continue to go about half dead?"

Another husky forty-four-year old Endeavorer was Dr. G. W. Haddaway, who organized the first Christian Endeavor society in the Methodist Protestant denomination, and who was made a life trustee of the International Society of Christian Endeavor.

Mrs. Clark Speaks Again

Mrs. Clark, the best-loved woman in the world, as she was called, stood on a chair the better to be seen and heard, and spoke in her own direct and beautiful way.

"Mr. Chairman and dear boys and girls," she said, "for you seem to me to be boys and girls, I thought I would tell you why I came to this convention. I felt like the old gentleman whose grandson asked him one day, 'Grandpa, were you in the ark?' 'No,' he said, 'I was not in the ark; but why?' 'Well, grandpa,' said the boy, 'if you were not in the ark, why were you not drownded?' Well, I was not in the ark, and I am not 'drownded,' either. I shall tell you why I decided to come here. Nearly fifty years ago I promised my Lord that I would try to do whatever He would like to have me do, and I believed that this was one of the things He would like to have me do. But now I am here you have made it so much easier for me with your kindness and friendliness. I am glad I came, and I feel that you have done me good.

"I read somewhere to-day that a one-cat power engine that is running all the time is worth more than a forty-horsepower engine that is standing idle. Now, I am not a forty-horsepower engine—I have thought that some of you have one thousand horsepower. Whatever power we have we can give to our Lord. Shall we not all try to know what our Lord's will is and do it?"

Two beautiful bouquets were presented to Mrs. Clark as a token of the love of thousands of Endeavorers from all parts of the country.

"Our Dan"

"Our Dan," as he was lovingly introduced (and his "better seventeen-eighteenths") again brought the audience to its feet. He struck a ringing chord when he avowed:

"God pity the organization that exists for the sake of the organization. Christian Endeavor never forgets that it stands 'for Christ and the church.'"

An Endeavor Pilgrimage

As he presented the cause of Christian Endeavor foreign
field work, help to weak fields, war-impoverished, he told of
Secretary William Shaw, years ago, on a pilgrimage for foreign
Endeavor, bringing back from the South Seas the garments of
an islander who had nothing else to give.

Envelopes were quietly distributed, and the thank-offering
will strengthen the hands of many a hard-pressed missionary and
Christian worker in foreign fields.

President Poling announced that in 1931, following the San
Francisco Convention, another pilgrimage will be undertaken to
the South Seas, Australia, Europe, and around the world, the
semi-centennial of Christian Endeavor's birth, to hasten the
bringing of Christ's world to Him.

A SATURDAY "NIGHT OF NIGHTS"

Madame Schumann-Heink Sings, Dr. Landrith Prophesies, and James Kelly Talks of World Peace

The great convention hall presented a pretty sight for the
evening meeting Saturday. The audience had been gathering
while the Fellowship banquet, at which 1,500 plates were served,
was still on. When the crowd from the banquet filed into the
hall, the seats reserved for them were soon filled with an earnest
multitude.

Homer Rodeheaver and the magnificent choir sang the audience into a receptive mood in a beautiful song service, deepened
by a brief devotional time that followed.

A special honor was conferred on the convention by the
presence of Madame Ernestine Schumann-Heink. She entered
the great hall led by Dr. Poling, the audience rising to give her
a rousing welcome. Madame Schumann-Heink is a smiling,
elderly lady, radiating good will and kindliness; gray-haired, it
is true, but youthful in heart and spirit, interested in everything
that was going on, smiling and nodding in manifest happiness.

Schumann-Heink Sings

Dr. Poling introduced Madame Schumann-Heink as a wonderful mother and a wonderful artist, one of the greatest con-
traltos the world has ever known. What a voice, strong and
vibrant, soft and gentle in the *piano* passages, yet with the
carrying quality that is the secret of only the greatest singers!
After singing the aria, "The Lord Is My Light and My Salvation," from "Elijah," she received a great ovation, and,
coming to the front of the platform once more, said, in her
delightful German accent: "I suppose you expect me to make a
big speech or to sing a long aria. I cannot sing more now.
I have given ten lessons to-day, and you know what that means;

and, although I have mighty fine pupils, 'Mother' has to talk, and sometimes sing for them. Don't I?" (And she turned to a group of her pupils.) Well, *the Lord decides what we can do.*"

Flowers were presented to the singer as she bowed herself out. And then came one of those interesting episodes that pop up unannounced in our conventions. Madame Schumann-Heink stood at the top of the choir steps, and faced the great audience, we believe the biggest yet, and a magnificent sight, while the choir and audience sang, "God Be With You Till We Meet Again." It was a sort of farewell, and a beautiful one. One more bow, and she passed from our sight; and the young people were left with an unforgettable memory.

The ovation she received, however, and the singing of that farewell hymn moved her to tears; and she said to Dr. Poling, "Ask them to pray for me that I may be strong." And this was promised.

A Prophetic Voice

Dr. Ira Landrith is probably the most popular speaker in America. The thought with which he started his eloquent address was that if the big things that should be done are not done soon, they may have to be postponed for years. The title was:

JUST ONE QUADRENNIUM FOR THE CRUSADE

By Rev. Ira Landrith, D. D.,
Citizenship Superintendent, International Society of
Christian Endeavor

"The Trinity of Triumph"—evangelism, citizenship, and peace— will become, instead, "The Dismal Defeat," so far as this generation of youth is concerned, unless it marches to victory inside the next four years.

Evangelism must succeed ninety-eight times in a hundred if it succeeds at all, before people are twenty years of age. Somewhere between twelve and twenty by far the most abiding decisions for Christ are made. Fail with the youth of sixteen, and four years hence he is out of reach; and fail with his nineteen-year-old brother, and you have lost them both, with few exceptions. The rule applies quite as relentlessly to the twelve-year-old, who is most likely to follow his brother of sixteen into or out of the church by the time sixteen has reached twenty.

Plainly and bluntly, we have no time to lose unless we are willing to fail in this greatest work in the world, the task of saving for Christ and the church this present flitting, imperilled, and much-maligned, because susceptible and easily salvable generation of youth. Since the average of our opportunity is but four years, why wait four hours? "Why stand ye here idle?"

If there be anything in the persistent rumor of the waywardness and skepticism of youth, may not the explanation be found in the religious complacency and evangelistic indolence of adults and the church? According to a recent interview with the author of "The Christ of the Indian Road," the anti-Christian leaders of both India and China were both in their youth determined to accept Christ, and had set about it in characteristically thorough Oriental fashion, when they were both thoughtlessly turned away from the cross by previously trusted and later perfunctory or inconsistent teachers, one in South Africa and the other in North America!

Whatever else may be true of modern youth, he has X-ray eyes for shame and what he calls "bunk." He is a trained and scientific— many think, a too scientific—truth-seeker. Is it strange that, coming home from high school or college, where he thinks he has learned to winnow the chaff of pretence from the wheat of fact and the zeal for truth, he should halt himself at the base of Calvary when he finds us there, our crosses flung down, and our unsandalled feet at rest and unwilling to attempt the ascent? In more modern phrase, think you not that our children will care for Christ if we are careless about his cause or our own conduct. Neither God nor youth is mocked. Whatsoever pleasure-worshipping, law-defying, self-seeking parents sow, that shall they also reap. We are accustomed in this modern and too modernistic age, to talk too much of the youth problem and by far too little of the adult problem, the example and training problem for parents, pastors, churches, and homes. Four years of burning soul-seeking would solve all these problems. Let's go.

*   *   *   *   *

But Christian citizenship, particularly in North America, and most particularly in the United States, is also a matter of four years-- not longer. There will not then be enough Christian citizens even to hold the balance of power in this republic unless we spend the next four years in hearty and heroic evangelism of, by and through young people, all crusading together with Christ. No word thus far spoken must be interpreted as absolving Christian youth from the vital duty of leading other youth to Christ in this threefold crusade. We grown-ups could never do this work; you can, young people, and you must, or it can never be done. This is a plea that the rest of us make haste and help you to get it done during this quadrennium.

Christian citizenship is largely the fruitage of education; and education comes easy in youth, harder in early manhood, and distressingly difficult in middle life and age. A single generation trained to crusader zeal for the slogan,

"My first vote for virtue,
And never a ballot for booze or boodle,"

would solve most of our civic difficulties. Knowing the truth about politics would soon make us free from the misrule of those politicians who never grow to the stature of Christian statesmen. For this generation this necessary education must come in a four-year course.

But tolerated civic vice likewise grows tall and irresistibly strong in four years. Consider law-enforcement of prohibition. Eight years ago it would have been easy; ten years ago its enforcement was expected by both foe and friend; four years ago the cupidity of iniquity and the indolent tolerance of decent people of both high and lower degree had made a dry nation the task of a more dauntless and gigantic statesmanship than we then had in power; and to-day and for the next four years this "noble experiment" must win, or it will never win. This is no pessimist's plaint. Three quadrenniums of experimentation with this overwhelming fiat of a free people at the polls may not be enough to force the repeal of prohibition, but paralysis is often worse than death. That the people responsible for the Eighteenth Amendment mean to have it enforced by its unafraid friends, and not defeated by criminals and their respectable allies, the too tolerant "otherwise law-abiding," should be, since the national election, plain enough to any wayfaring man, though a politician. We have faith in the President, and should stand by him, the more resolutely because our past patience permitted others to multiply the difficulties of his administration. Let's get it done.

For more than ten years we have dawdled and played politics with world peace. If we are to have an end to that hang-over of the Stone Age, war, that end must come before the close of this quadrennium. All peoples demand it.

The Pact of Paris voices this popular demand. It proclaims war an arch-criminal. America must now quit using the skulls of all who have paid the supreme price of war as the handballs of partisanship, and inside four years agree with the other nations of the world on a preventive punishment for such national criminals as seek the bloody ways of war rather than the blessed paths of peace. Let's get it done.

* * * * *

But who shall do this vast task, who insure within the next four years this "trinity of triumph?" Has not Christian Endeavor come to Christ's Kingdom for such a time as this? It has vast numbers at home and abroad, and informed numbers create and may control public opinion. It has the ear and the heart of the Christian world. It has never failed nor fooled. It can if it will, and it has demonstrated for half a century that it will if it can. It is the youthful, many-tongued testimony of the nations and the denominations. Unhindered by sect or section, party or creed or tradition, Christian Endeavor, ready to go, and already going beyond the limits of its too beggarly resources, seems to be God's own anointed to lead this crusade with Christ to its triumph.

Let's help Christian Endeavor to get it done.

Dr. Landrith then called for funds and subscriptions, which came in generous response that night.

A Musical Interlude

One of Madame Schumann-Heink's pupils, a Negro girl, Miss Inez Stevens, delighted us with a melodious rendering of the difficult coloratura song, "Oft Have I Seen the Swift Swallows," just another of those happy episodes for which we have learned to look. The appreciative audience gave an encore, and the response was, "I Do Not Ask a Rose to Bloom When You Are Near."

The splendid voice-control evidenced the efficient teacher.

Then an address:

PRO CHRISTO ET ECCLESIA

By Carlton M. Sherwood,

Extension Secretary of the International Society of

Christian Endeavor

It was the present American Ambassador to Mexico, Mr. Dwight W. Morrow, who recently uttered those intriguing words: "Youth is greater than age as hope is greater than history."

It was the spirit of such a conviction that brought into being the Young People's Society of Christian Endeavor; and it has been the strict loyalty to the society's motto, "Pro Christo et Ecclesia—for Christ and the Church," which has kept it a vital and growing force as an important enterprise in the establishment of the Kingdom of God.

The Christian Endeavor society has been primarily a religious movement. It has been educational and social in many of its features, but its primary emphasis has been upon personal loyalty to Christ

and service for the church He established. Though many have
doubted the probability of youth's response to such a strictly religious
appeal, the movement in the brief period of five decades, has trained
in its ranks nearly twenty millions of young people, and enrolls in its
present active constituency over four million members in eighty thousand societies in eighty-seven denominations in all the nations of the
world. Figures may be dry, but figures like that need no amplifica-
tion to demonstrate the fact that young people respond to a genuine
appeal for loyalty and service in a great cause. Many important
secondary results have followed in the train of Christian Endeavor,
and many other important influences have been advanced because
of it, but its constant emphasis upon personal loyalty to Jesus Christ
and definite loyalty to the local church has been pre-eminent. Many
movements have challenged the life-interests of young people to a
variety of worthwhile enterprises, but the Christian Endeavor society
has made its greatest contribution in church loyalty. After all is
said and done, the most important thing on earth for Christians, old
and young, is the church. Thus the Christian Endeavor society has
placed this first thing first.

Throughout America and other nations of the world, wherever the
society is found, there also are found the prospective active church
leaders, lay and clerical, of the next generation. The evidence of this
is demonstrated constantly. Take the list of the ministers of the
average denomination in which the Christian Endeavor society is
found, and it will be found that two-thirds or more of them came up
through the Christian Endeavor society and made their decision for
the Christian ministry in the society. Take the list of the local church
officers and the same is true. Take the list of the important
leaders of the great denominational and interdenominational movements, and the same is true. The moderators of most of the denominations to-day in the United States, and many abroad, are old-time
Christian Endeavorers. The society is clearly demonstrating that an
intense loyalty to the local church is not incompatible with a deep
devotion to the principles of the denomination or communion to which
the young person belongs. The finest denominational service rendered
in many places is by Christian Endeavor trained leaders.

This movement is also demonstrating that a deep devotion to
denominational principles is not incompatible with the great, broad
spirit of interdenominational fellowship. It may safely be said that
fully as much, if not more than any other force in America and the
world has been the Christian Endeavor society in the last half-century
in developing that broad spirit of interdenominational fellowship
which had led, and is increasingly leading, to the larger and greater
desire for Christian unity. This spirit has been developed by a sound
psychology. It has been a movement from the bottom upward rather
than from the top downward. It has united the young people in
common objectives and programs of service upon which they could
mutually agree and engage. Thus by the simple device of working
together they have come to know and understand one another and to
realize their common sharing of Jesus Christ and His task in the
world. This fellowship has allayed the differences which always
come from ignorance of one's fellow and fellow Christians. While
it has not lessened the earnestness of conviction as to essential principles of local churches and communions, it has brought in the important realization in the life of youth that the great ideals and service
which unite them are much more important than those other factors,
no matter how earnestly held, which divide and separate. Thus, by the
simple plan of living and serving together, young Christians in the
societies of Christian Endeavor have found the method and the spirit
of the unity of the church for which Christ prayed, and which their
elders were unable to find, if, indeed, to see.

Beyond this, the society of Christian Endeavor has laid great emphasis upon the implications of the spirit of Jesus in every avenue of life. Its message has been to declare that life is not lived in water-tight compartments; that there is no secular that is not also sacred, and that the Kingdom of God calls for better men building a better world. The outreach of this attitude has been a program of good citizenship and social endeavor heretofore unparalleled in the life of the church. It was the youth of the last generation that faced the age-long and increasing evils of the traffic in beverage alcohol, and it was that youth under the influence of these released Christian forces that finally decreed the elimination of the liquor traffic in the United States. Beyond all that has been achieved, there is still the greater achievement which is to come of not alone a sober America, but a sober world. We have brought up a generation of young Christians who have not been afraid to face social evils, no matter how ancient, and to will, in the spirit of Jesus Christ, that these evils must go. It is well known that it was the International Christian Endeavor Convention in Atlantic City in 1911 that first threw out the slogan "A Saloonless Nation by 1920." The same newspapers that now are fighting prohibition then called this slogan an ideal of youthful, fanatical dreamers. But before 1920 the dream was a reality. Before this generation passes from the scene, the prohibition of the traffic in liquor will be established, not alone in the Constitution and the law, but in the life and practices of the people generally as firmly as any other provision of the life of the nation and as solid as the Rock of Ages.

Christian Endeavor stands for church loyalty, church unity, Christian citizenship, the Christianizing of the social order and the bringing in of the Kingdom of God on earth.

WORLD VISION AND WORLD CHALLENGE

James Kelly's specialty seems to be world vision. Mr. Kelly, who hails from Glasgow, Scotland, is president of the European Christian Endeavor Union, and vice-president of the World's Christian Endeavor Union. "Youth and World Peace" was his theme, but it was prefaced by a brief description of the European field and by the greetings of our European brothers. In Great Britain and Ireland especially splendid progress has been made, and Christian Endeavor is now reaping the benefit of patient work done in the years following the war. Below we give in part the speech on

YOUTH AND WORLD PEACE

By James Kelly

During the last ten years one subject of vital and increasing interest has obsessed the minds alike of peoples and of statesmen the world over—the problem of World Peace. One hears this subject discussed from pulpit, platform, and press; from Senate, Parliament, and the great Assembly of the Nations, leagued together—partly for friendship's sake; partly through fear—to save the world and civilization from threatened annihilation. As a result peace treaties and pacts have been signed by the nations, but peace in any real sense of the word still eludes a disappointed, timorous, and suspicious world.

It is true that so far as appearance goes, the cause of peace seems to have progressed exceedingly, and to have secured the allegiance of nearly all countries, but anyone who has the very slightest knowledge of the Continent of Europe alone, has some idea how much bitterness—and justifiable bitterness—still exists between nations, and how there is a divided allegiance. Peace! Yes; but Justice first. Righteousness and Peace must go hand in hand, and Peace without Righteousness can obtain but lip service.

I believe it is because these two have been so lightly divorced that still to many men and nations Peace is but a beautiful word written upon paper. Once and again on paper Peace has been embraced; War has been renounced. Good people feel within themselves a glow of satisfaction, but, after all, it is a "paper Peace," and we have learned by bitter experience that a piece of paper is but a frail barrier to withstand the torrent of national ambition or greed.

By all means let us have pacts to renounce war, but let us not forget to undergird and secure these. We organize for war; we must still more organize for peace. We must educate, and educate, and educate, and organize for peace. The struggle for peace is one that must go on unceasingly, and in every nation, among every people, and it will be a very long and stern fight, for we fight against principalities and powers and spiritual wickedness in high places, as well as against levity, sloth, presumption, self-confidence, and thoughtless folly.

It is the wildest optimism to assume that we can rest on our oars and feel that War has now been definitely abrogated, and that we have entered on a period of more or less permanent peace. If that were so, there would be no meaning in the gigantic armaments which still exist, or in the feverish efforts of almost all nations to improve their warlike machinery and to invent even more and more deadly instruments of destruction. One is tempted to ask: Do the nations really want peace? Many certainly do, but, frankly, I believe that to nations who feel that they have been ruthlessly despoiled and treated with savage injustice, the very thought of peace without justice is an intolerable thing. Is it not to the interests of the whole world to re-unite justice and peace.

If peace is really the deep-seated desire of all nations, why do they not disarm? It is because, though peace is on the lips of peoples, it is not in their hearts. The nations, as a whole, have no great, deep-seated desire to sink their national pride, their national prejudices, their national advantages, and to look upon all men as brothers. Now, as heretofore, they are all out for personal advancement, personal enrichment, personal gain, and, as we all know, this attitude does not make for peace, but for estrangement, and, in extreme cases, War. Who can picture a stable peace founded on selfishness?

We have been slowly learning that in the world of industry, co-operation brings better results than strife. We must realize that this is true also in international life before we can secure the blessing of peace.

How, then, do the nations show their desire for peace? Are they willing to spend, and to be spent, for it? All of them spend colossal sums on armaments, and employ and pay armies of men to perfect their schemes of preparedness for war. How much in hard cash do they spend on perfecting the peace machinery, and how large is the band of men and women they employ and pay in the interests of peace? This is surely a just measure of their interest in war and peace respectively. No nation has a peace minister; all have ministries of war. All nations have spies, who risk life and honor and take all risks to find out the strength and weaknesses of their peaceful neighbors, not at war. I know of no nation whose government maintains and equips specially trained bands of men and women to go to neighboring countries in the interests of peace. What a mighty thrill would pulse through the world if some Christian nation would include in its cabinet a minister for peace instead of a minister for war.

Pacts of Peace! Covenants of Peace! Treaties of Peace! all of them filed on bayonets, and to those who have eyes to see, the biting steel is gleaming through. The pacts of peace are written on paper; the instruments of war are formed of shining steel and deadly vapors.

Will you not make it your business to organize and mobilize for peace; your only war being war against war and indifference and selfishness and all the other evils of the pit and the slime. We must mobilize for peace.

The World Alliance for the Promotion of Friendship through the Churches and the League of Nations are making steady and systematic progress to mobilize manhood and womanhood in the cause of peace, and this great world-wide organization of Christian Endeavor, and especially this section of it, has pledged youth to renounce war, and now we must mobilize for peace. We must by patient instruction prepare the mind of youth and childhood for the coming new day. Hating war is not enough; we must love peace. Our foremost task is to create a supporting public opinion by enthroning the world's conscience in its common sense.

Further, governments must be brought to see that there is a growing demand for the expenditure of money in the interests of peace. In war we do something more than encourage men to spring to arms; we have arms for them to spring to. And so, in mobilizing the world for peace, governments must have peace equipment ready. We ought to seek peace and pursue it with such intense concern that minor differences will be lost sight of in the common loyalty to our great Leader, the Prince of Peace.

I have not lived in Southern Europe and mingled with different races and peoples without realizing with a growing despondency just how much, or how little, the Pact of Paris means to some people.

And so let me stress once again: Our pacts and our treaties must become practical; they must become something more than paper. We must do more than desire peace, or disarmament, or the reduction of armaments. These are practical questions, and as such must be dealt with practically.

Young men and women, what is our duty in this great question? Shall we stand aside, and simply, with quiescence, watch the ebb and flow of the tide, or shall we put the whole energy of our youth, of our manhood and womanhood, into the great cause of world peace. It is the business of the followers of Christ to go ahead of the statesmen as pioneers who take risks for an ideal which the world will say is impracticable, until, through the releasing power of God, it has been accomplished. It is our duty—at least, so I believe—to declare that Christianity and war are incompatible. The duty of a Christian is to get done what the world says cannot be done. What is the Gospel? It is nothing else than that the end of human life is fellowship with God and fellowship with man. Our different Christian communities preach "Love your enemies," and yet to-day how much we see on every hand of racial prejudice, sense of superiority, and un-Christian nationalism.

Might I remind you that the principles of the Kingdom of God are:

Truth always—and never subterfuge;
Kindness always—and never violence;
Love always—and never hatred!
Trust always—and never fear.

One word more! There is one influence we can all exert; one power we can all set in motion. It is prayer. Prayer changeth things. Yes, it does, but it begins by changing us, and afterwards we change things. It makes of those who pray, people more just, more generous, more sincerely desirous of peace, more ready to cast out of their own minds the things that make for war. It corrects our judgment of one another, and clarifies our judgment of ourselves.

> "Then let us pray that come it may,
> As come it will, for a' that;
> When man to man the world o'er,
> Shall brothers be for a' that."

MARION SIMMS, JR.
Field-Secretary, Nebraska

FREDERICK L. MINTEL
Field-Secretary, New Jersey

WILLARD E. RICE
Field-Secretary, New York

HERMAN A. KLAHR
Field-Secretary, Ohio

CHAPTER VI

MODERN EVANGELISM

Evangelistic Oratory—Christian Endeavor Principles—
An Evangelistic Address
Sunday Afternoon, July 7

After an uplifting song service, under Percy Foster, Sunday afternoon, July 7, Dr. Haddaway, a life-trustee of the International Society, led in a period of devotions.

The first address was on

YOUTH AND HIS CHRIST

By A. J. Shartle,

Treasurer and Field-Secretary of the International Society
of Christian Endeavor

The conservation of youth in all lands is the largest piece of conservation we have on our hands. The story of the cross has always thrilled young lives. The lives of the ages seem to have converged in the present day. The program is complete. The cross is aflame. The call to the heart and life is clear. It is loud. It is insistent. The cry is heard: *Youth Wanted! Men Wanted! Women Wanted!* There is a crisis. Faith, and hope, and love, and sacrifice, inspiration, insight, courage, patience, and loyalty—these will come with the gathering of young people about the cross.

Youth to-day in the consideration of his Christ is seeking a place in the life of the church where they find opportunity to develop initiative and where they bear recognized responsibility. If you want to hold young people to the church, you must give them something to hold on to.

We believe we can supply this something to hold on to. Something with a standard of character. Something with an all-inclusive program. Something born in the heart of God—and that something is the ever-growing, intensely practical, deeply spiritual organization of world-wide *Christian Endeavor.*

Here is an organization that stands for religious training through constant religious service. It stands for conversion, consecration, evangelism, loyalty, and fellowship with all who love Jesus Christ. It believes in all rational, wholesome amusements, and is against those that lower the physical, moral, and spiritual tone.

If I Were a Pastor

—And had forty young people who, of their own accord, would promise to support the church in every way;

77

—And if those same young people, of their own accord, would meet weekly to pray and praise and give Christian testimony;

—And if they had their minds set on missions and the forward movements of the kingdom of God;

—And if they were eager to bring their associates into the church;

—And if they made it a rule to pray and read the Bible every day; I should get down on my knees every night and thank God for those forty young folks, and I should loudly bless the society which prompted them to do these things.

These are just the things that eighty thousand times forty young people have promised to do and are doing all over the world. Here is an organization that trains and leads a new generation of stalwart, praying, Bible-loving, hard-working young people who will put Christianity first and promote a Christian fellowship that shall extend to every land.

Christian Endeavor offers to youth in the worship of his Christ, some outstanding objectives, something of major importance for youth to hold on to.

First, Confession

A young person without religion is an exception. Heedless of tradition, he demands a religion in terms of his own life, and activities which have inherent value and interest for himself. When a youth decides to accept Jesus Christ as the King of his life, he is still a youth and loves youthful things. His decision is prompt and genuine. It should be as promptly accepted at face value by his church.

Christ is on trial before the world to-day and we are His witnesses. If we know anything in His favor, and we do, we should speak out, remembering always that our life, no matter how small and humble, is worth an hour of talk. Where can we find a more suitable place to consecrate our all at the foot of the cross and confess Him before men, than in meetings of Christian Endeavor, at the office desk or workshop bench or in the community where we live?

Second, Private Devotions, or the Quiet Hour

No movement however big, no Christian however gifted, can maintain spiritual life and spiritual strength apart from prayer and pondering the word of God.

The stimulating effect of Christian Endeavor upon the personal life is shown in the everyday life of its members. Here is an organization which provides methods, plans, and periods for private devotions,—a time set apart when the individual through prayer, Bible study and a closer personal walk with God, is inspired to "love mercy, do justly and walk humbly" before his God.

Third, Stewardship

Giving is a part of worship as much as is praying and believing. It is the fruitage of our faith and our thankfulness for the blessings received and our loyalty and love to Jesus Christ. The object of Stewardship is Possessions—life and money. The greatest and most priceless treasure is *your own life.* This is yours, but not to waste and abuse. You are guardian of it and must give an account of it. God has a plan for every life and has first call on your life. It is not a matter of self, but service is the magic word that should thrill and enthrall one early in life. Make your life count for good. That is the challenge.

Another possession is money. Money is crystallized personality. It is yourself in marketable form. You may have little of it and possibly you never will have much of it, but there is no one living who does not have *some* of it, little or much. God never relinquished or transferred His right of ownership over that which He created. It still belongs to Him. Man is a steward, holding and administering that which he has as a sacred trust, and must account for all that he has. God's ownership and man's stewardship are to be acknowledged by devoting a definite proportion, usually not less than one-tenth, unto the service of the Lord.

Fourth, Personal Relations

The personal relations of and in Christian Endeavor are many and outstanding in the life of youth. The fellowship found in the society, church, and union work plus our interdenominational Christian activities, make for a personal relationship that is of inestimable value. It affords a privilege of knowing youth of other denominations and clasping hands in a bond of Christian fellowship not found elsewhere.

Fifth, Evangelism

Christian Endeavor goes forward hand in hand with evangelism and helps youth understand the power of Jesus Christ in human life. A young lady, in writing to her teacher, said: "In church they say the same things over and over again, yet they don't seem to tell one anything. They talk of their love for Jesus and how happy it makes them, but they never say how they get it. Oh, I wish I could make them understand!"

Christian Endeavor, through personal work and personal decisions, prayer and intercession with the Master, brings the soul, sick and spiritually hungry, into relationship with God and a personal acceptance of Jesus Christ. Evangelistic Christian Endeavor is found in the slums of the city, the community, and the home. The thousands of Life-Work Recruits enlisted, the volunteers ready to serve, and those in the ministry, mission fields, social service, and kindred organizations reveal a spirit of evangelism in Christian Endeavor, and a definiteness of purpose as the impelling power actuated by consecrated Christian Endeavor.

Christian Endeavor presents these objectives to those who may not understand; and those who do understand and yet lag, it stimulates to increased activity. If we understand youth, then youth will continue to respond, accept the challenge, and ring true.

An Oratorical "Fest"

Paul C. Brown, who has had charge of the oratorical contests at this convention, introduced the six speakers, five girls and one boy, one of the girls a Negress. The topic was "Christian Endeavor and Evangelism." The speakers were Anna May Wheeler of Louisiana; Dorothy Symington of California; Harold Cox, Indiana; Marian Jackson, Washington, D. C.; Blanche Youmans, Kansas; and the sixth, Mary Jewell Ellis, Missouri.

Fred W. Ramsey Speaks

One of the men who is rapidly coming into intensified national fame as a great Christian leader is Fred W. Ramsey, a trustee of the International Society, a member of the executive committee, who some months ago was elected successor of John R.

Mott as general secretary of the National Council of the Young Men's Christian Association. Dr. Foulkes introduced him, not only as a personal friend, but as a zealous and successful soul-winner. No description in words can reproduce the eloquence and force of Mr. Ramsey's address, itself an ideal gospel sermon, powerful and appealing. He began with thoughtful and deliberate emphasis a speech, an abstract of which we give here.

THE CHALLENGE OF PERSONAL EVANGELISM

By Fred W. Ramsey,

General Secretary, National Council, Young Men's Christian Association

How rich have been the gifts that the hosts of Christian Endeavor have brought through the forty-eight years of its wonderful history and laid at the feet of the matchless Christ! But there never was a day when youth was bringing richer gifts than it is bringing now. I am overwhelmed by the richness of the contribution that has been brought to the cause of Jesus Christ by these young people that have just spoken to us; and, if I followed my own inclination, I should steal away to some quiet place to meditate upon the gifts and charm of youth to-day as it comes to the cross and lays before Him who hangs upon it its tribute of truth and love.

These young people have covered the range of my own thinking on this subject, and have presented it to you with infinitely more charm than I could have given it. I want them to know how deeply we appreciate what they have done for us, and what it has meant to us, not only to hear their words, but to see that inner glow upon their faces.

The Challenge of a Cross

The challenge of personal evangelism is the challenge of a cross. Nineteen centuries ago a youthful Man who loved life deeply, knowing the joy of life more than any of us ever did, passed through the gate of an ancient city to die, bruised and crushed and broken. Just before that He had said to a group of His disheartened friends, "Be of good cheer; I have overcome the world." And that lonely figure on a cross on a lonely hill through the years has been and still is a lodestone drawing men to God and to all the highest purposes of life.

The youth of America ten or twelve years ago came to understand, by a process that was deadly and terrible to contemplate, what the cross means in human life, and we are coming again to-day to a new apprehension of it. The World War taught us something of its meaning. Joyce Kilmer, the young American poet who went down to death in the mud and blood of the trenches, wrote out of the tragedy of Flanders fields a poem that showed that he understood, and that he realized that Christ was in the agony of tortured bodies and shattered souls. *"My shoulders ache beneath my pack,"* he wrote, as the shoulders of Jesus must have ached beneath the load He carried. I pray that we may not have to wait to face the darkness of some lonely Gethsemane or some black Calvary of our own before we feel upon us the weight of the cross of Jesus. Claim it for yourself now—the meaning and the mission of the cross in your own life. Let the obligation of the cross rest its full weight upon your heart. It will bring you into the company of men and women to-day who are under burdens, and it will qualify you for fellowship with the choice spirits of our time and of all times.

When we glimpse the meaning of the cross, all of life responds and yields to the high claims of God.

The Claim of the Living Christ

The claim of personal evangelism is more than the claim of the cross; it is the claim of a living Christ. We cannot leave Christ upon the cross. He comes down from the tree, and takes His place at the very centre of our lives to help us in our struggle for fullness of life and character. Thank God Jesus did not remain upon the cross. He descended from it, and He is here and everywhere that men and women are in need of help and sympathy.

Mr. Ramsey told how he came to realize the greatness of the problem of evangelism when a friend pointed out to him that there are in the world 320,000,000 boys and girls between the ages of twelve and eighteen. Marching in single file it would take this host years to pass a single point. One in every four of the marchers would be a Chinese; one in every five would come from India; and one-half of them would come from Asia!

These young people are hungering to know God. Millions of them have never attended school, and never will. Millions of children from six to ten years old will never know anything but unremitting toil all their lives; they will feel the pinch of famine and the sharpness of disease, and *we are their only hope*. For we can reach them in the spirit of love and brotherhood.

"I seem to hear the words of that great lover of youth," continued the speaker, "who went to His death outside the city wall, 'Inasmuch as ye have done it unto one of the least of these my brethren, ye have done it unto me.' Here is our task, to share with this great company of youth the world around the blessings that we enjoy."

Mr. Ramsey urged that we begin our efforts with *ourselves* and in our own homes. He exhorted the young folks to put a new spirit into their home life. "Go home and look at mother. You may see lines in her face that you never saw before. I remember," he continued in a burst of personal reminiscence, "the first time I realized what my father had been doing all through the years. He was a carpenter, and week after week, year in, year out, he brought home his pay, unbroken, to mother. I had not noticed that this was anything great. But I remember the day when, looking at him, I realized for the first time that my dad was breaking under this thing, and was going down under the load. I looked at him with eyes that saw and with a heart that understood. Then I resolved that although I never, as long as I lived, could fully pay back what he had done for me, I would begin to pay back what I could. Thank God, I was able to pay something, and was able to give him some joy and satisfaction before the end.

"It is no use talking about citizenship across this land, or peace across the world, unless we make Jesus Christ king in our homes everywhere.

"Learn to look at your Sunday-school class with the understanding eyes of Jesus, who is standing with outstretched arms waiting to share His best with you."

Mr. Ramsey spoke of a decision he had seen Dan Poling make when two paths lay open before him; one path that led to leisure and economic security, and one a path that would make immense demands upon his strength, but would allow him to serve the youth of America. And "Dan" chose the service of youth!

Mr. Ramsey closed with John Oxenham's beautiful poem:

Come, share the road with Me, My own,
    Through good and evil weather;
Two better speed than one alone,
    So let us go together.

Come, share the road with Me, My own,
    You know I'll never fail you,
And doubts and fears of the unknown
    Shall never more assail you.

Come, share the road with Me, My own,
    I'll share your joys and sorrows.
And hand in hand we'll seek the Throne
    And God's great, glad to-morrows.

Come, share the road with Me, My own,
    And when the black clouds gather,
I'll share thy load with Me, My son,
    And we'll press on together.

And as we go we'll share also
    With all who travel on it,
For all who share the road with Me
    Must share with all upon it.

So make we all one company,
    Love's golden cord our tether,
And, come what may, we'll climb the way
    Together—aye, together!

leaving us all moved to the very heart and with a new vision of the meaning of the cross.

Oratorical Awards

The judges in the day's oratorical contest based their opinion on content and delivery, fifty per cent. each. They decided that the first prize should go to Blanche Youmans of Kansas, and the second to Marian Jackson, a Negro girl from Washington, D. C.

JUNIOR WORKERS DEDICATE THEMSELVES

Mrs. Clark the Honor Guest—A Candle-light Service That Will Not Be Forgotten

Sunday Evening, July 7

Mrs. Francis E. Clark, beloved wife of the founder of Christian Endeavor, was the honor guest at a Junior Workers' dedication service held Sunday evening, July 7, at 6.30 P. M., in the Doric room of the Baltimore Hotel.

The program had been most carefully planned by Miss Mildreth J. Haggard of Minneapolis, Minn.

"Keeping Tryst with Mrs. Francis E. Clark" was the inspiring subject for a beautiful candle-light service.

The Scripture was read by Jack Eaton Miller of Oklahoma City, Fred Chubb of Pennsylvania, Miss Hilda C. Applebaum of New York, and Mrs. Myrtle Morris of Texas. Each read a passage of Scripture before each of the four verses of the song.

Mrs. Clark in her charming, sincere manner said:

I have been very much impressed lately in reading my Bible, how the Lord talked about common things, salt, patches, seed, etc.—all used to teach simple truths. I have some trees in my yard that I call my own, and I have named them. The largest and most stately I named Jabez, because Jabez was more honorable than his brethren. And then I found that Jabez prayed (mostly a selfish prayer), but when I look at Jabez out in my yard it reminds me to pray.

And then, too, to-night I was looking out of my window, and I saw queer and many-shaped shadows, and I thought of that passage in Luke about Peter. Peter was so like the rest of us, and I was reminded of our influence—shadow; we never know how far-reaching the shadow cast by our influence extends.

There was once a woman with a very hot temper. She had just bathed and dressed her very small daughter, but the daughter soon fell down and was dirty and dishevelled looking. The child came into the house expecting to be punished severely, but the mother had just finished a talk with God, and said, 'Come, darling, we will put on another clean dress,' and the little child replied, "Mother, if God is like you, then I love Him."

The influence Christianity has on our lives was beautifully illustrated by a personal story Mrs. Clark told. "When one of our own boys was four years old, we sat through a long church service. The child rustled the leaves of the hymn-books, then he dropped the book, then he got down on the floor and picked it up, then he played with my fan, then he dropped it, then he got down on the floor, and I was very impatient with him because I knew he knew better. I prepared a reproof for him and determined to say a few words to him on the way home, when suddenly two chubby little arms were flung around my neck and he whispered in my ear, 'Suffer the little children to come unto Me.' Although I had heard scarcely anything of the sermon, I preached one to myself all the way home."

At the close of Mrs. Clark's helpful words, about thirty State Junior superintendents walked to the front, lighted their candles from Mrs. Clark's candle, and the superintendents were followed by every worker in the room, each one lighting his or her candle from Mrs. Clark's candle. Mrs. Clark closed the service with a beautiful dedication prayer.

Cornet music was played by Wilbert Martin of Freeport, Ill.

AN APPEAL FOR LAW AND GOSPEL

Sunday Evening, July 7

The evening devotional period was led by Dr. Percy Hayward, director of the Young People's Section of the International Council of Religious Education.

An octette from the big convention chorus, with Mr. Rodeheaver, sang "In Heavenly Love Abiding," especially for Mrs. Clark, it having been a great favorite of Dr. Clark.

Stanley Printz, a grandson of Treasurer Shartle, of the International Society of Christian Endeavor, and honor student of Muhlenberg College, 1930, was presented by Dr. Poling as the speaker on

CHINA'S COVERED WAGON
By Stanley Printz

It was a living, lurid world-picture of one of the hugest migrations of the oppressed known to all history. As he graphically limned it: There trudges an emaciated yellow peasant in tattered blue denim over an endless, weary, dusty road or trail, his wife and smaller children following. The older daughters have been sold to lives of shame to finance the trek, and the older sons have been conscripted into the wrangling armies. The father is carrying on his back his own aged father, and wife and each child lug some household goods. Their name is legion. The way is strewn with skeletons--skulls with empty eyesockets stare up from the dust; leg-bones, ghastly hands beckoning to such a stream of distressed, affrighted humanity, starved, scourged by disease, desperate, fleeing China, pressing its flight into Manchuria to escape military tyranny, extortion, rapine, and death.

Water is doled out to them by the Japanese railroad officials, but what of food? They gnaw grasses, roots, refuse, anything that animals will devour. The way is strewn with their un-buried dead; yet on they go, riding the trains into Harbin.

Yet this pitiful remnant that survives, within a week after reaching its destination, has dug up the earth with sticks, and planted grain, and settled stoically down to the new life with a patient smile, trying to forget the pillaging war lords. And that pitiless, grasping Chinese general, who builds a million-

REV. PAUL V. CLARK
Field-Secretary, Oklahoma

Ross GUILEY
Field-Secretary, Oregon

dollar palace is one and the main reason for the trek of hordes and legions of Chinese farmers leaving the home land for Manchuria.

What is to be done? Can this yellow ebb-tide be stemmed that day by day is flooding into the new Land of Promise, with cholera and bubonic plague stalking behind them, as well as ruthless war lords?

The speaker compared this migration to that of the children of Israel from Egypt, and of the oppressed European peasants to America's Western plains. The hope, he said, is that to those enduring, seemingly indestructible coolies, some of whose kind our Western coast knew so well, a breathing spell will be vouchsafed in this new land long enough to give them a foothold and to plant a new nation, a Christian people; and the appeal is to Christian Endeavorers to second the missionary and relief work of their churches in this direction.

Then an address entitled

FROM SEVEN TO SEVENTY

By Rev. Stanley B. Vandersall,

Vocations Superintendent of the International Society of Christian Endeavor

The words of this theme are not the statement of an arithmetical progression from seven to seventy; nor are they connected, except in sound, with that beautiful teaching concerning forgiveness, where the numerals seven and seventy are both used. They rather have an interpretation intended to designate the scope of Christian Endeavor's influence in personal life. Freely translated, this theme means that Christian Endeavor has a place for every person from the child to the grandfather.

To provide an outline that may more easily be understood and retained, I am asking you to follow me in four imaginary episodes which will deal with different phases of Christian Endeavor's influence. The use of the personal pronoun is only to indicate that reference may be made an any individual.

"I am a boy of nine years. I am no different from other boys of my age, coming from an average family with only ordinary benefits in home and school. I am no better, nor am I worse, than any of my companions. I am an attendant in a Sunday-school class with a good teacher. But something unusual has happened in my life.

"A consecrated young lady in our church came to us one day, and suggested that a group of boys and girls—some older, some younger, than myself—were requested to meet in the church for the purpose of organizing a Junior Christian Endeavor society. In common with my companions I did not take the invitation very seriously, but went along with them and I found, to my extreme interest, that a program of work and service was outlined exactly fitting our lives. Those who are seven or eight years old are placed in a group by themselves and have a superintendent of their own. Those who are nine, ten, or eleven make up the regular Junior society.

"Little by little the different phases of Junior Christian Endeavor have been opened up to us. I found that there were meetings where boys and girls were given the opportunity to open the Bible to read and to learn its passages; that these boys and girls were encouraged to offer public pray and testimony, a thing which I never expected to do; and, more than that, I have found that these boys and girls are expected to carry on a program of activity in committee work, in social life, in leadership of meetings, and in giving, which has been a strong force in our lives and an attraction which we could not resist.

"Under the lead of our superintendent we have learned the important parts of the Christian life. We have gone out after other boys and girls, and have brought them to the same confession. We have happy social occasions, enthusiastic programs of work, and devotional meetings that touch our hearts and bring out the best there is in us. We give and pray for others, and have learned to think of the whole wide world in terms of the gospel.

"But this is not all. We have learned about other Junior Christian Endeavor societies in other churches, and we have gone out to some rallies and conventions where, in the company of many other Juniors like ourselves, we have appreciated the helpfulness of our organization. I, for one, am thankful for the day when I came to Junior Christian Endeavor. It helps me, and I like it."

*   *   *   *   *

"I am a lad of fifteen. When I was nine, I joined a Junior Christian Endeavor society in our church, but now I am too old for that connection, happy as it used to be. My friends and companions are now in high school, and although we are still interested in the things which we learned in Junior Christian Endeavor, we are not satisfied with the appeal of that society for us. Can you imagine, therefore, how eagerly we received the word that we should leave the Junior society and become Intermediate Christian Endeavorers?

"We now have a society of our own, planning our own meetings, raising our own finances, deciding all our committee work, applying the principles of Christian Endeavor to our particular needs as we see them, and keeping the Christian life ever prominently before us. We have two advisers, a man and a woman, devoted members of the old Christian Endeavor society, but they so skilfully give their advice that we know that we are doing the work.

"My companions in the society, both boys and girls, come from several different classes in our Sunday-school. We have different tastes and ambitions, but we meet on a common platform in Intermediate Christian Endeavor. We make good use of the things we learn and do in high school, having frequent essays, debates, and open discussions on themes which relate the Christian life to young people like ourselves.

"Among our greatest delights are those which come when we have contact with other Intermediates. We had a convention not long ago, and we frequently have Intermediate rallies in our city. In the convention and in the rallies the entire program is carried on by the Intermediates themselves, except for a few invited speakers and guests who help us.

"Our society makes much of reading and public speaking. We are interested in games and outdoor diversions, but we keep foremost before us that we are young Christians, and we mean to make of ourselves the best possible men and women. We try to excel in reading the Bible and in knowing its contents, and many of us are Comrades of the Quiet Hour. Intermediate Christian Endeavor, designed for us and carried on by us, means everything in our lives."

*   *   *   *   *

"I am a young man of twenty-one, having almost completed my educational preparation for life. I am a member of the Young People's Society of Christian Endeavor in our church. I was first a Junior, and in that society I gained the great blessings of Bible teaching and

Christian activity for boys and girls. Then I became, in due course of time, an Intermediate, where with the outlook of a youth I could bring some of my dreams into being, and where my youthful spirits were properly guided into Christian channels. Now, in company with my friends, young men and young women, I find great delight in the well-rounded activities of our society.

"Our meetings are extremely helpful because they open up to us every phase of modern life. Our activities through the different committees reach not only our own church and community, but through our missionary operations we thrust ourselves to the farther parts of the world. We have a wonderful spirit of helpfulness, and encourage one another in great service. We take seriously that part of our Christian Endeavor pledge which urges us to loyalty. Our pastor says that he puts every dependence on our society, because we become the backbone of volunteer activity in the church. Frequently he depends on us to carry on a part or all of the church service in his absence, and our members make up much of the choir, and hold other offices in our church and Sunday-school.

"As Juniors and Intermediates we had our minds and hearts directed toward Christ; but now, having decided for Him and realizing the near approach of our adult life, we earnestly work for others. I should not want, by any means, to take out of my life what Christian Endeavor has put there."

* * * * *

"I am a man of middle life. I look in both directions—forward with hope and backward with thankfulness. My own children now occupy the place which was mine a few short years ago. I was in Junior Christian Endeavor. In course of time I passed on to the Intermediate society, and still later, as a young man, I came into the Young People's society. Through these several steps of training in Christian work and activity I gained for myself, in common with many companions of like age, a wonderful foundation. It was in Christian Endeavor that I put into practice the principles I learned in my home. It was Christian Endeavor that gave us development in public expression. I have never forgotten how to pray, nor to put my thoughts into words, nor to lead in committee work or other executive capacity.

"But I outgrew the Christian Endeavor society. For a time, as an adult, I was in the adult society in our church. As a busy man I could no longer give it attention; and in common with the other men and women of our church, some of whom, like myself, had been trained in Christian Endeavor, I wished the young people success in their efforts.

"But a little while ago, we became aware of a new call to persons like ourselves. I read and was told of an organization in Christian Endeavor which maintains the connection and interest of former Endeavorers and friends of the society, the parents of growing children, and those responsible for the work in the church and community.

"Knowing what Christiain Endeavor has done for me, I would not for the world have my children deprived of similar benefits. How eagerly, then, I welcomed the suggestion that we might have a group of Christian Endeavor Alumni in our church!

"With the help of some friends of many years, and with the encouragement of the officers of the church, we have organized an Alumni Council. In this Council we have included as many of the people in our church as could be reached who have ever had membership in Christian Endeavor anywhere. We have likewise extended membership privileges to officials and those responsible for its many activities. We have brought Christian Endeavor to the forefront in our thinking, and we mean to give every possible encouragement to the young people in our church as they propose and promote their several active societies. Along with the younger societies we are now promoting a program ot fellowship, education, and missionary work.

"Some of our Alumni are already growing old, and will not be with us long. Some of us are still in the strength of adult life, and we intend to supplement our membership by these younger friends who will from time to time graduate from the Young People's society.

"Moreover, we have found a means of putting ourselves into Christian Endeavor. Here we find the real way for our activity in the Crusade with Christ. We have been invited to show our interest in the progress of this movement throughout the world. Eagerly have we welcomed the chance to become partners in world-wide Christian Endeavor. Our Alumni freely give some of our money, much of our prayers, all of our sympathy, to the cause of Christian Endeavor and in behalf of Christ and the church."

*   *   *   *   *

This is the interpretation of our theme. From seven to seventy literally gives an opportunity for Christian Endeavor to find its way in blessing boys and girls, young men and young women, and older people who would do service for Christ.

Missionaries to the Platform

In response to the invitation of Stanley B. Vandersall, Christian-vocations superintendent, fifteen missionaries, returned on furlough, and outgoing, came to the platform, and were introduced. Their names and fields are as follows:

Dorothy A. Linney (office assistant), Allison James School, president of a boarding-school for Spanish-American girls, Santa Fe, N. M.

Miss Mabelle Shaffer, general field-secretary for missionary work, Methodist Protestant Church.

Johanna Louise Graf, Turkey, Mesopotamia, kindergarten.

Sarah R. Charles, Menaul School, Albuquerque, Mexico and New Mexico, Presbyterian.

C. H. Suckau, Mennonite missionary in Indian since 1909. Home on furlough.

Mrs. C. H. Suckau.

Rev. and Mrs. Howard W. Cover, Bogra, Bengal, India, missionaries to the Moslems, Churches of God.

Dr. and Mrs. D. S. Lowe, Seoul, Korea. Sailing September 6, 1929. Presbyterian Board.

Miss Lea Blanche Edgar, Hangchow, China, Northern Baptist. Sailing August 5, 1929.

Miss Leta May Brown, India, Disciples of Christ, United Christian Missionary Society. Sailing August 28, 1929.

Miss Eva L. Smalley, Bible-teacher, Nanking, China, Presbyterian, U. S. A.

Laura K. Wolfe, Allison James School, Santa Fe, New Mexico. Work among Mexican girls. Presbyterian, U. S. A.

Mrs. Rodger Earl Winn, Pyengyang, Korea, Presbyterian.

A Musical Tableau

A pleasant surprise came to the vast audience in the form of a musical tableau. All were requested to turn facing the rear of the hall. Lights were snapped off, and on a stage opposite the speakers' platform there stood out under a spotlight a tableau of a Russian family, a scene depicting the birth of music. The composition was beautifully rendered with a violin obligato, and as an encore which the pleased listeners demanded, "A Little Bit of Love" was sung by the same exquisite voice.

Then followed the major address of the evening, by Raymond Robins, on—well, he gave it no title, but it will live as an awakening voice. We may call it

LAW AND GOSPEL

"Once in a thousand years or so," he began, "you feel that you would like to make a speech. This is one of the occasions. Such trying conditions as now face youth will not often happen to mankind."

He referred back to the Great War and its consequent horrors. And now, by a leap of a century in a decade, behold fifty nations have agreed to outlaw war; and two leading nations, one headed by a Quaker and the other by a labor leader, are seeking, not merely the limitation of arms, but the prevention of future wars. And the Christian world should seek in every way to further such a policy.

If it does, in time August 27 will become the World-Peace Day as Armistice Day never can be, because to half the world Armistice Day means defeat and humiliation.

"But," the speaker continued, "you have another great cause to espouse—citizenship. What place has citizenship in such a convention? I believe that the problem of clothing, housing, feeding the world's population, is a religious question. one of justice and righteousness."

Mr. Robins illustrated this thought by stating that one-third of his life had been spent in public service. It was but his duty to society. And he received a resounding response to the declaration that a citizen who would not take time to vote or serve on jury was a traitor to his country.

The greatest challenge to the citizenship of America to-day, he said, is the liquor question; our present high standards of living cannot be maintained if the wages of the working man are to be dissipated through 400,000 saloons, as they were before prohibition.

Preserve the Constitution

The new effort for better enforcement that our President has launched is bound up with the integrity of our Constitution. He asks the American people to validate their own action in voting prohibition, for only in this way can society be preserved from anarchy.

He holds a stronger hope of such an achievement; but the task is the more difficult because war, the rule of brute force, has left a psychology of violence and crime to be overcome. It is this state of mind that in Europe has made necessary dictatorships in Italy, Spain, Poland, Bulgaria, Russia.

America has escaped the bitterness, distrust, and desperation of this aftermath of the war because we rely on our Constitution to safeguard us; it is the greatest fabric of social government in the history of mankind.

There have always been two lines of attack upon our Constitution. One is the attempt to break it down by force, as in the first Whiskey Rebellion that Washington so summarily repressed, and the war for secession. The other has been by tacit or formal nullification—and that is treason. It traitorously strikes at law and order. It has been tried four times in history—what is known as the Hartford Convention, the South Carolina nullification, defiance of the fugitive-slave law, and the present "wet" campaign of ridicule and lies to bring into disrepute the Volstead law.

We need in this critical hour to bring before us again and often the stalwart attitude of Lincoln when some of America's most brilliant orators, men of highest character, were assailing the fugitive-slave law as unworthy of support. In that great meeting in Springfield, where three-fourths of his audience were against him, and his political future hung in the balance, his words rang out as sharply as the shots of the Minute-men at Lexington: "I have always hated slavery . . . but we have no right to interfere as long as it is in the Constitution. I am for honest enforcement."

Lincoln's Example

"O youth of America, if in that trying hour Abraham Lincoln stood against nullification, shall we, because of the appetites of men, or for gain or yielding to lax sentiment of some who ought to know better, shall we in an easy-going fashion consent to practical nullification, or shall we count as foes to be feared and fought those who ignore a law they do not like, while it is lawfully a part of our nation's Constitution?

"We are under a great President, who believes that poverty can be mitigated, if not removed, by economic laws. The issues of this hour are more economic than political. Herbert Hoover has the best economic intelligence of any public man in the world. He needs your support to outlaw the liquor traffic and to eradicate the liquor curse."

The Gospel Needed

Mr. Robin's impassioned conclusion was a plea for youth to take religious work, as he had done for one-third of his life, as companionship with and service under Christ. Without this moral passion and self-control civilization would die. The greatest factor in solving to-day's problems is not intellectual or physical, but the sense, the understanding, the willingness, and vital force of prayer.

"Men say to me, 'Robins, I don't want outside help to fight my battles.' They think that is courage, but they forget that the persons who have made the deepest dent in human destiny have prayed."

He cited the Galilean, Paul, Luther, Knox, Cromwell, who was laughed at by the Cavaliers, but who won fifty-four battles, and at Marston Moor flung back the courtiers with their sneers and curled locks.

"For myself," he said, "my prayer is, 'God, I don't want You to help me when I ought to help myself.' But a man can get to the limit of his strength pretty quick. Then I don't want to bluff myself, or lie. I want the help I can get from the dominant Power of the universe."

Mr. Robins held his hearers breathless, reporters' pencils suspended in air, while he related an instance of an unanswered prayer for just one more vote needed in the Illinois Senate to pass a child-labor law. He had done everything he could, and leaned his head against the wall in discouragement, pleading, "If I have overlooked anything I might do, God, show me now."

"Friends passed, saying, 'Robins is tired; he needs sleep.' But I wasn't sleepy; I was praying. And then I remembered a Senator, a corrupt Irish boss who yet had a soft side for children. I sent for him, and told him what was needed, and appealed to his Irish chivalry for childhood. And when the roll was called, he answered, 'I vote, "Aye." ' Instantly politicians and lobbyists rushed to him exclaiming, 'You don't mean that; your vote will pass the bill, and we can't have it so.'

"And he faced the speaker, and demanded a second roll-call; and when his name came again, he bawled out above the din, 'I vote, "Aye." '

"I don't claim to know much about prayer, but I think I know what it is to lean back on the Infinite. I would rather you Endeavorers had the power of prayer than any other gift."

Singing, "I Would Be True," the greatest Audience of the convention melted away into the streets impressed as it had not been before with an overpowering sense of the reality of God in human destiny.

WARREN G. HOOPES
Field-Secretary, Pennsylvania

E. F. HUPPERTZ
Field-Secretary, Texas

CHAPTER VII

A "PRIZE" SESSION
Monday Morning, July 8

A Korean boy protégé of Mr. Rodeheaver, Chai Myung Hyun, who is on his way back to his native land after several years' musical training in Chicago, was introduced and sang in his native translation, "Nearer, My God, to Thee."

Succeeding this the following State field and denominational secretaries were introduced: Mrs. J. Q. Hook, Idaho; Rev. Frank P. Wilson, Illinois; Miss Elizabeth Cooper, Indiana; Mr. Everett Robie, Iowa; Mr. Harold Lovitt, Kansas; Mr. F. C. Dixon, Maryland, West Virginia, Delaware; Mr. Ernest S. Marks, Michigan; Mr. Alfred C. Crouch, Missouri; Mr. Marion Simms, Jr., Nebraska; Mr. Frederick L. Mintel, New Jersey; Mr. Willard Rice, New York; Mr. Herman Klahr, Ohio; Rev. Paul Clark, Oklahoma; Mr. Ross Guiley, Oregon; Mr. Warren Hoopes, Pennsylvania; Mr. E. F. Huppertz, Texas; Miss Louella Dyer, Washington; Mr. Clifford Earle, Wisconsin; Rev. Frank Getty, Presbyterian, U. S. A. Rev. S. S. Morris, D. D., African Methodist Episcopal; Rev. E. W. Praetorius, Evangelical; Rev. Harry Thomas Stock, Congregational.

Others were in attendance on the convention, but are present at this moment.

A special prize, a two-foot cocoanut cake, was presented to Mr. Klahr, Ohio field-secretary, for securing the largest number of Society Boosters for THE CHRISTIAN ENDEAVOR WORLD.

The oratorical contest on Peace was next on the program, with the following speakers: Lorraine Wallace, Mesa, Ariz.; Edna Walker, Ossining, N. Y.; Richard Eakin, Tulsa, Okla.; Evelyn Zwicker, Marshfield, Ore.; Rolande Teide, Redfield, S. D. These had successfully run the gauntlet of local society, and local and State union elimination, and had thus earned free trips to the International Convention. The two prize-winners in this final test were: first, Richard Eakin, Oklahoma, and second, Edna Walker, New York.

The prize-winners in the citizenship contest were Gwendolyn Gaskill, Michigan, and Paul Rhoten, Nebraska. The winners in the evangelism contest were Blanche Youmans, Kansas, and Marion Jackson, District of Columbia.

Reality in Life

Dr. E. L. Reiner, pastor of Waveland Avenue Congregational Church, Chicago, a trustee of the International Society, and one of the most valuable advisors and "peppiest" speakers and conference leaders, was introduced by Dr. Poling as "Dad" Reiner, without whom no convention would be complete.

He led the convention in a study of "Reality in Life," using the International Society's book, "Acquainting Youth with Christ." First, he said, there must be intellectual reality. He told of how his little daughter had to be reasoned with to convince her that God was giving her daddy a square deal, because of certain minor misunderstandings in the parish. She insisted, "You are the bestest man in the world." So he had to show her that these things that troubled her were not real, but only seeming.

In the spiritual life, too, there must be a sense of reality; things must be reasoned through. He read from the text this definition: "The Christian life is daily life lived in the spirit of Jesus by the help of His unseen presence." Life is not always the same. "When I go into the pulpit, I am not what I am then, but what I was when I prepared the sermon. It is well if life can be so constant as always to seem real.

"No young person can resist the genuine holy life in another. An ounce of deed is worth a ton of creed. The finest point of contact in leading youth is friendship. What is friendship? Take the stories of David and Jonathan, of Jesus and John, of Damon and Pythias. A friend is one who loves and understands you." Dr. Reiner told how his young girls shyly say, "Let me introduce Mr. So-and-So, my friend." It means that acquaintance has grown into friendship, and may go on to another "ship" whose first syllable is different.

"All human friendship is a type of friendship with Christ. If you want a friend you must pay the price, with Christ the price is walking with Him and trusting Him."

He illustrated trust by the story of an emperor who had been maliciously warned that his court physician meant to poison him with medicine. But when the doctor presented the draught the emperor looked him confidently in the eye and drank it.

Prizes Awarded

Harold Singer introduced the secretary of the awards committee, Miss Louella Dyer.

The first prize, a framed copy of the autographs of the speakers, was presented to Mary Elliot, representing the Belmont Christian Church, Kansas City.

The second, a religious picture, went to the Park Avenue Evangelical Church. Honorable mention was made of Jackson Avenue Christian Church, West Side Christian Floating Endeavor Society, Independence Boulevard West Side Christian, and Walker's Tabernacle. These awards were for poster displays.

The young daughter of Professor Jones, chorus-leader, sang charmingly "The Last Rose of Summer." This was followed to the delight of all by a unique trio in which Miss Jones sang, her mother whistled, and her father accompanied on the piano.

Denominational Rallies

The various denominations that met at the Christian Endeavor Convention in Kansas City held individual rallies on Monday afternoon. Between 300 and 350 Disciples and Congregational Endeavorers had a royal get-together time, with speeches and luncheon. The Seventh Day Baptists had a splendid rally. The United Presbyterian and the United Brethren each met for times of fellowship and inspiration. This was also true of the Presbyterians and other denominations. The Reformed Church in America and the Reformed Church in the United States combined forces in a delightful luncheon hour. The denominational rallies proved to be a popular feature on the program.

A GLORIOUS ENDING

The Purpose Meeting—States Tell of Aims in a
Great Closing Meeting

Long, long before the opening hour on Monday evening, "the last great night of the feast," Endeavorers from all parts began to march toward the convention hall.

They sat in delegations, and as most of these delegations wore special insignia of some sort, the scene became more and more colorful as the hall filled up.

The Iowa group in bright red blouses made a large splash of color in the hall; and they carried the invitation "tall corn," with tassel on the end, that they had used in so striking a way in the parade.

California with their yellow caps made another splash of color, but one might say the same for practically all the delegations.

Percy Foster led the song service and had everybody in the hall singing with gusto, and a meeting that begins with sustained happy song cannot fail to be successful.

Thanks to Kansas City

A resoluion of thanks to Kansas City for the splendid hospitality shown the delegates was passed, and mention was made of the wonderful co-operation of all who in any way have had to do with the convention, directly or indirectly.

"The Lost Chord"

The great convention choir, led by John R. Jones, which has done such splendid work all through the convention, moved every heart by its superb singing of "The Lost Chord."

Then a telegram: "*The Luther League of America in session in Omaha, offers fraternal greetings. May the present Christ make His fellowship felt in every session.*

"A. J. TRAVER,
"General Secretary."

Devotions (Phil. 4) by James Kelly of Scotland were followed by an announcement by Dr. Poling of the World's Convention next year in Berlin, Germany. A collection was taken to provide the World's Christian Endeavor Union with funds with which to help, perhaps, some European as well as American Endeavorers to attend that meeting.

Making Life Count

Dr. John Timothy Stone, introduced by Dr. Poling as a great educator, a great man, president of McCormick Theological Seminary, amply justified this description, when in charactistic style, without preface, he launched into a gripping evangelistic address. He is a great preacher, but more, a great, warmhearted soul whose intense and flaming zeal is only matched by his moral earnestness and sincerity.

The subject he chose was, "How You Can Make Your Life Count for Most." The "how" as the address progressed proved to be "by soul-winning," for one not only is blessed one's self in winning souls, but reaches out to a multitude of lives through those one wins.

This idea was developed with great force and eloquence, with many illustrations taken from our common life.

Well-Deserved Praise

Mr. Charles D. Williams presented the members of the Convention Committee, who made a splendid array of young men and women, and gave an idea of the tremendous amount of work entailed in putting over a convention like this.

Dr. Poling called to the front the boys and girls that had done the ushering. They came marching down both sides of the hall under tumultuous applause, and presented a striking scene in their red scarfs. They made a small army as they arranged themselves in front of the great platform.

Mr. Gates was asked, "What about them?" and replied that he had never seen a convention where, as far as details are concerned, things had been more satisfactory than in this Kansas City Convention. He had nothing but high praise for the Convention Committee, the ushers, the Boy Scouts, and the choir, which he declared was the best convention chorus we have ever had. As a matter of fact, the choir added immensely to the success of the convention. Dr. Poling pointed out that the service rendered was all voluntary, and showed the spirit of Christian Endeavor.

THE MARCH OF THE STATES
Purposes and Aims Expressed

W. Roy Breg, Southern secretary, was in charge of the next part of the program, "The Purpose Meeting," when a representative of each State stepped to the front and in a few words declared the purpose of the State for the coming two years.

Pennsylvania pledged allegiance to Jesus Christ for the next two years, with whole-hearted devotion for the Crusade with Christ.

New Jersey will be found doing its utmost to make the principles of the Crusade with Christ real in the hearts of the young people of the State.

Wisconsin's reponse was, "Trusting in the Lord Jesus Christ for strength, we shall strive to show ourselves approved unto God, workmen that need not be ashamed."

The representative of *North Dakota* brought greetings, and said, "We are taking home the gleam so that we may better crusade with Christ."

The representative from *Minnesota* also brought greetings, and said, "It is our aim to be in on the great crusade with the Master."

Connecticut promised to take back home the spirit of Kansas City, and inspired by it seek to do better work in the future than in the past.

Virginia, we were told, stands ready and willing to help the youth of the State to a higher and better life.

Kansas expressed the intention of being loyal to the cause of Christ and the church.

Nebraska expressed need for leadership-training in Christian Endeavor, with special emphasis on Junior work.

The State of *Washington* will seek to make Christian Endeavor more Christian and to exalt the Christ.

Indiana pledged allegiance to the principles of the crusade.

Oregon repeated a statement made by Dr. Poling, "We will see this thing through!"

The State of *Illinois* promised to do its part in the Crusade with Christ for truth and righteousness.

Florida, the land of sunshine, sent hearty greetings, and promised faithful service in the crusade.

The representative from *Kentucky* said, "If Kentucky will, she can; and if she can, she will," indicating the State's aim to do great things for Christ.

Iowa, the State where the tall corn grows, is going back to crusade for Christ and seek to put the twelfth chapter of Romans into practice.

As for *Ohio* we were told that the challenge of this convention will be found in thousands of lives in that State.

After being a part of such a great convention, the *Oklahoma* delegation could not but go back home thrilled to do service for Christ in Christian citizenship, evangelism, and world peace.

The *Texas* representative said that the eyes of 10,000 or more Endeavorers in Texas were on us, and that they would join in crusading with Christ in Texas.

Delaware delegates declared that they were going back to their home State with a greater vision than they had ever had before. The allegiance of 40,000 was promised when we celebrate the golden anniversary of Christian Endeavor in 1931.

Michigan delegates, we were told, are going back home to do their best to win Michigan for Christ.

Forty thousand Endeavorers of *Missouri*, it was declared, are saying: "God bless you. We accept the challenge to crusade with Christ!"

Arizona's aim was expressed on her banner, "Consecrated Workers Trained for Service." They return to do greater things for God.

Colorado pledged its support in the great Crusade with Christ.

In *New York*, it was stated, 130,000 Endeavorers pledged themselves to press on in the Crusade with Christ, and to bring a large delegation to the Golden Gate in 1931.

Washington, D. C., promised to try to do a creditable job for Christ and the church in the coming two years.

Alabama pledged herself to back the program of Christian Endeavor, and promised to seek to make the next two years glorious in the history of the movement.

The *Massachusetts* delegate spoke of the Christian Endeavor power-plant of Massachusetts, serving more than 50,000 young people, and stated that it has found new power in this convention.

Idaho pledged itself to a greater crusade for Christ and the church.

The Endeavors of *Maryland*, it was said, have been taking Jesus first, others next, and self last.

The Endeavorers of *Utah* will go back from this experience to service as more loyal crusaders.

New Mexico is for world evangelism. "We invite you to join us."

Arkansas, the Wonder State, earnestly promised to crusade with Christ.

West Virginia Endeavorers are ready to accept the challenge. "And you can count on us," they said.

Paul C. Brown, Pacific-Coast secretary, said "Aloha," meaning "greetings" from the *Hawaiian Islands,* where he has been visiting on a Christian Endeavor trip. His word of greeting was "Kohua," which signifies co-operation.

The delegate from *Canada,* Dr. Mactaggart, said that Canada stands loyally shoulder to shoulder with America, and will fight together to make this whole continent bone dry. "We shall work and pray to keep our borders without a gun and free from the liquor traffic."

Dr. Finlay brought greetings from bonnie *Scotland.* He said he would carry back to the young people there the story of this convention and of the great and noble youth that had attended it.

Mr. James Kelly represented the *European Christian Endeavor Union,* which includes twenty-two nations. He said that he would pledge the union's co-operation with America in the Crusade with Christ, and emphasized the invitation to come to Berlin in 1930, and show the world that Christian Endeavor stands for Christian brotherhood and for world-wide peace.

New Hampshire sent greetings, and quoted the Scripture passage, "We love Jesus because He first loved us."

Mrs. Clark Speaks Again

Mrs. Francis E. Clark, wife of the founder of Christian Endeavor, was called to the front. She said: "Once more I want to thank you, every one, for all you have done for me in this convention. Every friendly word has helped me and given me new courage to go back to my home to do what I can, wherever I can, for Christ and the church."

Closing Moments

A brief talk by Dr. Poling closed with his calling for Life-Work Recruits, and a host of them from all over the hall rose to their feet. A call to confess Christ as Lord and Saviour also brought a number of earnest young people to the front.

Dr. Poling asked all to rise who would pledge themselves to see the Crusade with Christ through, and the audience rose to a man. He asked them to give a salute to the incomparable Son of God, to throw both hands on high and repeat, "Trusting in the Lord Jesus Christ for strength, I will see this thing through."

A reverent prayer by Dr. Foulkes to the divine Redeemer, the vision of whose face we have seen and the love of whose life we have felt, brought this part of the meeting to a close.

The audience joined hands and sang, what has come to be a Christian Endeavor hymn, "Blest Be the Tie That Binds."

The gavel fell, and the thirty-second International Christian Endeavor Convention ended.

CHAPTER VIII

RADIO HOURS

On four days at noon Dr. Poling conducted a radio-question hour. The question period was prefaced each day by a short address by Dr. Poling. We give below some of the questions answered.

* * * * * *

Do you believe in kissing-games? Have you ever played them?

Well, I never played as many as I wanted. Now, of course, I do not want to be misunderstood. I agree with Booth Tarkington that kissing to be properly appreciated should be an event, and never become a habit. Another writer has said something else that I am reminded of just now, that familiarity with the sublime is deadening. Through too much intimacy the beautiful may be made common. Sometimes it is done unwittingly until it is no longer beautiful, until it is just common. I think that is all I need to say to this wonderful crowd of understanding young men and women. Kissing to be appreciated should not be a habit, but an event. As to the kissing-games, Christian Endeavor is finding games that are immeasurably better than kissing games.

* * * * * *

A friend of mine refuses to become a Tenth Legioner because he says, "Everything belongs to God; the tenth is only one tenth." What can I answer?

I can give you a good answer that comes from a St. Louis Bible class. A friend from over there made a similar statement, saying he was not giving one-tenth because he was giving everything. The man to whom he made the statement said he believed God would be profited if he could discount the fellow ten per cent for cash. What do I mean? I mean that we have to have a starting-point; we do belong to God; everything we have belongs to God; but we must have a starting-point, and ten per cent is a mighty good starting-point. Christian Endeavor has discovered that it forms habits, that it leads one to become methodical and, more than that, that there seem to be attendant blessings as a result of that kind of consistent every-day giving. I recommend the tenth to you, not because of anything that may have been enjoined under the old dispensation, under Israel, but because of its efficiency, because of what it does, not only for the church and the world generally, but because of the habits it forms that are worth while in the life of the individual.

*   *   *   *   *   *

What do you think of prize-fighting?

I think it is a mistake. I am very sure it would be a mistake for me. There is, however, a very distinct difference between prize-fighting and boxing. Prize-fighting is utterly demoralizing. Gene Tunney indicated that he was a real fellow, not when he whipped Jack Dempsey, but when he turned his back on the prize-fighting ring.

*   *   *   *   *   *

What is the most important Christian Endeavor committee? I am always on small committees.

I will tell you which is the most important committee—it is *your* committee; and, if that is not what it ought to be, then it is for you to make it what it may become.

May I illustrate that? Some years ago a young man who was a graduate of Oberlin returned to his home town, and was added to the membership of the good-literature committee. He tried to find out what the committee was supposed to do, and no one seemed to know. He went to his minister, but neither did he know. The young man decided to make it a real committee, and started by preparing a reading-list for that society. He found out that they were not reading good books, largely because they were not acquainted with good books. He prepared a reading-list for them, and eventually it became such a help that the ministers' organization took it up, and the lists were widely distributed. That is what I mean when I say that your committee is the most important. Remember that when you go back. Decide to study your committee. Decide to put into it your enthusiasm, all that you have. Make it the biggest thing in your society.

*   *   *   *   *   *

What do you think of amateur tennis-players who turn professional?

They have a perfect right to do so if they desire. It does seem to be a mistake, because the field is restricted. Some brilliant amateurs who have become professionals have spent a great deal of time trying to re-establish themselves as amateurs. Certainly there is nothing wrong about turning professional if they desire to do so, but the amateur would seem to have much greater opportunity.

What denomination has the largest number of Christian Endeavor societies?

You will be interested to know that the church having the largest number of Christian Endeavor societies, including the Old World, is the Methodist Church in its various branches. The church next in line is the Presbyterian; the next is the Christian Church. If we go to Australia in 1931 we shall be entertained very largely by the Christian Endeavorers of the Methodist Church, out of which the largest constituency comes.

* * * * * *

I recently attended a Christian Endeavor convention, and while there wanted to accept Christ as my Saviour, to become a Christian. In fact, I had to leave the consecration service because the inward urge was too great. However, my father told me if I do so he will kick me out of the house. I am too young to leave home. What shall I do?

This is a very great question. What shall I do? There is only one thing that you can do, follow the gleam. Make your decision for Jesus Christ. I think if you will go to your father directly, as many another young person has gone to his father directly, you can bring him to an understanding. I shall very earnestly pray that he may understand. When you are called, as Peter was called by the sea long ago, there is only one answer to make, "Here am I, Lord."

* * * * * *

My fiancee and I mutually love each other. However, I am studying for the medical profession, and have two years of college work still to complete, as well as four years of specialized work. Shall we be married now or wait until my training is completed?

I know a young girl who married the man of her choice and went into the community where he was studying, went to work as a stenographer, and for the first two years helped along, and they managed to get along famously. It seems to me others could find the way out in just this way. On the other hand, it is always unwise to decide too quickly on such a matter. It is generally better to wait. I wish I might talk personally with the one who asked this question.

* * * * * *

Do you think there will be any more books added to the Bible?

No. In the first place, the Bible is a library, as you know. There are sixty-six volumes in this library. Many other books of devotion, of course, will be written. They are coming from the press every week, but they are not part of the Bible. It is finished; it is complete.

When would you say a person is old enough to be married?

Some people are too young to marry when they are thirty. Some people are old enough to get married when they are twenty-one. I was in my twenty-first year when I was married, but I was out of college and had just a little money in the bank —enough to buy a kitchen stove. When it can be accomplished satisfactorily from the standpoint of preparation for practical living, I am very happy to see young people get married. Nothing rejoices me more than to watch a young man and woman march down the aisle of the church to take their covenant vows and enter into that holy relationship, but what a sad thing it is to rush away from high school and into marriage, which if not understood becomes the tragedy of all tragedies!

* * * * * *

What should our attitude be toward other religions?

In every religion there is good. We appreciate that increasingly now. Our good friend, Dr. Cory, told us he regretted the empty temples to-day, because from the temples, once crowded with worshippers, the people had gone out into the ways of atheism. You see religion is essentially man's search for God. Man is incurably religious. Christianity is more than that, however. Christianity is finding God in and through Jesus Christ.

* * * * * *

Do you believe "the meek shall inherit the earth"?

Yes, I believe it; but who were the meek referred to in that statements? The meek were those who, in terms of the Master's great statement on the mountain-side, gave themselves in complete surrender to the will of God.

Do you recall that the term has been used in literature of horses? They were referred to as "meek" horses. What did that mean? That meant they were trained horses. The chariot horses of the ancients were "meek" horses. Why? Because they were trained; they were subject to the will of the driver. They went forward under his direction. It did not mean they were pale, pallid, and supine. There's the difference; we misunderstand the meaning of the word "meek."

* * * * * *

Are older people a help or a hindrance in the young people's society?

It depends on the older people. I am glad that we have graded Christian Endeavor. In my own church we have graded societies, and I am quite sure they so understand the message and opportunity of Christian Endeavor that they would not consent to the amalgamation or the union of the groups except as they may come together on certain occasions.

Of course, in smaller societies again and again older people have made a very happy contribution to the life of the Christian Endeavor society in the local church. The ideal is to give the society to the young people; to make them responsible for it; to make the obligations theirs, and the opportunities as well.

* * * * * *

To what denomination do you belong?

From the standpoint of this convention we are not concerned chiefly with the denomination to which an individual may belong. Here you are before me, Methodists, Baptists, Presbyterians, Congregationalists, Friends, Evangelicals, members of Christian Churches, and all the rest, and you all look alike to me. That's the way I feel. I am a minister of the Reformed Church in America. I would rather not say that; not because I am ashamed of it, thank God, but because I do not care to see you emphasize that. I believe I am a better member of the church, I know I am, because of what this movement has put into my life; because the privilege of knowing you and other Christian friends around the world has given me a better understanding; it has enabled me to see what you and others are doing. After these experiences I always go back to my own church with new inspiration. That's the way I feel about it and the way you ought to feel about it. We accept this matter in the terms of the great message we heard this morning.

* * * * * *

What kind of young women do young men like to marry?

Just the kind, if you please, who are here. Christian Endeavorers. Those who are really alive, happy, and attractive. Yes, that would be my answer, and I wish that you who are listening in could look into the faces of the young ladies gathered here and the young lady who presides so graciously to-day.

* * * * * *

Do you believe young people are interested in politics?

I know these young people are. You have heard the resolution that was adopted. You have read the pledge that was signed here by more than 8,000 of them, in which they declared their support of the government; in which they announced they would co-operate with the President of the United States in terms of law-observance and enforcement! If we are not citizens of to-day, we are citizens of to-morrow. I cannot hope to be a true Christian, it seems to me, unless I am doing my level best to be a loyal Christian citizen to my own country.

* * * * * *

What do you think of the argument of personal liberty as used against the Eighteenth Amendment?

Personal liberty is a great and precious thing. It is only

when personal liberty is misunderstood; when it is mistaken for license, or rather when license is mistaken for personal liberty, that trouble comes in. We can have no true, democratic government until people are willing to sacrifice their personal liberty in the interests of public welfare, and we have had demonstrations in each generation of men and women who have been prepared to sacrifice their personal liberty in order that the State and community might be happy and safe and free. Personal liberty must be subordinated to public welfare. Is it not a fact that the community always reserves the right to take away the personal liberty of the individual who, by asserting his personal liberty hurts society?

Let me illustrate that. I was born in a frame house and I have always been impressed with frame houses and prejudiced in their favor, but in the city in which I live to-day I cannot build the best frame house on earth. Why? Because of fire hazards. Frame houses would endanger the community, and my personal liberty to build a frame house is denied because of the right of the community to protect itself. Yes, I believe in personal liberty, but personal liberty is not license, and must be secondary to public liberty and welfare.

*   *   *   *   *   *

Do you believe that belonging to the Christian Endeavor union takes young people away from their local churches? The pastor of our church does not approve of the union for that reason.

The Christian Endeavor union should not take people away from their local church. I am happy to have my own young people act as union officers, and I am glad to surrender them from time to time to do the work of the whole community. It is only when from time to time some of us overemphasize the place of the union that we get into this difficulty, I think.

*   *   *   *   *   *

I am in love with a young lady. Her parents object to our marriage. They do not, however, object to me as a man. What shall we do?

Now that depends. I must know, of course, why they object to your marriage. I am glad they do not object to you as a man. If you will be patient and strive to find the viewpoint of the parents of the young lady, I believe the proposition will work itself out. Perhaps she is too young to marry; perhaps her education has not been completed.

*   *   *   *   *   *

How can I develop a spirit of reverence in my young people's group?

First of all, by being reverent yourself, as I am sure you are. I wish all of you could attend a meeting in the Oakwood School in New York, the school of our friend Reagan. There the very atmosphere is reverent. Do it by your own poise; do it by leaving a pause in the meeting; do it by prayer, silent or audible; do it by reading the Scripture; by offering a testimony, and by speaking directly and personally. Take advantage of every opportunity. Some of your group may not have been properly introduced to the reverential, and much will depend upon your own attitude.

* * * * * *

Will you please give your opinion of college fraternities and sororities? Are they wrong, or can one belong to one and still be considered on the same basis religiously as non-fraternity people?

You are the answer. There are fraternity and non-fraternity people in this great auditorium, many of them. Frankly, I would personally prefer to see the fraternity idea abolished in the high school. That is my personal conviction in regard to the matter.

I went to a non-fraternity college, and I am glad that I did, but some of my friends who are great Christian leaders, great figures in the Christian movement, have their fraternity ties, and have had their lives enriched by them, and we shall judge not that we be not judged.

* * * * * *

What is personality? Is it inborn, or can it be attained? If so, how?

Personality is *you*. That is the answer. Personality is you. Is it inborn? Yes. It is a gift to an individual, to be developed, to be enriched, to be educated, to be trained, and to be released. Personality may be debased, can be debased, but personality can also be mastered until it approaches more and more to the image of the Lord Jesus Christ Himself, as we come close to His will and into the heart of His purpose.

* * * * * *

Last night my roommate and I had an interesting discussion on world peace. I read in Matt. 24:6: "And ye shall hear of wars and rumors of wars. See that ye be not troubled, for all these things must come to pass, but the end is not yet." Will you please explain this verse, as I want to be true to my pledge, and at the same time have the right understanding of this verse?

It does not say that you shall not take a pledge to do your level best to end war. That doesn't bring an indictment against the Christian testimony of the church in terms of the great word of Jesus, "By this shall all men know that ye are my disciples, if ye have love one to another." By this we do not escape the implications of this other text, "They that take the sword shall perish by the sword." The pledge is in harmony not only with the Scripture, but with the will of the Father and with the will of Jesus Christ.

*   *   *   *   *   *

At what age should a girl be allowed to go with boys without a chaperon?

I cannot answer that question for you. Some young people are older at fifteen than others at seventeen or eighteen. I say to you that none of us should turn ourselves away from the advice of those who know us well and love us dearly, our parents and our friends, and decide arbitrarily on these points. I like to feel that Christian Endeavorers in this intermediate period, in this youth-time of joy, are having more of the wide friendship; that we have real friends, and many of them, who make up our circle, rather than in terms of an isolated friendship, if you please, with an individual person, that removes us from the richness—well, from the richness we would have in a convention like this, for instance.

*   *   *   *   *   *

A young man tried to tell me that Niagara freezes over in the winter. I said, "Bolony." Who is right?

"Bolony" as you use it is not right. Niagara does freeze over—not every winter, of course. Can you imagine it? That mighty stream of water freezing solid—freezing solid so that multitudes can go out on the ice? Many lives have been lost because of risks that have been taken when the thaws were on. It doesn't freeze solidly every winter, but again and again it does freeze solidly, and when the searchlights are played upon it, it is a wonderful spectacle.

*   *   *   *   *   *

What is your opinion of organic church union? What is the Christian Endeavor viewpoint?

I gave expression to what I believe to be the Christian Endeavor viewpoint with regard to organic union on the opening night in the presidential message. We are not outside the church. We are in the church and of the church. We are not a young people's church. We are loyal to the churches to which our societies belong, so we give support to the union commissions that have been organized. We do not have a commission on organic union in the Christian Endeavor movement for the reason that has been suggested. I believe the time is coming, however, when the churches of the great denominational families, Presbyterian, Methodist, and Baptist, will unite within the bounds of these church families first, and then in God's own time, if it is well, shall go on to the larger expression of organic union. I do know, too, that young people are impatient of delay when it becomes apparent that there are vital economic, spiritual, and missionary losses due to schisms and separations.

How long a time should a young man go with a girl before giving her a Christmas present?

Evidently this young man is saving up a long time ahead. It is not so much a question of how long a time you go with a girl, but how deep your feeling for the girl is. It is also somewhat a question of how deep your pocketbook is. The question, after all, is the spirit of the matter, is it not? It is a beautiful thing to give Christmas presents. I have always suggested to young men that they speak with their sisters, or mothers, or if they do not have sisters that they speak with some one with the interest of a sister, and who can give good advice. The important thing is not the present, as I am sure you will all agree, but it is a matter of spirit, a matter of heart, and last a matter of financial ability. Sometimes young people are tempted to do perfectly foolish things because of the enthusiasm of the moment.

*   *   *   *   *   *

Do you favor high-school and college students having their own automobiles while away at school?

I think it is almost invariably a mistake for high-school and college folks to have their own automobiles while they are away at school. It takes a lot of time to handle an automobile properly and keep it in proper shape; it means too much time from study and other affairs. I have always appreciated the wisdom of school authorities who have kept automobiles off the campus during school years. It seems to me there are ways of taking care of those times when an automobile may seem necessary, and that it isn't necessary for us to have automobiles to run around in while we are supposed to be concentrating on the curricula and the educational programs of our lives.

*   *   *   *   *   *

Do you favor the woman in public life?

I favor the woman in public life. Thank God for the woman in public life. I was for suffrage for women before I had any power to express myself at the polls, and everything I have seen since has convinced me that until we had the contribution of women in citizenship, the expression of woman's leadership in public life, the leadership of women like Justice Allen, our democracy went forward hopping on one leg.

CHAPTER IX

QUIET HOUR SERVICES

The Shrine Temple was crowded morning by morning for the Quiet Hour service conducted by Dr. William Hiram Foulkes.

[Dr. Foulkes chose for the general theme of his Quiet Hour services, "In the Upper Room with the Master." On account of a temporary illness he was unable to present in person the topic for the opening Quiet Hour. His long-time friend, Dr. A. E. Cory, responded as a substitute, taking Dr. Foulkes's general theme and following his particular suggestion for the day.]

LIFTING OUT THE SOULS OF MEN

By Rev. William Hiram Foulkes,

Vice-President of the International Society of

Christian Endeavor

In the second Quiet Hour service Dr. Foulkes presented the dialogue between Jesus and Judas, as well as that between Jesus and Peter as the central incidents of the morning's message. He said in part:

Once again in the early morning we gather in our upper room with the master. We shall not be ready to crusade with Him unless we become intimate with Him. We shall not readily follow Him into the busy world and upon the field of world-conquest unless we become imbued with His spirit in the upper room of friendship and surrender. The upper room presents not merely a contrast between the hurried, noisy world without, and the spirit of peace within. It also suggests a contrast between the outward lives of the disciples and their true and inmost selves. The Master's deepest concern with them was, as His deepest concern with us is, with what is really deepest. He seeks to find what is really underneath, what is regulative and vital.

The setting of to-day's incident is simple but dramatic. He who had laid aside his garments to become the servant of all takes His garments again, and is seated in the midst of the disciples as their Master. He who had stooped to conquer now sifts their souls before the judgment-seat of His Lordship. We first saw love on its knees in humility and service and into the uttermost. Now we see love seated in its true dignity. It is the fault of our easy-going times that we want Jesus' Saviourhood without being willing to submit to His Mastership. We are willing to accept Him as a divine drudge appointed to take away the disagreeable things of life.

We hesitate to make Him the Lord and Master and to give complete control of our lives into His keeping. He will not long continue to be Saviour of those who will not permit him to be Lord and Master.

As we reverently ponder the message and expose our hearts to the ministry of the upper room, we come face to face with Jesus' longing for human friendship and sympathy. "He was troubled in the spirit," not much because of the evil designs of His enemies, but because of the fickleness of His friends. Nor did He despise what they had to offer. Although they, like ourselves, were leagues removed from the holiness of life, the serenity of purpose, and the deathlessness of the love that was in Him, they did not offer Him in vain any measure of affection or confidence. Nor do we. Jesus had a creative imagination. He could see what was not yet there. He penetrated the heart of Peter, and saw powers and steadfastness that had not yet come into being. He fathomed the depths of doubting Thomas' heart, and found a faith that no one, least of all Thomas, suspected. He sounded the abysmal depths of Judas' perfidy, too. When the nakedness of His own soul loomed before them, their souls became bare before Him. Their very best came to the surface and their very worst, too.

Judas went out, and it was night. Let the curtain of divine mystery fall upon that scene. Calvary is not a tragedy, but the apostasy of Judas is the world's greatest and most poignant debacle of soul. It was not until Judas had gone out that Jesus uttered His valedictory of love, His love and their love, each for the other. His new commandment He could not give them until Judas had gone out.

Let us remember, too, that we cannot dally with the temptation to betray our Lord without the certainty of final exposure staring us in the face. What doom befell the apostolic apostate. What a wreckage of wasted souls is scattered in His pathway through the years!

Jesus saved Peter. He made him over into a new man. He took the crumbling sand of irresolute and vacillating impulses, and made them adamantine. What He did with Peter He can do with us. What befell Judas may befall us. What does Jesus find underneath all our pretence and lip service? Does He find lustful hearts? Does he discover pictures on the wall of memories that defile His holy temple in us? "But I am President of my Society." "I'm an officer of the District Union, or a State Officer."

Oh, my friend, that is only your badge. Other people pinned that upon you. Whose hand do you wear on your heart? Are you jealous and suspicious Are you proud and vainglorious? Do you bear the badge and keep what is put therein? Do you profess the truth with your lips and live a lie in your heart?

Do we, rather, sincerely love Him in our inmost hearts? Judas could not have said it, for he hated Jesus. Peter first boasted of it, and then after his tragic denial was given his chance humbly to confess his love for the Master. We, too, have our chance to-day to hear and heed the two great words with which the glorified Jesus moves out of the Gospel record "Lovest thou me?" "Follow thou me." Upon this searching question and upon this loving commandment have the destiny of our souls. Do we love Him? Shall we follow Him through thick and thin and all the way?

The third Quiet-Hour address was on:

MY BODY FOR YOU

The most wonderful thing in the visible universe is the human body. So far as our scientific knowledge goes the body is the apex of creation. It outranks all the masses of matter, however vast they may be. It surpasses every other known form of organic life. It overtowers all the other known embodiments of physical and chemical forces.

Our whole moral universe is fabricated of the threads of bodily functions and activities. What people do with their hands and their feet; what they say with their tongues, the visions to which they summon their eyes, the voice to which they open their ears, the thrills to which they yield their sensitive nerves, the burden they bear upon their backs or the problems with which they rack their brains constitute the greatest element of moral life.

I have every warrant, religious and scientific for asking you to center your thought upon the most wonderful thing in all the world—your bodies. Scientific warrant, I say, because we must judge life not merely by a study of its simplified form, but by an analysis of its must complex product. If we would be ultra scientific we must learn the meaning of the most ultimate forms of life, not merely of the most primitive.

There are only three possible attitudes toward the human body, and I make bold to outline them to you in some detail. One is registered in the creed of the voluptuary and the sensualist, which he expresses in these words: "My body for myself!" This creed underlies no little of a modern philosophy. It is blazoned both in film and press, in magazine and book. It is the saturating spirit of modern cynicism. It is the breeding passion of criminal indulgence in deadly drugs, running the whole gamut from cocaine and heroin to equally devastating alcohol. It is the proud boast of the glutton. It is the loophole through which vermin-like bootleggers crawl into the homes or through which our so-called respectable citizens sneak into speakeasies or into the contraband lockers of clubs and cellars. "My body for myself! That is, my body is an end in itself. I can do with it what I please. I can do in it what it suits me to do. I can indulge its every appetite. I can say 'yes' to every caprice. My body for me!" To the boundaries of a certain great barrier this form of modern paganism must be permitted to live. It is time that people who want to wallow in the slime of lust and intoxication must be permitted to do so, unless and until their indulgence disturbs the rights of their fellows. They must not wallow in public places, on your doorstep, in my parlor or office. While folks may do all of these things they are only indulging themselves in a horrible and morbid burning of the flame of passion. All too soon the flame subsides and all that is left is cinders and ashes. Hospitals, asylums, institutions of penal correction are full of the victims of this creed of self-indulgence which carries with it the unescapable verdict of self-destruction. Sow the seeds of gluttony and intoxication, and you will reap the whirlwind of debility and death. Sow the seeds of unrestrained and unspiritualized sensuous indulgence, of sexual perversion, and you will reap the ghastliest harvest of diseased bodies and doomed souls that it is the tragic lot of human eyes ever to behold. "My body for myself" is a glittering creed. When its dishonest lustre has worn away it appears to be what it really is—the galling chain of physical disintegration and moral decay.

There is a second creed concerning the human body. It is the creed of tyranny and despotism. It runs thus: "Your body for me! My body is not big enough for my own hurts and desires. I need your body, too, and I must have it." This cruel creed is the taproot of economic and industrial injustice. It is responsible for all of man's inhumanity to man, and for what is worse, man's inhumanity to woman. It is the "big stick" that herds the morally helpless into the prison camp of unrequited labor and that extorts from them their life-blood, that my body may be made comfortable and ecstatic. The story of the writing of this creed carries us back to human beginnings, to the caveman and the jungle. It sweeps us past the mighty pyramids and the great engineering project of antiquity. It pushes us over the thresholds of sweatshops and down into the dark recesses of damp and foul-aired mines. It drags us into twelve hour a day, seven day a week factories, where under-privileged folk wear out their bodies. This is the creed that bids men reach out their hands and immolate tens of thousands of helpless girls upon the pagan altars of their own appetites every year. The taproot of this creed is the vitalizing center of every form of unrewarding economic and social toil, of the traffic in intoxicants and other poisons, of gambling and prostitution, of every phase of human indulgence at the expense of other people's bodies—and rising to its most appalling form in the carnage of war, wherein greed, rapacity, chauvinism, social hatred, pride of opinion and even religious bigotry have thrust the bodies of millions of our fellow human beings into the hot hell of the front line trenches, or if death is averted, into the horror of maimed and broken lives. Such a philosophy as this is even deadlier than that of mere self indulgences. The latter classes one's own body as an end in itself; the former must have yours and mine and a hundred or thousand others to gratify its desires.

Into the face of these pagan philosophies some two thousand years ago a young man flung his strange and, at first, inconceivable creed. It is the mysterious aftermath of self-sacrifice. "My body for you!" Why, the whole universe seemed upside down when that word was first uttered. "My body for you!" It was in a quiet upper room; a young carpenter turned wayfarer, just on the edge of thirty years, is saying good-bye to a little company of men who had followed him for a bare three years of glorious adventure. He took his hands, the gentlest and most wonderful human hands that had ever touched human flesh, and first of all, with those hands, washed tired, and it may be, bruised feet. Then with those same hands, He took bread and broke it, and gave it to them and said, "This is my body which is for you!" Bread broken for them, "My body for you!" What a body it was! Beautiful in its holiness, its wholeness. Those hands had never laid a lash upon the back of any struggling child of man. Those feet had never ridden rough-shod over the souls and bodies of the weak and helpless. Those lips had never cursed or led astray the erring and the fallen. Those eyes had never, by a glance or a gleam, brought shame to the heart of a woman or doubt to the heart of a little child. Those hands had healed the blind and the lame, the lepers and the demoniac. Those hands had wiped away the stain of sin from defiled faces and had lighted the lamp of hope in the breast of the despairing. What a wonderful body that was, "holy and harmless and undefiled." Every nerve must have quivered with the fullness of life. Every muscle must have responded to a holy impulse. Every heart-beat must have been directed toward some holy purpose of being. Yet in but a little while and that beautiful body would be spat upon, crowned with thorns, buffeted and at length nailed to a cross, hands and feet. Bloody sweat would burst forth from that tender flesh—that gentle voice that had never whispered aught but the holiest truth would be parched and cracked in the agony of crucifixion thirst. "My body for you!" This is the creed of Christ and of all Christ-like souls. This is the creed with which the spirit of that young man of two thousand years ago has won other young men and women in every age of the world and with which it would win you. That creed has been the philosophy of one of the noblest men I have ever known, a man knighted by the British Government, a man whose Christ-like human hands have probably treated more blind eyes into sight than any other pair of hands on earth, since Jesus was here among men. I refer to Sir William J. Wanless, M. D., the founder of that great Miraj Hospital in India. This glorious creed, "My body for you!" is the creed of all the martyrs, whether like Dr. Maguchin, in the field of science or like the ill-fated pioneers in the art of aircraft. Such men and women all, so far as they have been moved by sacrificial impulses, have heralded their holy creed, "My body for you!" What a heroic creed it is! How it drives out our cowardice and dissipates our fears! How it challenges our faith and summons our love! How it nerves our courage and embodies our purpose! What a premium it puts upon these bodies of ours in making them the servants of the holiest and the highest!

Youth is at the cross roads. A self-indulgent age, mad with pleasure, with its hand upon the throttle of power, wonderful when controlled and yet terrible when undisciplined, challenges you to-night. It literally wants to eat up your flesh and to drain your soul of its life-blood. Will you let it fasten its gilded chains of ease and indulgence around your bodies and let it teach you by goad and spur its pagan creed, "My body for myself?" Will you let it lash and drive you at the chariot wheels of tyranny and abuse of others and compel you to make others pay toll to your desires by the yielding of their bodies to you? Rather listen to the voice of One who will never set you free! The One who girded Himself with a towel and who washed the tired feet of the toilers! Will you let Him teach you how to wash the bruised feet of lifes' toilers? The One who gave His body to be broken for the sin and sinners of the world? Will you let Him have your body to be broken again for the hunger and need of the world?

In the words of the great Apostle of old, I beseech you, therefore, O beloved young men and women, most of you like Jesus as he began his great career on the sunny side of thirty, with your careers just ahead of you. I beseech you that you here and now *present your bodies*—your beautiful, glorious, serviceable bodies—a living sacrifice on the altar of human need, and that you make Jesus' philosophy of life your deathless creed, "This is my body which is broken for you!"

MRS. REX A. FULLAM
Field-Secretary, Vermont

LOUELLA DYER
Field-Secretary, Washington

CHAPTER X

CLOSE-UP VIEWS OF THE CONVENTION
THE TRUSTEES MEET ONCE MORE

California Wins the 1931 Convention

In the meeting of the trustees of the International Society of Christian Endeavor, postponed till Friday, the officers of the International Society were elected. Mr. E. C. Sams, of New York, was elected a member of the executive committee, and a number of new trustees were also named.

Dr. Poling introduced Mid-West Secretary Singer, who is responsible for many of the details of the present convention. He presented his report of work in seventeen States, visiting board meetings, conferences, conventions, and institutes. The theme of all conventions in these States this year has been, "Crusade with Christ." There are ten field-secretaries in these Mid-West States, all but two giving full time to the work. Christian Endeavor work has been built up, and several States have been lifted out of debt. Some of them have won fine recognition, Oklahoma and South Dakota winning first places in the registration contest, in the order named.

The Jubilee Convention, 1931

Washington, D. C., and San Francisco, Cal., both desired that the 1931 convention, the jubilee of Christian Endeavor, be held within their borders. Each city was given fifteen minutes in which to present its plea.

Milwaukee, Wis., and Indianapolis, Ind., each wanted the convention in 1933, and each of these cities was given eight minutes to place its arguments before the trustees.

San Francisco Wins

It was not only the eloquent peroration of the lady president of the Golden Gate county union, Miss Reis Deihl, that won the convention of 1931 for San Francisco, although her closing words struck a responsive chord, "Bring the Golden Jubilee convention to the Golden State by the Golden Gate." California had practical arguments, and offered facilities splendidly adapted to such conventions. Dr. Poling facetiously told the

113

Californians that they were sentenced to entertain the 1931 convention; and it was a happy, singing crowd that accepted the "sentence."

A Golden Pilgrimage Year

The Golden Jubilee idea, however, was greater than could be confined to one convention. Dr. Foulkes, speaking for the executive committee, described a plan to make the golden anniversary year the greatest of all years. The plan was to make 1931 a Golden Pilgrimage year; to make a pilgrimage to Portland, Me., to the shrine of Christian Endeavor; to go from Portland, perhaps, to Washington, D. C., for a couple of days and gather enthusiasm as well as spread our message in the national capital; to move farther west yet for meetings for another day or two, and so to San Francisco for the official Jubilee convention. The idea of thus sweeping through the country to a grand climax in San Francisco, and seeing embark there for Australia the group of delegates who will attend the Australasian celebration in 1931, captured the imagination; and the executive committee was empowered to make plans to carry these projects into effect.

A brief prayer by Mrs. Clark brought the meeting to a close.

WORKSHOP PERIODS

Conference Work in the Shrine Temple

Christian Endeavor conventions are more than loud huzzahs! They are not devoted entirely, or even largely, to inspirational meetings, but are given for the most part to practical conferences on Christian Endeavor work.

On Thursday morning, July 4, the various halls of the Shrine Temple were filled with earnest groups of young people anxious to listen in on conference work and take part in it.

These conferences were divided into age groups. A host—several hundred—of Endeavorers between eighteen and twenty-four met in one hall; a group of Endeavorers under thirty met in another hall; yet another group of those more than thirty held their meeting in another hall; and there were conferences for Junior leaders, for those under eighteen, and for those under thirty; all groups discussing "How Can We Crusade with Christ for Peace?"

After fifty-minute conferences on this theme leaders and speakers were changed, and the conferences reassembled in the various halls to discuss "How Can We Crusade for Christian Citizenship?"

The third theme of the Crusade with Christ, "Evangelism," was the topic of a series of conferences on Sunday afternoon, and attracted large audiences. The question discussed was "How Can We Crusade with Christ for Evangelism?"

There is no doubt about the interest of the young people. They believe in Christian Endeavor, and want to know how to increase their usefulness. They are not merely out for pleasure. They have set their hearts upon great things.

The same general scheme was followed Friday, Saturday. and Monday, the subjects, of course, being different. There were conferences on citizenship, vocations, stewardship, world friendship, Junior Christian Endeavor work, Intermediate work, Expert Endeavor, the prayer meeting, music in worship, recreation, missionary methods, leadership, prohibition, the rural church, publicity, Christian Endeavor in the city church, successful societies, "Progressive Endeavor," how to lead singing, and so forth. This brief list will give some idea of the rich fare prepared for the delegates, and the bulging conferences demonstrated that the program was appreciated. The chairmen and speakers at the conferences were for the most part our own field-secretaries and denominational young people's workers.

Day after day the young people gave hours to these conferences. There was little or no sight-seeing. The great convention halls had a wonderful attraction to these Endeavorers. They had come, some of them hundreds of miles, not to have a good time, but to learn something of Christian Endeavor and its methods, that they might go back home to their churches to labor more earnestly and more intelligently, as well as more efficiently, for their Master and their Lord.

Everywhere one went at these conferences notebooks were in evidence, and one may be perfectly sure that the young people carried back to their home places many ideas that they will seek to put into operation. The conference feature of the convention was one of the most practical and most valuable of all the features.

THE BIGGEST FEATURE OF THE KANSAS CITY CONVENTION

The Work for Juniors

Mildreth Haggard and Co-Workers Plan Future Program

The Junior features of the convention program at Kansas City represent the contributions of a surprising number of individuals and groups over the country, and their success was due to these contributions to the willing and generous help of Miss Cora B. Wells and the other members of the Kansas City Junior Committee; to Miss Lagineu Latimer, the city superintendent; to the tireless devotion to detail of the Junior staff and their helpers, and to the whole-hearted co-operation of the fine corps of State superintendents and their official representatives, who were present in the convention. Twenty-nine of this group were entertained at dinner in honor of Mrs. Clark.

met for conferences, and had tea together on Sunday afternoon.

More than one hundred and fifty Junior workers "Kept Tryst" with "Mother" Clark on Sunday evening, and none will ever forget her personal message on "influence shadows," or her dedication prayer.

There was a conference for union Junior workers, with a very scholarly and valuable presentation by Mrs. A. A. Alexander of Wisconsin.

The conference hours for society superintendents, who met each day in the spacious lounge of the Shrine Temple, were planned to allow time for questions and personal conference with the speakers and State superintendents.

The conference room was a fascinating place on Monday morning, with its wealth of exhibit material on World Friendship and Christian Citizenship, with the wonderful privilege of listening to the pioneer African missionary, Dr. Royal J. Dye, and the opportunity of gleaning practical help from Mrs. Elliott of Kansas City, Mrs. Morris of Texas, Mrs. Sproull of New Jersey, Miss Babcock, Miss Holloway of Nebraska, Miss Blakney of Minnesota, Miss Lindahl, Miss Cole, Mrs. Martin of Illinois, Miss Seaver of Massachusetts, Miss Clodfelter of Illinois, Miss Mable Shaffer of the Methodist Protestant Board of Missions, and Miss Eva Callarman from the United Christian Missionary Society.

Few people, studying the exhibit of Junior activities and participating in the conference hours, could know how many individuals and groups over the country had contributed to the Junior features of the convention program, nor how much appreciation was due the tireless devotion to detail of the Junior staff—Mrs. William V. Martin of Illinois, Miss Charlotte G. Babcock of Wisconsin, Miss Edna C. Smith of California, Mrs. J. W. Miller of Oklahoma, and Mrs. Ethel S. Petri and Mrs. D. J. Lane of Minnesota—and the willing and generous help of Miss Cora B. Wells, Junior chairman for the Kansas City Convention Committee, Mrs. Nellie G. Sproull of New Jersey, Miss Sadie Seaver of Massachusetts, Miss Mayme Clodfelter of Illinois, and all the members of the Martin family, Mr. Martin, Wilbert Martin, Mr. and Mrs. Howard Butt.

Mrs. Petri presented the survey of State program and promotional material, representing Junior work in many States. This analysis and summary had been made by an educational expert, Miss Gladys McAlister of Minneapolis. All of the source materials were bound for reference and study by State leaders.

The conference hour for union Junior workers on the afternoon of the third was of especial interest to State leaders, because of the consideration of the building and promotion of the Junior program. Standards for Junior work were discussed, and Mrs. A. A. Alexander of Milwaukee, State superintendent for Wisconsin, gave a very practical and scholarly presentation of motivation and attendant learnings, challenging all to restudy the incentives we use.

State superintendents gathered in conference on Friday afternoon also to consider the adaptation of the Junior program to the needs of rural societies with Mrs. Lane, herself the superintendent of a rural society, who not only listed the limitations of rural groups in general, but pointed out the advantages to be capitalized and the principles to be followed in planning for rural fields. Wisconsin has outlined and promoted a leadership-training course, based on the "New Junior Workers' Manual"—to be used on the extension course plan,—and this outline was studied with the author, Miss Babcock, Wisconsin's associate Junior superintendent.

The Juniors had the glad surprise of meeting Mrs. Clark and hearing one of her inimitable stories on Sunday afternoon. This hour, presided over by the charming Kansas City Junior superintendent, Miss Lagineau Latimer, was the Junior Session of the convention and brought to the Juniors Mr. Homer Rodeheaver with his trombone, Dr. Daniel A. Poling, and Mr. James Kelly.

Two periods were given to the consideration of prayer-meeting participation with Miss Mamie Gene Cole, director of religious education, First Presbyterian Church, Fort Smith, Arkansas, and to a brief discussion of expressional activities for Juniors, with an explanation of the exhibit panels in the arcade at convention hall, which units illustrated in order of decreasing importance the ten most important activities of Junior Christian Endeavor as related to the lives of the Juniors. Our publication manager, Mr. C. C. Hamilton, arranged to get into the Junior conference on this morning to present the JUNIOR CHRISTIAN WORLD—verbally and actually—since all received copies.

The last morning—Monday—was the busiest of all and some thought the most interesting. The conference room was occupied, wherever one looked, with exhibit material on World Friendship and Christian Citizenship,—the beautifully constructed model of the Moneika Mission Station in Africa, brought by Miss Florence Lye from her Juniors in Dayton Ohio, posters, pictures, books, maps, villages, curios, especially those brought from the Holy Land by Mrs. Sproull, who described them.

The Junior workers were rarely fortunate in their luncheon programs: the Fourth with the Cornet Trio (Faith and Howard Rutt, Wilbert Martin), General Secretary Gates presiding, and President Poling speaking; the Fifth with Miss Wells, the local chairman, presiding, and Mr. James Kelly speaking on the important theme of training Juniors in appreciation (the lovely picture by Copping, "Christ and the Children," which hung in the Junior exhibit, was the gift of Mr. Kelly to the convention); the Sixth, Missouri Day, with Mrs. J. A. Chapman, State superintendent, presiding over a beautiful service in appreciation of Miss Dora Clemens' thirty years of service for the girls and boys. The delightful decorations and favors for the several meals, as well as the badges, for which the registration cards were exchanged in the conferences, were prepared by our artist, Mrs. Martin. The menagerie, which she made and sent to make the dinner for Mrs. Clark "a howling success," came from Miss Frances Sibley of Seattle, Washington.

[One important omission has been made in the above report, namely, the fact that Miss Mildreth Haggard of Minneapolis was the leading spirit in all the splendid work for Juniors. Her contribution to this part of the program cannot be over-estimated.—*Ed.*]

EMBRYO "CAPS AND GOWNS"
Extraordinary High-School Convention

International Christian Endeavor has been running a six-day intensive leadership-training school in Kansas City. It was suggestive of "caps and gowns" in more ways than one. It was real class work that in most summer training-schools or camps leads to credits and ultimately diplomas. It will come to that sooner or later in Christian Endeavor. We used to fear that such a "grind" would be "too heavy" rations for our young people; but, bless our timid souls! they just ate it up at Kansas City and were hungry for more.

But there were actual caps and gowns to lighten the heaviness. A perspective of the Shrine Temple auditorium each morning from 8.00 to 12.10 revealed touches of bright head-coverings: scarlet caps of Missouri Endeavorers, olive-brown caps of Kansas, orange caps of California; caps with tassels, overseas trench caps, Turkish fez caps, green and white visors—a flower-garden of State union head-gear. That, in the amphitheatre of the Shriners' auditorium, with the "faculty" on the stage, backed by painted scenery picturing lakes and forests and verdure and clouds, was the setting of a real, earnest struggle to wrest a better preparation for the work of the Kingdom out of the hours that could be snatched from busy, bread-winning, housekeeping, teaching, student lives.

Principal Frank Getty, scholarly, virile, keen, experienced in dealing with young people's problems through the sixty-seven Presbyterian young people's summer assemblies of which he has oversight, held the reins in a masterly hand. His lieutenants were Lawrence Little, secretary of young people's work for the Methodist Protestant Church, with a score of summer assemblies to plan and man; Paul Clark, executive secretary of the Oklahoma Christian Endeavor Union; E. F. Huppertz, field-secretary of the Texas Christian Endeavor Union; Frank

P. Wilson, field-secretary of the Illinois Christian Endeavor Union; William J. Reagan, principal of the Oakwood School. That's the set-up, a sample of the other similar sections of this great summer high school with twelve thousand students. Only they called it a High-School Convention. The students in one section were majoring in peace, citizenship, evangelism. In another of the sections it was missions, vocations, recreation. Note-books? In earnest? Too intent even to chew gum. Drinking in lectures as calves drink milk when you put your fingers into their mouths and force them to. You should have listened to the rapid-fire machine-gun quizzes that poured in from the seats at the professor's desk. No, usually it was a give-and-take encounter. "We want to know rock-bottom facts," was the attitude. "We must have something that will get results."

SUMMARY OF SERVICE TALKS AT THE HIGH SCHOOL CONVENTION
By Prof. William J. Reagan

(Professor Reagan delivered a service talk at the close of the high-school convention each day.)

Present Day Superstitions and the Mind of Jesus

We have inherited many superstitions from the past. We are afraid of black cats, of the number 13, of Friday, of ghosts, and these superstitions are perhaps more potent influences on our lives than we realize. They are not, however, the really dangerous superstitions which confront our present generation.

The first and perhaps the most fatal superstition of to-day is the belief that young people and older have that they can get some place without going there. We are willing to admit the operation of law in connection with the automobile, the radio, and in fact with all machines, but in spite of the information which the new psychology is giving us as to law working in our minds we fail to realize that law operates always and everywhere; that we pay for our vices and are rewarded for our virtues. We do not seem to realize that real freedom cannot possibly be reached by following our whims; by yielding to passions; by complete self-expression. Real freedom is reached by substituting voluntary obedience to fundamental and inward law, in the place of external or forced obedience to artificial, temprorary, or man-made law. We need to see that self-realization and not self-expression is the only adequate and challenging goal.

Rights and Duties

The second superstition resembles the first. It is the belief that "our rights" and "other people's duties" are more important to us than "our duties" and "other people's rights." As life grows more complex and at the same time more intimate, it is increasingly important that we realize the significance of obligation. "Your rights and my duties" is a significant Christian Endeavor slogan. The word sacrifice is almost obsolete in these days. A selfish humanism has taken the place of a vital, virile Christianity with a cross at its centre. Cheap nationalism, racial superiorities, industrial conflict, exploitation of our fellows, is the inevitable result of this philosophy of pleasure-seeking humanism. However, it does not satisfy. It is incomplete. Its challenge is inadequate. We must follow our great present-day leaders, Herbert Hoover and Ramsay MacDonald, leaders who have the far vision; who prefer being right to holding office.

Do Ideas Matter?

The third superstition is the belief we seem to have that activity may be made a substitute for thought. "Your creed does not matter, what you *do* counts" is only half true. Both young people and older need a renewal of faith in truth. We need to see that what a person really believes is one of the most important things we can know about him. An adequate philosophy of life; a renewal of interest in facts, these are the needs of our generation. We boast loud and long about our friends, our abandonment of outgrown creeds and customs, and yet we quickly yield to the New York *Times* or the Chicago *Tribune* or some other daily. The difficulty of prohibition enforcement is partially due to our failure to find out and know facts. We must know the truth if we would be free.

Science and Worship

The fourth superstition is the belief that scientific thinking can be made a substitute for worship, for appreciation. We fail to realize that wisdom is infinitely superior to mere knowledge. This superstition is perhaps more dangerous than any of the others because it makes all of the others possible. There is, however, evidence that we have discovered the danger of this present attitude and are trying to find a way to change it. Great scientists are themselves pointing the way.

In the past we have talked a great deal about the faith of Christ. In recent years we have emphasized the life of Christ. We need to place beside these two emphases an emphasis on the mind of Christ. None of these superstitions can remain if we have the mind of Christ.

Playtime Starting at 7.00 A. M.!

Did you ever hear of a Christian Endeavor convention studying how to play? Yes, there was a "Playtime Breakfast" for this high-school group.

Then there were "recreational demonstrations" to a roomful of eager searchers after the secret of perennially fresh socials. They were sent moving rhythmically around the room in unison, in games that would take the fret and restlessness all out of "bad" children in two minutes.

That's a sample of the recreational course that Carroll M. Wright conducted. And so citizens, pastors, Junior workers, Sunday-school teachers, all got their share of help in this new-fangled training-school. Yes, the teachers were taught by experts how to tell a Bible story, how to dramatize the truth.

Twelve thousand Christian Endeavorers gave their vacations to go to school to learn how to be better workers, better leaders, in a thousand churches and communities. Talk about cutting melons, there's going to be a rich coupon-cutting in the affairs of the churches that are thus fitting their best young people to step into the shoes of those who must soon lay down the burden.

Is it the dawn of the millennium?

Well, it's the "mill" of the millennium. You've got to have the mill before you have the grist. The mill is grinding. Keep it oiled and powered.

IMPRESSIONS OF A SEASONED CONVENTION-GOER

No matter how convention-hardened one was, Kansas City had much to bring new thrills, much that no other International Convention has ever offered. For instance, styles of dresses have changed radically and added a new element of colorfulness to the audience. Whether one sat on the floor or high up in a balcony, everywhere the eye swept across acres of bright-tinted millinery and dressmaking, not to mention hosiery, that made a picturesque spectacle.

Much of it was what passes in review on our fashionable boulevards; yet there were added the brilliant-hued State caps, sashes, badges, armlets, and after the wonderful flower-garden parade, parts of gorgeous regalia that would make an Oriental rajah's city look drab. It surely was the most colorful convention that Christian Endeavorers have ever held in America, not excepting the poppy-embowered convention in San Francisco in 1897.

A Convention of Youth

Another impressionistic touch that lent virility and gladness was the youthfulness of the constituency. It was remarked on the reviewing-sand for the parade by some of those who have been attending conventions since Minneapolis, New York, Boston, and Montreal, "I believe that Christian Endeavor is growing more youthful with every big convention I attend."

It stands to reason. In the early days only mature pocket-books could meet the strain of cross-continent trips. To-day youth controls more money, and added to that, it has automobiles and good roads; and so travel is possible that once was not.

Then, again, the Junior society and the Intermediate have been reaching down nearer where the cradle-roll of the Sunday-school catches childhood. Christian Endeavor is undeniably, exuberantly, audaciously, self confidently, happily younger than it ever has been since Mother Endeavor Clark passed the cookies in Williston parsonage. Thanks be!

"When do we eat?" was not a momentous question, nor, "Where do we eat?" By a commissary scheme never before equalled in a convention the local convention committee and the headquarters management raised the matter of feeding the outer man to a dignity and perfection never before attained. Practically all the meals were provided for in the wonderful Shrine Temple banquet-hall; tickets were issued to officials, speakers, and others in that class; and all delegates were invited to buy tickets and enjoy the fellowship and cheer of the large gathering with its feast of song and wit and fun, at only what solitary meals in less hospitable and cheery public cafes would have cost them. So almost the whole convention dined as a family. It was a wonderful idea that never should be allowed to get away.

An Impromptu Spiritual

To sit at one of those meals with Homer Rodeheaver as guest and song-leader, and see him marshal the white-jacketed Negro waiters, whom he had drilled previously, to sing with him

> "I wan' to be ready,
> I wan' to be ready,
> I wan' to be ready to walk in Jerusalem,
> Jes' lak John,"

was a delectable dish that no outside caterer could add to his menu.

It was pre-eminently a *singing,* a musical convention, as delightfully tonal in character as it was colorful. Professor Jones, the trainer and leader of the choir, was the very soul of music. To sit near him while leading in one of those grand oratorios, and watch the play of expression on his mobile face, and hear his jubilant notes, was to feel the contagion of a great wave of emotion poured out by thousands of voices. There were great soloists, great pianists, great orchestras. On Friday there arrivad, all unannounced, the Memphis orchestra, which had paid its own expenses to the convention, and gave a wonderful treat of instrumental music.

It was pre-eimnently a *student* convention. Well, for one thing, the spiritual environment of the student body the church sends out every year to colleges and universities received more systematic consideration than ever before. At the college luncheon half a score of well-filled tables mixed viands with questions, answered by such experts in work among college students as Raymond Veh of the Evangelical Church, with experience on the campus of the University of Illinois and Evanston; Frank Getty, head of the young people's educational work of the Presbyterian Church in the U. S. A.; Gordon Howard of the United Brethren; S. S. Morris of the African Methodist Episcopal Church; Floyd Shacklock of New York; and Principal Reagan of Oakwood School.

But it was a "student convention" primarily, because every morning session was devoted to the seminar method of procedure, classes studying specialties under experts, as against the old-time "hurrah" mass convention where we were shown abundantly what to do, but trained in precious little of the how to do it.

It was an *evangelistic* convention. Every day the Quiet Hour under Dr. William Hiram Foulkes tenderly stressed the surrendered life. And every day the evangelistic truck, loaded with Paul C. Brown's California singers and workers, went to the open places in the streets to proclaim and sing into the ears of the people the old gospel of love and salvation.

Sharpshooting Bible Contest

One of the most interesting features Sunday afternoon in the Shrine Temple was a rapid-fire Bible-turning contest. This work has been splendidly promoted by Florence Kinney, Oklahoma State Intermediate superintendent, who acted as announcer for this contest. W. Roy Breg, Southern-States secretary, had charge of the drill. The three contestants were Wilna Milburn, Durant, Okla.; Harold Bachelor, Provo, Utah; and Josephine Davis, Washington, D. C.

The triangle test took place on the Temple stage. "Ready, aim, fire!"

Scripture references in succession were announced by book, chapter, verse. The sharpshooters sat with Bibles closed in their laps, and the first to stand and begin reading the passage called for won the point.

Sometimes two jumped up almost at once, but referees decided which was first, or whether it was a tie. The interest of friends of the contestants was so keen that request had to be made to refrain from applauding, and even then hand-clapping burst bounds when some especially swift work was done. Often the passage was found almost before the announcing was completed. Marvellous results are achieved with frequent drills.

The first and second in this contest were Wilna Milburn, fourteen points; Josephine Davis, nine.

Probably few adults in the audience could have done half as well. Those Intermediates will not waste minutes fumbling pages when they want a Bible verse. They learn the order of the books, and open to them like lightning.

Publicity Contest

In a country-wide effort to utilize the press in behalf of Christian Endeavor, and gain other publicity, the following showing was made: Pennsylvania, in group A, secured 31,608 inches. In group B, Kansas, 7,872 inches. In group C, Maryland, amount not received. In group D, Florida, 5,740 inches.

Another contest, arranged for counties, resulted as follows: with 50 to 100 societies, Northampton County, Penn., 7,254 inches. 25 to 50 societies, Carroll County, Md., 6,997 inches. Less than 25 societies, Daytona District, Fla., 2,259.

The International Publicity banner was awarded to Washington, D. C. Honors in the National Publicity Exhibit in the lobby of the convention hall were won by Pennsylvania. A ring

was awarded to the Pennsylvania State publicity superintendent, Mrs. Dorothy Rooker, Easton, Penn.

Those Twenty "Eats Together"

"The more we eat together,
The more we eat together,
The more we eat together,
The happier we are."

The thirty-first International Christian Endeavor Convention
was emphatically an "eat-together" affair. There were sched-
uled something like a score of premeditated breakfasts, lunch-
eons, banquets, most of them in the Shrine Temple banquet-
room. Not only was the menu good, but plentiful. Frequently
it was announced, "Second helpings for those who want them";
and, whether it was chicken or ice-cream that was called for,
the "seconds" were cheerfully and liberally forthcoming.

It was not just a matter of feeding, either; the following
names of some of these "feeds" will indicate the double purpose served.

Always there was enlivening music led by Foster, Rodeheaver, or some acknowledged song-leader, and quips and
bantering from table to table made feasts of wit and repartee
as well as of calories.

There was the "Recognition breakfast," the "Junior
Workers' luncheon," the "Fellowship banquet," the "Playtime
breakfast," the "College luncheon," the "Intermediate banquet," the "Christian-Vocation breakfast," the "Sunday-
School Workers' luncheon," the "Official breakfast, luncheon,
and dinner," the "Trustees" and Field-Secretaries' banquet,"
and last, but greatest of all, the great "Convention banquet,"
for which every inch of table space was in demand, and many
turned away weeping and wailing because they had delayed
making reservations.

"Go; you'll pick up something worth while," some one
urged. And the spontaneous droppings from kindled, happy
minds were often the richest pickings of the convention, which
gushed riches like a Texas oil-well.

Sunrise Praise Service at Liberty Memorial

On Sunday morning people had been gathering from all
directions by automobile, buses, street-cars, on foot, near the
base of the tower on the commanding plateau, which Kansas
had spent $20,000,000 to transform into a beautiful and striking
monument of liberty and peace. They sat on the stone steps
and sood on the grass, conversing quietly and reverently, while
the risen sun struggled through clouds, until Homer Rodeheaver's trombone broke forth in "Praise God From Whom All
Blessings Flow."

Rev. William Washington led in a fitting prayer, after which the strains of "Holy, Holy, Holy," led all thought upward.

Dr. Poling's address pictured the assembly as on a mountain, soon to descend with new courage and zeal for service. It reminded him of a fishing-trip, when no fish were caught, but the beauty of the scene made the fishers says, "It is good to be here."

The mountain is no place for permanent abode such as Peter suggested on the mount of transfiguration. The mountain is made for the plain. Those who go to such a mountain as this must go back to the plain, its needs of service and of sacrifice.

There was a new fervor in the closing song, "I'll Go Where You Want Me to Go."

It was one of those rare, genuine spiritual uplifts to which charm of setting, freshness of the morning hour, intimate heart fellowships, and the mystic presence of Him who sweetens and gladdens every place where He is found, all contribute to a climactic experience of following closely.

An Eye-Filling Jaunt Around Convention Hall

What went on inside the convention hall is told elsewhere. But sights to be seen in the corridors encircling the auditorium make an entrancing tale. Nearly seventy booths, most of them colorfully decorated, and many unique and striking, enticed the stroller down the winding lane. Besides the usual literature, registration, information, and public-service booths such as street-cars, telephone, telegraph, post-office, etc., there were scores of inviting denominational, local-society, State, and other booths, dressed up in yellow, red, purple, and rainbow-colored crepe-paper ribbons (all fire-proof material, by the way), and refreshment booths, and booths that fed the mind and soul.

Every denomination and many a State union did itself credit, and it is impractical barely to mention all of the fifty and more. One of those that most struck one was the booth of the Missouri State union, conspicuous for the large dynamo that Missouri's float carried in the parade, labelled "The Power behind Missouri's Activities."

California's booth was as purple as a pansy-bed with the "San Francisco, 1931," folders that played so large a part, with the California "sunshine" songs, in winning the decision, on Friday afternoon, to go to the Pacific Coast in two years with the first International Convention at the Golden Gate since the epochal first one in 1897.

The Moody Bible Institute had a display in which motion-pictures of street and rescue-mission work featured. Scores of conversions reward this work and the radio broadcasting of the gospel message which it does.

Something Exotic

New Mexico's booth, while not so spacious as some, displayed interesting handiwork of the Indians; it was in charge of the Indian Christian Endeavorers.

The national poster contest cut a large figure with gayly colored attractive posters from all over the country, the prize-winners of many a hard-fought contest. A pocketful of ideas on how to advertise by hand-made posters could be gained in a few minutes there.

The Central Christian Seniors of Kansas City had thoughtfully fitted up a comfortable rest-room with davenport, Morris-chair, reading lamp, and other creature comforts appealing to the weary-footed.

The African Methodist Episcopal Zion Church had a telling Tenth-Legion exhibit with a spot-light thrown upon it, where the lime-light is needed.

Graded Christian Endeavor of the First Presbyterian Church, Tulsa, Okla., had a long section of the curved wall, and Floating Christian Endeavor was in evidence with a model of a United States battleship, and a list of the ports where it throws out the life-line.

One gripping set of pictures and display heads was that of the Italian Institute Home, a Protestant mission of Kansas City that maintains clubs for boys and girls, gives meals to the needy, and uplifts the life of its community by close contacts.

The Raytown, Kan., and the Jamestown, N. J., Endeavorers exemplified on the assigned wall space the possibilities of the rural church. The Independence Boulevard Endeavorers had a most appealing collection of Chinese curios, as another had the flags of all nations and a collection of curios from missions in Africa.

The Third Presbyterian Endeavorers had a hard-hitting way of picturing the important work of the lookout committee—a huge pair of spectacles on the wall, with the words, "Lookout Committee" beneath.

The Birthplace of Endeavor

No creation of the many original and impressive booths probably held attention more strongly than did the large-size models of the "Birthplace of Christian Endeavor," Williston church and parsonage, real gems of architectural reproduction, colored to life, and in their natural setting.

World-peace literature covered a large section of the wall, and the "Crusade-with-Christ" colored window was a thing of real beauty and a joy and inspiration to thousands.

It would be easy to go on using high-powered adjectives to describe the many others as worthy of mention, like the six-foot globe of the Independence, Mo., Christian Endeavorers, which typified the world-conquest of Christian Endeavor and the world's need of it.

One other motion-picture entertainment in the Shriners' Auditorium was a five-reel prohibition story, with a newspaper-office setting, laying bare the criminal plotting and devilish cunning with which the bootlegging syndicate of the underworld and its disloyal scofflaw patrons may be fought to a finish.

Delegates to Kansas City, 1929, will not soon forget the fascinating "Avenue of Bazaars" with their wealth of scenic interest and information.

Rodeheaver's Musical Clinic

"Rody" got a job he'd been itching for—a chance to teach song-leaders in Endeavor and other church services how to make song a much more carefully planned and skilfully executed part of the program.

Every morning from 9.50 to 10.35 he had the choir-loft in the convention hall packed, with a spill-over into the first balcony at each end, of Endeavorers willing and eager to be shown how by one of the greatest leaders of mass-singing in America to-day.

This is how keen they were for a chance to improve. "I want volunteers who will come down here and lead in a song, and have any faults pointed out. Who will come?" This was responded to immediately by a young man and a girl. They in turn undertook the test, nervously, of course, and then submitted gracefully to corrections, the benefit of which went to all.

Mr. Rodeheaver answered questions from the class. "What have the facial muscles to do with good singing?" He gave a demonstration by singing with rigid and then with flexed mouth-muscles. It is a new venture in Christian Endeavor Convention work, with promise of being a very popular and potent one.

The accompanist was shown what a prelude is for, an interlude, and how to get back always to the opening chord. Long live Rody's music clinic!

CHAPTER XI

A BATCH OF RESOLUTIONS

Thanksgiving

The Thirty-Second Convention of Christian Endeavor, in session at Kansas City, Mo., unites in thanksgiving to God for guidance during forty-eight glowing and growing years. We believe the movement came providentially into the world to inspire and help young people serve Christ and the church. Its record among a vast multitude of eager-hearted youth surely bears witness to the stamp of divine approval. It came like a life-giving current into the religious life of the world, and to-day perpetuates and reproduces the regenerating experiences of the early years.

We reaffirm our faith in this mighty movement of youth, which has girdled the world with its golden ministry, and still calls insistently for young men and women, boys and girls to find in discipleship of Christ the supreme fact and joy of life. We believe that Jesus Christ, the acceptance of his person, and the application of the spirit of His principles, remain the unchallengeable solvent for the increasing complex problems of life.

We rejoice for the God-given leadership of Christian Endeavor since its inception. Our hearts are filled with affectionate memories of Dr. Francis E. Clark, our founder, the beauty of whose Christian character and the splendor of whose gifts and consecration remain our cherished possession. His life lives on in the gracious ministries he inaugurated and in young life still helped by the vision that came to him in Portland, Me.

We do not forget Mother Endeavor Clark, who partnered him in Christian Endeavor. We give thanks for her gracious presence at this convention, and unite in presenting to her our loving greetings and the assurance of our prayers.

We are increasingly grateful for the radiant leadership of our president, Dr. Daniel A. Poling, whose rare qualities of mind and heart have made him one of the heroic figures of national and international life. We view with pride his ever-increasing influence, and are confident that under the standard he raises this great movement is going forward to ever-enriching achievements. We pledge him our allegiance, our loyalty, and our co-operation. He is our beloved captain in a modern crusade, and we pay our tribute to the unstinted devotion of his work for Christ and the church.

Citizenship and Law-Enforcement

The Thirty-Second International Convention of Christian Endeavor, speaking for its four million members, as they have expressed themselves in the home, school, the church, and at the polls, declares that prohibition is making good. In terms of health, economic welfare, safety, the protection of the home, America's great adventure is proving practicable and necessary.

We believe that the Eighteenth Amendment constitutes the greatest moral reform in the corporate life of the nation within the present century. It is a noble effort to free people from the age-long curse of the liquor traffic.

Through the courageous crusading of our elders, our generation of youth has inherited a land free from the legal sale and distribution of liquor. This is a blessing difficult for some of us to realize who have never seen a saloon. We pledge ourselves to work for the preservation of this reform, the benefits of which are so manifest.

We have noted with deep concern the repeated declarations of President Hoover on the question of lawlessness. "It threatens the foundations of the republic." This constitutes a challenge which cannot be overlooked. People who break this law have destroyed the very fabric of our democracy. Christian Endeavor, through its voice in this convention, assures the President of its earnest and enthusiastic support in his publicly announced purpose to establish an increasing respect for the law throughout the nation. We believe his leadership in this matter marks a new era in the progress of law observance and enforcement.

The highest form of patriotic and Christian citizenship demands our using every possible resource in calling America to the conscientious obedience to the Eighteen Amendment and its enforcing acts. We support every effort toward this end. There is necessity for the co-operation of the home, the school, the press, and every religious organization. We must obey and observe the law and let it be known we believe in it.

We pledge ourselves to total abstinence from intoxicating beverages. We urge all good citizens to register themselves in this fundamental way against alcoholic liquor. This is educational work of the greatest value.

There are vicious forces which for personal desire would betray this great cause. They are united and unscrupulous. We must be united, untiring, and zealous; for this reform is forwarding the highest good for our human kind.

We repudiate the veiled suggestion that youth in our educational institutions are flouting this law in large numbers. With peculiar satisfaction we note an uprising of student life to deny this accusation. While minorities may selfishly violate this law, ignoring their own best interests, we unhesitatingly affirm that the overwhelming majority of students are law-abiding and idealistically inclined.

Christian Endeavor is with the President of the United States in his efforts, because we believe the moral health of the people, the highest spiritual welfare of our citizenship, demand that a new respect for law be created in the hearts of men and women. We join hands with all other agencies working in this field, praying that soon we may witness its complete and final triumph.

Loyalty to the Church

The patriotic celebration of the Declaration of Independence called to mind the unexampled material progress of American life. The vast natural resources in the United States and Canada, coupled with inventive genius and persistent energy, have brought wealth beyond the dreams of the early years. We give thanks to Almighty God for this glorious heritage, which has made possible higher standards of life to vast numbers of people.

Material wealth brings its temptation to forget the unseen moral virtues which have been so evident in American history. Concrete may crumble, steel rust, and bank deposits dwindle, if those inner qualities of honesty, virtue, and honor are not being constantly cultivated and produced.

We believe that our country to-day needs nothing so much as a revival of vital religion. The church of God through the years has been the inspiration and guardian of religion. It was founded to produce that kind of life and living which alone can exalt a nation. It is the eternal and everlasting institution. It ever renews its youth and power to meet the demands of the hour.

We pledge our loyalty and fealty to the church, our church. We feel its need in the national life as we feel its need in personal life, and this convention declares its abiding devotion to the church.

International Golden-Rule Sunday

Recognizing the education and spiritual, as well as financial and philanthropic, values of International Golden-Rule Sunday, we strongly commend and indorse the observance of Golden-Rule Sunday, on behalf of underprivileged children throughout the world, and urge our societies wherever practicable to co-operate with the duly constituted State and local committees in promoting international observance of this day.

The Missionary Task

Christian Endeavor believes that Christianity is international. It believes the world's need can be met at Calvary. It believes that men and women everywhere need Jesus Christ. The thrilling challenge of the Jerusalem Conference found an instant response in Christian Endeavor.

The lands and peoples into which missionaries have gone have changed, but the fundamental need of the missionary is still unchanged. We find this position supported by the keen anxiety of those in mission countries that there should be no slackening of our interest and co-operation.

The missionary is still needed for inspiration and friendly counsel, going along side by side with the Christians of these countries as their church moves to larger service in the kingdom of God. Thousands of Endeavorers have gone as missionaries to distant shores. Their dedicated lives have been one of the chief glories of this movement. The investment they have made is ever a perpetual stimulus to finer devotion on the part of those who remain at home.

We feel we are interpreting the mind of this convention aright when we unite in declaring that we will give ourselves with abandon, passion, and purpose to the missionary tasks ahead.

Church Unity

Christian Endeavor in convention assembled recalls with unbounded joy the blessings that have characterized our work by reason of its interdenominational fellowship. We have found a spiritual unity in our common tasks. The tides of young life of the various denominations have crossed and recrossed, and the contacts have helped to prepare the way for larger union. Youth is especially eager to emphasize the things that unite rather than the things that divide.

The movement hails with delight the fact that so many denominations and communions by official action, are moving towards organic unity. The great principle of union and unity is one to which Endeavorers by their very history and organization find themselves under peculiar committment. We are part of the church and loyal to the church, and as a youth agency of the church we call upon the youth of the church to give enthusiastic support to denominational leadership in this effort to bring nearer fulfillment the prayer of Christ that they all should be one.

Enrolment of Former Active Endeavorers

This convention enthusiastically indorses the proposal to enroll during the next two years one million former active Endeavorers. There are countless men and women in every realm of activity who remember with joy and pride the beginnings of their Christian life in this movement. They first learned to serve God and their fellows under its auspices. Without that initial experience the first step might never have been taken. Their hearts are filled with joyous gratitude for this agency of the church, which led them in youthful days to stand for Christ and the church. They constitute an asset of immeasurable value.

We recommend to the executive committee that this enrolment be inaugurated at the earliest possible moment.

"Crusade with Christ"

This convention is convinced of providential guidance in the Crusade-with-Christ program which was adopted in Cleveland two years ago. No appeal has more profoundly and deeply stirred the hearts and minds of Endeavorers. It has had a far-reaching influence. Forty associated groups and ten millions of young people have joined to develop this great enterprise. Young people are always crusaders; they have ever been through the centuries. To crusade with Christ, the matchless leader of youth, for definite tasks seems to have gripped the imagination of young life in a truly marvelous way. Evangelism, citizenship, and world peace are truly, as our president has said, a trinity of triumph, "Myself, my country, and my world."

The accomplishments of the past two years make a thrilling story. We give thanks to God for the uprising of response to this crusade call. We are more than ever convinced that as yet only the initial stages have been taken. The greatest work lies ahead.

Evangelism must ever remain the permanent, inescapable, and pre-eminent responsibility of Christian life. The duty of projecting the ethic and principles of Christ into citizenship we feel a growing obligation. The problem of world peace seems particularly the special challenge of this generation.

These three issues call us as powerfully now as at Cleveland. We want to share in this service with youth everywhere, and we pledge ourselves in the spirit of prayer and by personal vow to this conquering program.

Cigarette-Smoking

This convention views with apprehension the pernicious growing habit of cigarette-smoking among the young life of America. The recent colossal campaign of cigarette-advertising in magazine, on bill-board, and radio, exploiting adolescent youth and womanhood, fills us with disgust; and we will campaign to arouse public opinion to demand its abolition.

Racial Relations

Christian Endeavor from its beginnings has recognized no distinctions of race or color. We believe that this stand is fundamental to the progress of civilization. It is the only basis on which world brotherhood and peace can be established. It is the only principle that satisfies the definition of Jesus, "By this shall all men know that ye are my disciples, if ye have love one to another." Christian Endeavor is of all evangelical churches, all races, all colors, and all tongues.

The Paris Pact and World Peace

Christian Endeavor has committed itself to work for a warless world. We have been filled with gratitude as we have witnessed during the past years how the peoples and the nations of the world feel the essential urgency of this matter. In his inaugural address President Hoover made articulate this universal sentiment: "Surely mankind is old enough, surely mankind is mature enough, to advance the cause of peace in our generation."

We hail with enthusiasm the coming into effect of the Pact of Paris, under the terms of which nations condemn recourse to war for the solution of international controversies. We rejoice, too, that the nations who signed the pact have agreed that they will seek the settlement of all disputes that may arise among them by pacific means.

We are resolved in the light of the pledges of this treaty to maintain the peace of the world. We set ourselves to the task of creating the will to peace. We do not believe that war is inevitable. We believe, on the contrary, that world peace can and will be accomplished. To this high purpose we hereby dedicate ourselves.

We believe that the Pact of Paris witnesses to the political solidarity of the world, that business witnesses to the economic solidarity of the world, that education witnesses to the intellectual solidarity of the world, that the Christian religion witnesses to the spiritual solidarity of the world. Recognizing, as we do, this unity of mankind, we highly resolve to live at peace with the nations of the world.

We observe with gratitude as an organization representing Canada and the United States the efforts now being made by the United States and the British commonwealth of nations looking toward a substantial reduction in naval armaments. We express the hope that the diplomatic exchanges now taking place will result in a reduction-of-armament conference, and will include all the powers that have naval and military establishments.

We further believe that the United States, in order to make effective its pledges under the Pact of Paris, should become a member of the World Court of International Justice, and respectfully hope that without delay the Senate of the United States will complete this relationship.

There is now before the Senate of the United States an inter-American treaty of arbitration which will pave the way for lasting peace between the United States, Mexico, and the sovereign nations of Central and South America. We respectfully urge the early ratification of this constructive measure of international amity by the United States Senate.

Resolution of Thanks to Kansas City

It is utterly impossible adequately to express our thanks for the wonderful courtesy and hospitality of Kansas City. No greater cordiality has ever been shown to the hosts of Christian Endeavor in any previous convention. We have learned to love the "Heart of America," which has simply overflowed with gracious kindness. We carry away with us affectionate impressions which will last throughout life.

We should like to mention the name of every person who has contributed to the success of this gathering. That would take an entire session. We must say, however, to Mr. Charles D. Williams, his committee, and to all who have so unselfishly labored to make us happy and comfortable, that we are eternally in their debt.

We think of the efficiency in the organization of the parade; the glory of the music, and the minute care in all the ushering arrangements. We were especially encouraged by the whole-hearted co-operation of the Epworth League South, Epworth League North, the Baptist Young People's Union, and other groups. Everyone seems to have excelled themselves.

We can never repay what we owe to the Convention Bureau of the Chamber of Commerce, Mayor Beach, and the municipal officials; the pastors and the churches, and the kindly homes of this kindly city. We cannot name everybody, but thoughts of everybody are in our hearts. Honored and beloved friends of Kansas City and Missouri, we have been shown; you have conquered; we thank and love you.

CLIFFORD EARLE
Field-Secretary, Wisconsin

The Endeavorer's Bible

QUIET HOUR EDITION

The Christian Endeavor Emblem is stamped in gold on the cover.

These Bibles, specially printed for us, contain articles by Dr. Clark, Dr. Wells and Rev. Anderson, also the Quiet Hour Pledge, a Presentation Page and twelve colored maps. Printed with large, bold-faced type. Many societies will purchase these special Christian Endeavor Bibles for all their members to use in their prayer meetings, paying for them out of the society treasury.

No. 0349C.E. Black cloth, square corners, red edge, gold title $1.75

No. 0357C.E. French Morocco Leather, overlapping cover, round corners, red under gold edges, headbands and silk bookmark $4.50

No. 0327C.E. Same as 0357C.E. with addition of a complete concordance $5.00

Endeavorer's Pocket Testament

QUIET HOUR EDITION

These vest-pocket size Testaments are clearly printed with black-faced type. They are only ⅝ of an inch thick. The Christian Endeavor emblem is stamped in gold on the cover. They contain special articles by Dr. Clark, Dr. Wells and Mr. Anderson. Every Endeavorer should carry one always.

No. 01C.E. French Morocco, overlapping cover, round corners, red under gold edges, colored frontispiece, 7 black and white illustrations, silk headband and marker $0.75

No. 02C.E. Moroccoette, overlapping cover, round corners, gilt edges $1.25

No. 03C.E. French Morocco, overlapping cover, round corners, red under gold edges, gold title, silk headband and marker, boxed $1.50

No. 04xC.E. French Morocco, overlapping cover, round corners, red under gold edges, leather lined, India paper . . $2.50

C. E. Books, C. E. Pins and Rings, Convention Badges, Topic Cards, Felt and Silk Banners, Bibles, Etc.

International Society of Christian Endeavor

41 Mt. Vernon Street　　　**17 N. Wabash Avenue**

Boston, Mass.　　　　　　**Chicago, Ill.**

ORDER FROM NEARER ADDRESS

www.ingramcontent.com/pod-product-compliance
Lightning Source LLC
Chambersburg PA
CBHW021156020426

42331CB00003B/92